THE EVERYDAY LIFE IN AMERICA SERIES

EDITED BY

RICHARD BALKIN

For Susan

THE UNCERTAINTY OF EVERYDAY LIFE

Bᴇᴛᴡᴇᴇɴ 1915 and 1945 Americans experienced two world wars, an unevenly distributed but nonetheless impressive economic boom, and a severe economic depression. Making sense of the changes bedeviled both professional analysts and ordinary Americans of all classes. The alterations in everyday life were not simply those of the material sort but also in the realm of consciousness. Moreover, looming over the day-to-day comings and goings of people was the perception that the rate of change in their lives had accelerated.

Technological innovations in the movement of information enabled people, governments, and businesses to communicate almost instantaneously. Revolutionary changes in the manufacture of goods provided consumers with a diversity of inexpensive goods heretofore unknown in human history. Matching the production with the market also brought forth a newly important and expanding segment of the economy, the advertiser, whose job it was to convince wary or gullible consumers to buy new things and goods they did not need. These new advocates discovered that they could most successfully get their job done—or convince their clients of their success—if they traded on the vulnerable parts of Americans' collective consciousness. Uncertainty about the present, the future, or about interpersonal relationships increasingly came to characterize successful advertisers' strategies because the rules of the economic game seemed to have changed. Instead of the Protestant virtues of hard work, steady accumulation of wealth, and prudent and

limited expenditure, nearly instant riches and risky swashbuck-
ling stock market manipulation were proffered as the way to
wealth. But even in times that seemed economically beneficent
for many—the 1920s—an undercurrent of doubt lingered. If
money and good times could be had with relative speed and
ease when compared with people's perception of the past, they
could also be lost with just as much rapidity.

The rules of the social game, be it sexual or more tamely
interpersonal, changed too, identifying new trials to be overcome in order to succeed with others. New "social diseases"
such as halitosis and body odor were invented by advertisers
and manufacturers trying to sell new products or recast old
ones. This strategy revealed a new emphasis on maladies that
offended others—and were imperceptible to the bearer. Dale
Carnegie's *How to Win Friends and Influence People,* first published in 1936, became one of the largest-selling books of the
1930s, in spite of its late start in the decade. Carnegie's message
was simple and direct: Discover the best way to "fit in" with
others' expectations of behavior and one would stand the best
chance of succeeding. Productivity had been replaced by the
more subjective and unmeasurable qualities of personality and
personability—being able to "get along."

Farmers—trumpeted by many for generations as the bedrock
of the nation—for the most part did not enjoy the fruits of the
great economic party in the interwar era. Prices for agricultural
products collapsed almost immediately after World War I
ended in 1918. In the boom times and boom culture of urban business America they became "hayseeds," "hicks," and
"rubes." For them the sound of the Roaring Twenties was the
howl of the wolf at the door.

When the great crash came in 1929 it did not immediately
shatter all those dreams and ideas of prosperity that many
Americans of the middle and wealthier classes treasured. Many
thought that it was a temporary setback. But when the Depression deepened until one-third of the work force was out of work
completely and one-third had their hours reduced, the sense of
uncertainty that had hovered over people for decades sharp-
ened. When confronted with the reality of unemployment and

hopelessness, multitudes hit the roads or the rails looking for an environment where they might live easier without a job or on part-time wages (hence California's attraction). Others stayed at home and tried to endure the shame of being newly poor and the uncertainties of the availability of their next meal or their ability to pay the rent or mortgage. Before the crash, advertising executives and strategists had discovered the underbelly of American consciousness: Pride and self-worth were based on quantifiable signs of material well-being—goods—and the unquantifiable scale of social acceptance.

The first war in Europe began in 1914, when Archduke Ferdinand of Austria-Hungary was assassinated. The Great War has with some justification been considered a watershed by historians, and it had considerable temporary and long-range impact on the everyday lives of most Americans, especially after the entrance of the United States in 1917. Farmers enjoyed higher prices for a time. Families of soldiers worried about their men abroad. Some intellectuals and politicians opposed an American presence in corrupt Europe's madness. The Russian and other European revolutions frightened many—and encouraged a few. But unlike Europe, the United States did not lose an entire generation of men. Ancient monarchies did not fall. The war was "over there." Change in the rhythms and routines of everyday life in the United States generally occurred gradually, altered little by the death of national leaders or the invention of revolutionary products. The Wright Brothers' flight did not immediately result in skies crowded with airplanes or the faster delivery of mail. When President Warren G. Harding died in 1923, life changed somewhat for Vice President Calvin Coolidge and his family, but not much for most Americans. But it is possible to locate important events in and around 1915 that mark the year as a useful line of demarcation for a consideration of everyday life in the United States.

Emily Post's book *Etiquette* first appeared in 1915. Hers was not the first publication to advise Americans about their behavior. Such books had been published for centuries, and as improved power presses and cheap paper made for inexpensive printing after 1840, hundreds of such volumes appeared. But

Post's book struck a more responsive chord in Americans than did others of the genre after 1915. It went through five editions by 1937, and still sells. Like Dale Carnegie in *How to Win Friends and Influence People*, Post stressed the importance of manners and pleasing others, of developing one's "personality," rather than one's "character," which had been the center of attention for advice writers of the nineteenth century.

Her book appeared in the same year as another important popular cultural breakthrough of more ominous meaning. D. W. Griffith's film *The Birth of a Nation* opened on March 3, 1915. As a part of cinematic history, Griffith's motion picture deserves attention because it was the first feature-length film. It also broke free from the conventions of the stage: Griffith used long-distance shots, switchbacks, fade-outs, close-ups, and panoramas in his rendition of Thomas Dixon, Jr.'s novel of 1905, *The Clansman: An Historical Romance of the Ku Klux Klan.* The film cost $100,000 to produce—an unprecedented amount for its time—but it grossed more than $18 million over the course of its multiyear run. But technological innovations played only a small part in the success of *The Birth of a Nation.* The film's racist history of the United States, and in particular its glorification of the Ku Klux Klan, made it a profitable and popular fund-raiser and recruiting instrument for the reborn KKK. Fifty million people saw it, especially in the Old South, the Midwest, and the West, where the Klan was most successful. In late November 1915, William J. Simmons and fifteen other men had met in Atlanta, Georgia, to establish a memorial organization to the Ku Klux Klan of the Reconstruction era. The "Invisible Empire, Knights of the Ku Klux Klan" received a charter from the state of Georgia in a week. On December 6, 1915, *The Birth of a Nation* opened for an unprecedented three-week run.[1]

The Klan's renascence coincided with and furthered a huge migration of African-Americans from south to north. As the demand for labor grew quickly in northern cities, especially the automobile, meat-packing, steel, and other heavy industries, recruiters and the African-American press brought to southern black people news of a way to escape the threats of the Klan and the unending cycle of poverty wrought by the sharecropping and tenant-farming systems. Between 1910 and 1920, the African-American population of New York City increased from 91,709 to 152,647 (66%), that of Chicago from 44,103 to 109,458 (150%), that of Detroit from 5,741 to 40,838 (611%), and that of Cleveland from 8,448 to 34,451 (400%).[2]

African-Americans were not the only Americans moving from place to place. The U.S. Department of Agriculture estimated that between 1920 and 1937, 30 million people moved from farms to towns, villages, and cities, and 21 million from towns to farms. Immigrants continued to enter the country in large numbers until 1924, when revised quota acts (based on the percentage of ethnic minorities in the nation in 1890) were enacted, thereby severely limiting the number of immigrants from southern and eastern Europe. By 1930 the 40 million first- or second-generation immigrants constituted one-third of the population of the United States.

For most of the 14 million first-generation immigrants in 1930, family and neighborhood were most important, as they had been for the previous generation of immigrants—those who had arrived between 1890 and 1910. Immigrants typically formed their own enclaves within cities and towns, and their shared race, language, foodways, religions, and festivals served as bulwarks against the discrimination and suspicion with which they were commonly regarded. In New York City, for example, thirty-seven languages were spoken in 1920, and only one in six residents was Protestant. In Chicago in the same year, out of a total population of 2.7 million, more than 1 million residents were Roman Catholic, 800,000 were foreign-born, 125,000 were Jews, and 110,000 were African-American.[3] Foreign-language newspapers, stores, and shops abounded. The newcomers often had little choice but to take some of the most difficult and physically taxing and dangerous jobs in industry. To many middle-class and wealthy Americans, they also seemed the most receptive to "alien" ideologies of revolution, anarchy, and syndicalism than were the more "established" Germans, Dutch, and Scandinavians. Anglo-American elites worried that "American" civilization—which they identified as growing from a "pure" English stock—would not survive the onslaught of these different people and ideas.

By 1915 the United States had become an urban culture. In 1910, 54.2 percent of the population lived on farms and in villages of less than 2,500 inhabitants; by 1920, 48.6 percent lived in such areas. By 1933, one-half of all Americans lived within a half-hour drive of a city of 100,000 or greater population. Southern cities were in general smaller than those in the Northeast. In 1920 only New Orleans exceeded 300,000 population; Atlanta had over 200,000 residents, and eight other cities had more than 100,000 inhabitants. In the West, excepting Seattle, San Francisco, and Los Angeles (which annexed part of the San Fernando Valley in 1915), cities were small and compact. Salt Lake City had grown slowly, but other cities such as Denver, Boise, Butte, and Cheyenne remained small.[4]

The ways in which Americans earned their livelihood changed dramatically between 1915 and 1945. In 1776, 90 percent of the population worked on farms; in 1900, 32 percent were so employed; and in 1935, 20 percent tilled the soil or raised livestock.[5] Industrial work and management and clerical jobs replaced farming. Industrial productivity increased 40 percent in the 1920s, although the boom was unevenly distributed. The textile and coal industries and agriculture either stagnated or collapsed. The value of real estate showed the largest gain, followed closely by consumer goods and automobiles. New industries producing new products such as rayon and Lastex (a mixture of rubber, cotton, and rayon or wool) expanded dramatically. Burlington Mills, a rayon manufacturer, made $1.8 million worth of goods in 1927; in 1933, in the depths of the Depression, the company produced $16 million worth of goods; in 1936 the value of Burlington's production had risen to $25.4 million. U.S. Rubber Company increased its production of Lastex from 32,000 pounds in 1931 to 1.2 million pounds in 1933.[6]

Technology and science had been sources of great hope and inspiration for Americans throughout the era. Electricity, a source of energy and power available only to the urban dweller (and the wealthier of that sort) in the early twentieth century, reached farmers and other isolated Americans by the 1940s, in part through the efforts of the Rural Electrification Program of Franklin Roosevelt's New Deal. Government-sponsored projects dammed rivers and aided the irrigation of lands previously unavailable or impractical for farming. A new source of information and entertainment—the radio—was by the 1930s inexpensive enough to be owned by most Americans. The development of the cheap compact electric motor made practical the mass production and consumption of a myriad of household labor-saving devices that had been invented as early as the 1840s. These made housework tasks less demanding and time-consuming, but did not necessarily lighten the total work load. More jobs and more elaborate production were often the result of these innovations.[7]

Between 1915 and 1929 the widespread application of mechanization to the production of consumer goods and the increasing sophistication of advertising accompanied a substantial increase in real wages for white- and blue-collar workers. After virtually no gain between 1890 and 1915, wage earners' purchasing power increased 20 percent between 1915 and 1926. Income rose in these eleven years for nearly all segments of the work force, albeit unevenly. Farmers profited briefly between 1915 to 1920, when food prices doubled. But prices fell precipitously in the autumn of 1920 to a point 35 percent higher than that of 1915, where they remained for ten years. Income for farm workers and those in related industries—farm machinery, for example—remained relatively stagnant. Wages of other workers grew steadily, especially for those not in the heavy manufacturing or the extractive industries (mining, lumbering, and fishing), in which work was sporadic throughout any given year.[8] Poverty among nonfarm workers did not disappear in the 1920s, or reappear rapidly with the Depression. Many workers on farms and in mills, factories, and sweatshops struggled throughout the era, in unsafe workplaces for long hours and in difficult home environments. Thirty-three percent of all Americans had no running water in 1940, 67 percent had no central heat, 47 percent had no built-in bathing apparatus in their homes, 48 percent had no interior access to automatic or other washing machines, 48 percent had no refrigerator, and 33 percent cooked with wood or coal.[9]

American consumers—primarily the middle class and the wealthy—who had these conveniences were the targets of manufacturers and advertisers, who were continuously trying to broaden their sales. The federal government aided these efforts by expanding the categories of statistics it collected in each census; private polling organizations began to conduct regular surveys to identify "average" Americans and discover their habits. All were attempting to provide clients with data that could lead to more rationalized and predictable social and economic decisions. New magazines such as *Time* and *Fortune* and advertising firms such as the J. Walter Thompson Company surveyed readers or random samples of the population.[10] So great was the demand for survey information that *Fortune*'s poll of 3,000 Americans representing a "cross-section" of the population, initiated in 1935 on a quarterly basis, became a monthly feature by 1939.

Between 1915 and 1930 industrial production promised the virtual elimination of most homemade goods from the lives of all but the poorest and technologically isolated Americans. The Depression and the exigencies of the war effort after 1941 only stalled that effort. Enormous growth in the chemical, electrical, automobile, and food processing industries after World War I brought more goods to the populace at less cost and in more sophisticated packaging. The increased consumption of radios, cars, motion picture entertainment, and other goods and services helped create what historian Loren Baritz has called a "specific national culture based on artifacts, news of the latest style of rumble seat or shade of lipstick," and a society "saturated by mass-produced and mass marketed goods . . . and an ethic, a standard of living, and a power structure centered on consuming." Commodities became "keys to personal welfare."[11]

Manufacturers and advertisers traded upon this culture of consumption, producing goods in a variety of forms and colors irrelevant to the basic function of the product. Beginning in the mid-1920s, typewriters, lipsticks, cameras, plumbing fixtures, towels and bed linens, suspenders, underwear, and cheap silverware were offered in colors. Advertisements for goods for the home increasingly stressed the look of things rather than their function, implying that their technology was up to date and that they worked. Even the cheapest goods were pitched as better than those that had been available to royalty and the nobility in previous ages. The implication was that technology rendered unnecessary and pernicious any schemes to level inequities of class and income.[12] Even in the Depression, continuous references to the rich using cheap products served to reinforce the idea that technology and mass production had brought a revolution to the United States that had outstripped and rendered useless the political and economic revolutions that had occurred in Europe and that "alien reds" had tried to foist upon Americans.

Multiple consumption—two or more radios and even automobiles—became a tactic to fuel the consumption boom of the twenties. The two-car family would, the advertisers said, free the woman of the house from isolation. (It probably did some of that, but it also made her into the chauffeur and errand-runner of the family, thereby helping to end the careers of delivery boys and alter the practices of businesses that made house calls.) Similar pitches were made for multiple radios (avoiding battles with the kids about what to hear), telephones (avoiding running for the phone, or, if rich enough, avoiding having to contend with others for the line), swimsuits, and wrist-watches.[13]

The era also embraced the nation's greatest attempt at regulating behavior and transforming the social fabric since the abolition of slavery in 1863. Prohibition of the production, sale, and transportation of alcoholic beverages became an amendment to the U.S. Constitution in 1919. It was part of a larger reform effort to counter the changes that seemed to endanger the established order. Jazz, the movies (as yet uncensored), radio, "new" women, "flaming youth," and the "crime wave" in corrupt mobster-ridden cities and the nation's small towns were—to those who wished to see it—the proof of a culture that was out of control.

On the most personal and mundane level in everyday life uncertainty seemed a matter of course. The working class struggled to budget or borrow for a house, and jobs and wages were unpredictable. Workers often reported to work only to find the workplace closed or their jobs eliminated. Layoffs for a day or week could stretch into months if management found it necessary or profitable to do so. Women had the responsibility for maintaining their homes in order whether they worked outside the home or not and on finances that were unstable. And this had to be done in from one to four rooms, often with boarders, relatives, or acquaintances from the old country joining the family while they got their bearings in the new land.

The middle class and the wealthy had other problems with which to contend. Essentially freed from the crush of people and domestic space that the working class endured, the middle-class man (few women could get positions in management unless they owned the company) also wrestled with job insecurity. There were few objective methods to measure productivity or effectiveness in the office environment, and judgments were often based on unquantifiable personal characteristics. What colleagues said about white-collar workers behind their backs mattered, and failure to succeed was often characterized as a correctable personal failure that was never discussed with the offender. These flaws were reminiscent of late-nineteenth-century worries about "nervousness" or neurasthenia, and they increased the trade of psychologists and psychiatrists. The power of these new experts grew dramatically after Freud's trip to the United States in 1912 and the subsequent popularization of his ideas in magazines and periodicals.[14]

Some reformers pushed efficiency and rationality as a solution to some economic and personal problems. The ideology of Progressivism—that combination of science, Protestant rigor, and crusading reform identified with the first two decades of the twentieth century—informed the advocates of "scientific management." In 1915 Mary Pattison's *Principles of Domestic Engineering: The Business of Home Management* was published, and in 1920, Christine Frederick's *Household Engineering: Scientific Management in the Home.*[15] The idea of woman as business manager and chief executive officer of the household was not new: Catherine Beecher and other domestic advisors had used this analogy in the middle and late nineteenth century. The novelty of Frederick's and Pattison's books was in their enthusiasm for motion study and science and their commitment to the future.

Americans' faith in science and technology made popular heroes of Henry Ford, Charles Lindbergh, and even Al Capone (for his use of guns and fast cars). Futurism and technological wizardry informed art deco and "jazz moderne" styles of everything from buildings to radios and dinnerware. The American World's Fairs of the decade—the Chicago "Century of Progress" (1933) and the New York "World of Tomorrow" (1939)—worshiped the gods of science and technology, and presented Americans with a variation of the promise that religion had offered in previous centuries—a future with no problems.

But skyscrapers, "machine art," space heroes such as Flash Gordon (found in new entertainment media, the film and the comic book and strip), and futuristic cityscapes with complex bridgeways and whizzing transportation were but one part of the cultural accommodation to the pace and mode of life Americans encountered. Equally powerful for the middle class and the wealthy was a yearning for the past that they thought simpler, and therefore more comforting. Images of idyllic rural small towns of harmony and unity coexisted with the new world of the future. By the 1930s advertisers were promoting the traditional as much as they were hawking the new. In the mid-1920s Henry Ford—the man linked to the assembly line and the car for everyone—was busily organizing his paean to the past, Greenfield Village. (The name itself cleverly mixed images of the lush, cultivated farms and quiet, gentle small towns.) At the same time the Rockefellers were engaged in the restoration of Colonial Williamsburg (to open in 1935), and the Metropolitan Museum of Art was gathering together materials for its "American Wing." By the mid-1930s a reinvigorated "colonial revival" was in full swing (it began as a broad-based movement in the 1880s). The popularity of expansive western motion pictures in the late thirties and New Deal projects to record the genius of

American folk art and design manifested the desire for an alternative answer to that of the technocrats.

For the most part, the heroes of the era who represented the popular culture equivalents to Ford's Greenfield Village luminaries were sports heroes. Baseball players Babe Ruth, Joe DiMaggio, Rogers Hornsby, and Ted Williams; boxers Jack Dempsey and Joe Louis; tennis players Bill Tilden and Helen Wills Moody; sprinter and long-jumper Jesse Owens; all-around athletic star Babe Zaharias; football player Red Grange; and golfer Bobby Jones dominated their games and the media. The exception to this pattern was Charles A. Lindbergh. His solo flight across the Atlantic—the first successful crossing—made him an instant celebrity, a symbol of American individuality, enterprise, and daring.

But the achievements of a few could not erase the ambiguities and uncertainties of the modern age. In *The Modern Temper* (1929), Joseph Wood Krutch argued that science had failed to be the panacea for human problems that many advocates had promised it would be. The rootlessness and aimlessness that the Columbia University professor found characteristic of modern American urban middle-class culture was a product of the excesses of production and consumption that economic boosters had trumpeted throughout the twenties. The multitude of consumer choices had not liberated Americans, Krutch thought, but paralyzed them. In that sense Henry Ford and Krutch agreed: Ford was certain that there was no need for cars other than the basic black Model T, and that advertising campaigns were a waste of money. But Ford finally succumbed to the competition from Olds, Chevrolet, and others. In 1927 the Model A appeared in a choice of colors.

Krutch's lament applied only peripherally to the everyday lives of the working class. Immigrants gave up their homeland and its customs, but they did not yearn for its repression or poverty. Ranchers and farmers may have wished for better times or the open range, but not the labor of the past. These people did not share in the excesses of choice that characterized American consumer culture because in most cases they had little money to spend beyond that needed for the bare necessities. Even those with a little extra cash tended to keep their business within the ethnic or racial enclaves in which they settled or were miles from large stores. For the working class, the rootlessness of the Depression era was not the malaise of the intellectual or cultural sort; it was that of poverty and homelessness, desperation and shame.

Yet Krutch had identified a critical philosophical problem for everyday life in the United States between 1915 and 1945. His questioning of the millenarian promise of science and technology harmonized with a nearly contemporaneous revelation from one of pure science's own. In 1927 German physicist Werner Heisenberg reasoned that the electrical and magnetic nature of the atom precluded any ultimate accurate measurement of subatomic particles. The tools of measurement were themselves electrical, and the act of measuring subatomic particles altered their velocity and energy level. In the uncertainty principle Heisenberg exposed what at the time was the chink in the armor of scientific exactitude and promise. There were limits after all. This realization did not necessarily stop efforts to measure and control the economy, world events, or the everyday uncertainties most Americans faced. Decisions about colors of bathroom fixtures or how to get food on the table generated anxiety, although the latter concern was clearly of greater elemental significance. Pollsters, statisticians, sociologists, and government bureaucrats continued their surveys of Americans rich and poor during the Depression, trying to predict behavior or solve the crisis. But the information unearthed and interpreted was transformed by the observer's equipment and angle of vision, just as Heisenberg had argued.

The coming of World War II might well be thought of as a "certain" uncertainty. Surely, as Hitler began to absorb and disembowel other nations and Mussolini strutted about, occasionally pistol-whipping (with some embarrassing difficulty) a disorganized ancient monarchy in Ethiopia, Americans thought that they would be "drawn into the conflict," which suggested that it might be a reluctant entry. But if entry into the war was inexorable for many, the outcome was uncertain, especially against adversaries such as the Axis powers. Simply returning alive or physically and mentally complete from battle was an uncertainty, as family members and participants in both wars attested.

Some readers will wonder about the selection of information and the people to be considered in this book. The concentration on uncertainty as an informing mode of discourse may omit too much for some; for others this may weight seemingly less important groups, events, or individuals at the expense of those traditionally considered most important in American history between 1915 and 1945. Analysis of everyday life for the mass of the population necessarily examines both those activities and phenomena that endure over long periods of time in a relatively unchanged state, and those that change quickly. The former, which often characterize life in a limited region among a relatively homogeneous class, are usually termed *traditional* by anthropologists. The latter are often geographically widespread among most of the population, and are usually termed *horizonal.* Both horizonal and traditional practices are examined to the extent possible within the limitations of this publication series.

This analysis is also informed by the conviction that the material base of society—houses, artifacts, the visual world—is a key signifier of a culture's ideas, identity, and intentions.[16] These elements of material culture can provide clues to the lives of people who ordinarily left no written evidence of their beliefs, thereby opening up some of the details of American working-class and middle-class existence, as well as those elements of the lives of the few who did leave some written records of their lives.

Sources of information about everyday life and the culture of ordinary Americans are varied, including first-person reminiscences, artifacts, fiction, popular entertainment forms, advertising, and prescriptive literature. Each form has its limitations: The oral interview is powerful yet suspect because of the accuracy of memory and the tendency to blend wished-for pasts with actual occurrence; artifacts are mute and could have had multiple meanings for their users; artifact survival may indicate that a thing was not used, whereas the common was often "used up" and destroyed; popular fiction and entertainment forms may be formulaic and at best indirectly measure cultural norms and desires; advertising reveals patterns of promotional pitches and hoped-for successes in the marketplace; prescriptive literature tells us what critics wanted people to do, not necessarily what they did. Taken together, however, these forms can be examined and interpreted to develop an analysis that, like the object reconstructed by an archaeologist, creates form from fragments. Other analysts with more and different information may construct other forms; this is my best construction.[17]

This volume will attempt to investigate basic human behaviors that constitute the nature of everyday life. The next chapter examines work for blue- and white-collar workers, including farmers and ranchers and those engaged in the extractive industries, as well as the work of the home—housework. Some discussion of the dangers of the workplace and the contentiousness of the working world will be included. The economic cataclysm of the 1930s and the voluntary and governmental efforts to alleviate suffering are the subject of Chapter 2, and the third chapter considers the architecture and environs of the home in both city and country, and how Americans furnished a family's needs.

Education and religion in both formal settings and in the home, the processes of raising a family, and those of growing up and finding a mate are the subject of Chapter 4. The fifth chapter investigates health, medicine, and science, the foods Americans ate, and the attempts to reform eating habits. Chapter 6 analyzes playing inside and outside the home—games, sports, vacations, and nightlife. The epilogue considers the meanings of both the 1030 World's Fair and the atomic bomb.

1

WORK, STRUGGLE, INTOLERANCE

HISTORIANS and economists argue about when the industrial age began in the United States, but it was certainly ongoing by the end of the Civil War in 1865, and a dominant force in the everyday lives of nearly all Americans by 1915. In some parts of the nation, notably the South and most of the Midwest and intermountain West, industrial production of goods was a less important part of the regional economy than in the Northeast and the cities of the upper Midwest such as Chicago, Detroit, or Grand Rapids. Finding work, enduring long hours, and the uncertainty of keeping a steady income dominated the lives of many and perhaps most of the working class, whether on the farm or the sea, or in the factory, the forest, or the mine. Ever present for many workers was the possibility of injury, either immediate and possibly fatal, or the gradual, insidious work-linked lung and other diseases. Those who worked most closely with the natural world—especially farmers, ranchers, fisherman, and loggers—also had to contend with the vagaries of rain, drought, sea changes, forest fires, and technological shifts that could wipe them out economically for a season or forever. The uncertainty of the workplace environment often provided much of the impetus for workers to organize to try to obtain a more secure, safer, and less demanding and demeaning work environment, and the three decades here considered were witness to furious and protracted strikes and lockouts, as well as a new form of labor resistance, the sit-down strike.

The world of work in the home remained the responsibility

of women and children (although many also worked in factory and field). Housework—cooking, cleaning, child care, laundry, and some religious and secular instruction—occupied the lives of all women except for the small minority wealthy enough to hire out all or parts of it. Only after 1915, when the mass production of small inexpensive electric motors made it possible for many consumers to obtain devices that truly reduced household labor, was there any sort of revolution in the household. Those with the money to hire out housework had a more difficult time doing so, since for many of the traditional domestic work force, factories were more appealing and better-paying options and some ethnic groups thought domestic service demeaning. To some extent the shrinking pool of willing domestic workers was supplemented by African-American women who moved north in the great migration of the post–World War I era; racial prejudice kept them from higher-paying jobs.

Office Work

EXPANSION

The number of white-collar jobs increased dramatically between 1915 and 1945, as the economy began to shift toward a service orientation and as management became a more important part of the business and government sectors. Work in offices in large and small business drew Americans into an environment that was more rewarding financially, cleaner, less dangerous, and less physically demanding than that of the factory, farm, or home. Expansion in the white-collar segment of the economy was responsible for most of the expansion of the middle class that occurred between 1915 and 1945. While the total number of gainfully employed people rose from 41.6 million to 48.8 million between 1920 and 1930, the number of people in the extractive industries declined from 12.2 million to 11.9 million workers. The number of manufacturing workers remained about the same throughout the period, at about 11 million. The middle-class occupations grew steadily, increasing from 11.5 million to 16.7 million.[1]

Few middle-class women worked outside the home in the first half of the twentieth century. Robert and Helen Lynd found that 2.5 percent of Muncie's middle-class married women did so between 1920 and 1925. Those women in "lace-collar" jobs with few exceptions worked as clerks, typists, and secretaries. The only professional jobs open to women in any significant numbers were those of teacher, social worker, and medical nurse. All were jobs derived from what had originally been women's tasks in the home. College teaching, however, remained the province of white males, as did all the other professions.

Some working-class men did enter the space of the white-collar world, if not the power structure. Errand boys, couriers, and clerks most often came from the white Anglo-Saxon or northern European working class, and they hoped, like Andrew Carnegie or the heroes of Horatio Alger novels, to get ahead with hard work or a stroke of luck, or both. As the American economy became more bureaucratic and service and sales oriented, the managerial and sales segments of the work force mushroomed. The great age of advertising began after World War I, and the duties of financial control, personnel management, and planning expanded as industries did. The irony in this growth was that as the numbers of workers not directly connected with the tangible production of goods increased, the office environment was being brought closer to the mechanistic world of the plant or factory. Time clocks were introduced to offices in about 1915, with assurances from advertisers that punctuality and late hours were the best indicators of efficient and "profitable" employees.

SCIENTIFIC MANAGEMENT AND THE IMPORTANCE OF APPEARANCE

Office work was also altered by the application of the principles of "scientific management." Frederick Taylor was the high priest of this crusade, which had first been applied to the study of workers' movements on assembly lines. Taylor expanded his research to the office, proposing that efficiency would be enhanced if employees did one job only, such as opening mail, carrying papers from one desk to another, accounting, or sales. The masterwork on the topic was Taylor's *Principles of Scientific Management* (1911).

The principles Taylor and others promulgated directly attacked the nineteenth-century office system of the somewhat independent clerk and his private office within the office, the locking rolltop desk with its myriad pigeonholes and drawers big enough for filing papers. Scientific managers termed this behavior wasteful and potentially dangerous, since clerks could mislay or hoard papers vital to the smooth running of the firm. By 1915 the rolltop desk was disappearing from larger urban offices, replaced by the flattop seven-drawer desk for midlevel executives and the three-drawer flattop for clerks and typists. Files were centralized for access by the entire office, and even the occupants of seven-drawer desks were urged not to keep papers. Runners routinely collected and filed papers throughout the day, and speed and ease of handling paperwork became an important measure of success in the offices of corporate America. Pigeonholes and privacy were gone and discouraged, and some offices had rules commanding strict silence during the work day to avoid "distracting" workers. Desktop neatness and cleanliness and the ability to find paperwork at a moment's notice were openly equated with productive work habits. The hierarchy of writing instruments recommended by the scientific managers reinforced status differences. All clerks were to use the same nib on dipping pens (which tied them to their desks to write and discouraged individuality). Mid- and high-level executives were permitted more freedom, since they could use fountain pens, which allowed them to move about and write presumably important words.[2]

The visual distinctions in desks also applied to desk chairs. Executives at the highest level earned upholstered chairs; those a level downward got caned seats and chairs that swiveled and tilted back like the padded ones of their superiors. Clerks and typists were issued wood saddle-seat chairs with slat backs. These generally could be rotated, and some provided flexibility for the back by means of a spring steel connecting band. Eventually steel replaced wood as the material in many pieces of

office furniture, allegedly because it was lighter and more dura-
ble, but it may have been popular because it transformed the
office into an environment that looked more like a factory.
Office machines—typewriters, addressing machines, mechanical accounting machines, and dictating machines—were in
widespread use by the 1920s and resembled industrial machines until the 1950s, when the concept of the most effective
office environment was altered to a more "modern," fashionable, and perhaps domestic scene, allegedly to attract more
women into the office labor force.

The obvious message of this revolution was that appearances
mattered as much as—and perhaps more than—did performance, since measuring the latter was problematical. In the
factory in which workers were paid on a piecework basis, measuring success was easy. In the factory in which workers were
paid on an hourly basis, it was punctuality and the surveillance
of foremen and others that was supposed to guarantee productivity. In the office, the amount of paper passed over a desk
might be one measure of worth, and for typists the number of
characters typed per hour (on typewriters equipped with counters) would work for supervisors obsessed with quantification.
But so much of the work of the office was intangible that the
superficial characteristics of dress, deference, collegiality (at the
proper times, and only then), and the appearance of one's desk
became important measures of worth. (Salesmen had the pressure of the easily quantified number and amount of sales, but
most of them worked on a commission basis, unlike office management workers.)

White-collar workers' socioeconomic aspirations and egos depended on their ability not only to maintain their material way
of life but also to advance to higher-paying jobs. But the chance
of moving up also carried with it the possibility of falling back,
and white-collar workers' anxiety levels were constantly in flux,
whatever their situation. Subjective judgments by superiors determined success and failure in the business office, and confor-
mity in nearly all aspects of work life became highly valued.
Typical "successful" middle-class male dress included the dark
business suit and tie. The suit was best if it was double-breasted

with wide lapels and padded shoulders. With the ideal slim-hipped body, the man so dressed appeared to be even broader in the shoulders than he was, thus sending the signal that he was an aggressive athletic type not to be trifled with. Fedoras and borsalinos, not boaters, were the required headgear for these men, and their hats covered hair slicked straight back with no part. The body as streamlined machine had no facial hair. That was either for the old-timers of the nineteenth century (who were allowed their beards because of the poor shaving technology of the day) or perhaps for "alien reds."

ADVERTISING AND WHITE-COLLAR ANXIETY

The best clues to the insecure and uncertain nature of middle-class office life can be found in the patterns of advertising of the age. Beginning in about 1915, advertising shows a new strategic pattern. Ads focused on consumers' alleged or feared failings and then demonstrated the ways in which the right vacuum cleaner, toothpaste, breakfast food, or automobile could eliminate the flaws. The older tactic of describing the appearance of the product, what it did, and how it worked gradually disappeared, replaced by the advice and solace of the new corporate "friend" who could help one get that promotion or, for women, that socially desirable invitation or healthy child that other parents had. Feelings of inferiority, noted J. Walter Thompson Company advertising executive William Esty in 1930, were "a valuable thing in advertising."[3]

The consumer rather than the product became the focus in ads, primarily because distinctions between the same genre of products were minimal. The new tone of these ads was that of the counselor, one who might somehow understand the trials and uncertainties of the urban, bureaucratic middle-class lives to which the goods were to be pitched. An army of personal advisors were invented, of which "Betty Crocker" was only the most famous. "Mary Hale Martin" worked for Libby; "Ruth Miller" for Odo-ro-no; "Dorothy Dix" for Lux soap; "Mary Pauline Callender" for Kotex; and many more fictional characters toiled for companies making all sorts of products. With all this help readily available, blame lay with the victim for failure.[4] The strategy did not ignore the working class, who constituted by far the largest single segment of the public, because the advertising standard-bearers accurately assessed that the dreams, aspirations, visions, and hopes of both workers and the middle class were substantially those of the latter.

To succeed in convincing consumers to buy newer and more goods—and to define themselves by the goods they could own—advertising executives had to overcome centuries-old Protestant values. Thrift, disciplined work, delayed gratification, and contentment with one's material lot had to be replaced with beliefs implicit in quickly acquired wealth, installment buying, immediate pleasure, and dissatisfaction with the goods one already owned. Guiltless discard of things that still worked or that could be fixed was necessary in this new calculus of consumption; otherwise the economy could not continue to expand. Important too, especially in the world of the office, was the implied power of new and expensive clothes and other accessories. To these ends, companies spent ever-increasing amounts on advertising throughout the 1920s, trying to convince consumers to spend and white-collar households in particular to adhere to standards of consumption that stressed the superficial. In 1914, American firms spent $682 million on advertising; in 1919 they spent $1.4 billion; and in 1929 nearly $3 billion was devoted to promotion of goods and services.[5]

The most common advertising appeals centered on guilt, status, and celebrity. Even Henry Ford, who detested the idea of spending money on what he considered nonproductive elements, finally in 1924 approved an ad campaign that promoted the Model A because of its stylish colors and alleged associations with the wealthy. Ford cars were depicted in front of estates and mansions, and the idea was to give a "look" or a sign that the car meant success. Celebrities were used more and more to offer testimonials for products. The testimonial was an old technique, dating to at least the last quarter of the nineteenth century, but the extent to which the celebrity's importance replaced that of the product was the new component in the twenties and thirties. Rudy Vallee, a popular singer of the era, was one of the chief pitchmen for Fleischmann's yeast, which by 1919 had begun a major campaign to convince Americans that they ought to eat two to three cakes of the stuff for health reasons.[6]

Magazines and the airwaves were filled with hawkers for cosmetics, foods, clothing fashions, and hygienic products, who indicated that social ostracism and shame were the prices for failure to use the product. The ads placed women in a situation full of responsibility but with little real authority. They were portrayed as ultimately responsible for their husbands' successes or failures. They were expected to understand clothing fashions and to make certain that their husbands were well dressed. Failure to make a good impression at the office because of fashion anachronism or ignorance was identified as a potentially critical factor for securing a promotion or a new job. Another element in the formula for success was the wife's knowledge and acquisition of the right soaps, sock garters, breakfast foods, laundry detergents, laxatives, and other goods that were essential for her husband to be "at his best" in the competitive world of business in which many worked and to which many aspired. With the exception of the hunting, fishing, mechanics, and other male-oriented popular magazines, nearly all advertisements for these goods were directed to women.

The world the ads portrayed had no problems that the right products could not solve. A new pharmacopoeia of "diseases" appeared: halitosis (bad breath), body odor ("b.o."), bromodosis (odiferous feet), homotosis (furniture in "bad taste"), acidosis (sour stomach), dandruff, constipation, and others. The victim never knew why he didn't get the girl or the job or the promotion; or why she never got asked to the best parties or her children were playing alone. Since even one's "best friends" often would not tell the offender of a problem, how could the aspirant know why good fortune seemed to be so elusive? There was no answer except to be safe. It was a little like what the eighteenth-century French philosopher Blaise Pascal had figured about the existence of God: It was certainly more intelligent to be safe than to risk damnation.[7]

In a menacing reference to Darwinian biological theory, advertisements stressed that in the struggle to survive and thrive in the capitalist system, the line between success and failure was thin and the competition keen and close. Failure to achieve the middle-class goals of material success was the individual's fault alone. But the relationship between appearance, effort, and material success could be altered at any given moment by forces that were unknown or out of control, adding constant uncertainty and anxiety to the equation. This paradox remained unresolved for the entire era, and is a basic element of middle-class corporate culture in the United States as the twentieth century closes.

In the early twentieth century, a culture of personality that emphasized appearance and "fitting in" emerged among the growing American middle class. This replaced the emphasis on morality and work discipline that had constituted the proper "character" identified in nineteenth-century advice books. This became a formulaic strategy both for domestic advisors invented by advertisers, such as General Mills' "Betty Crocker" (1924), and counselors such as Emily Post, who continued churning out successful etiquette books.

DISCOVERING THE MIDDLE CLASS

Americans wanted to be or thought themselves part of the middle class. In March 1939 George Gallup's poll of American class identification found that 88 percent of his sample thought themselves to be "middle class." When asked to define their "income class," 68 percent thought they were in the middle, 31 percent in the lower-income sector of the country, and but 1 percent considered themselves in the nation's upper income group. The discrepancy is explained by the responders' conviction that the hard times they were experiencing were temporary. The small percentage that thought themselves at the top of the pyramid probably reflected the declining fortunes of some and a reluctance to boast of their status when compared to those they knew with more money. The same poll found that 90 percent of those whose income put them in the middle class thought they belonged there, and that 75 percent of the rich identified with the middle class.[8] Perception was tricky, however. The 1940 census found that one-third of the population was living in poverty, and in 1934 the advertising trade journal *Advertising and Selling* had found that less than one-third of the population was living on more than $1,000 annually, a figure the magazine's editors established as the minimum amount needed to participate fully in a "consumer society."[9] Left out of the consumer society were most immigrants, American Indians, farmers, African-Americans, single women in the work force, and workers in the extractive industries and domestic service.

Laborers

EMPLOYMENT AND UNEMPLOYMENT

For the working class, employment was probably even more uncertain than it was for their white-collar colleagues, but for different reasons. Even in the boom times of the 1920s, roughly 10 percent of the work force was out of a job at any given time; about one-half the men and two-thirds of the women were unemployed for more than ten weeks. With little or no formal insurance to fall back upon other than limited state and municipal relief funds (usually in cooperation with private agencies such as the Red Cross) until the passage of the Federal Unemployment Relief Act in March 1933, unemployment meant very hard times.[10] In the Depression the conditions and the suffering were exacerbated beyond anything workers had encountered before.

Finding a job was a trying experience for many in the working class, especially immigrants. Workers interviewed by John Bodnar for his book *Workers' World* remembered how connections worked and how the rules were bent. For some the path was eased by a parent. Ray La Marca started work at the Fort Pitt Spring Company when he was sixteen, able to land a laborer's job because his father got it for him. Later, during the Depression, he paid an agency to get him a job at Union Switch and Signal. Stacia Treski, from Nanticoke, Pennsylvania, had a harder time. She remembered that "every morning you would make the rounds from one [of the three silk mills, the cigar factory, and the sewing mill] to another. You just stood there and maybe they would hire someone." Eventually she went to New York City to get a cleaning job after she married her husband, George. Dock worker Charles Oliver's experience was similar: "To get a job on the docks men would line up each day. The bosses would hand out numbers and give you slots." Steve Kika's father got him his first job as a water boy in the mills when he was thirteen in 1914. He worked a ten-hour day and commuted between Reading and Philadelphia.[11] Sometimes corruption greased the wheels of employment hunting. "There used to be lots of payoffs to foremen for jobs," according to John Sarnoski, a laborer in the coal mines in the 1920s. Louis Heim, son of a German-born Lutheran family, recalled that in the 1920s some men in the Bethlehem Steel plant "would give the boss money; some farmers would bring in potatoes, chickens, eggs [to get special treatment or a job] . . . until the union came in." Occasionally a service organization helped. Ray Czachowski got his first job through the Boys' Club in Pittsburgh.[12]

Loggers, farm workers, miners, and others who worked in geographically isolated occupations were sometimes recruited by men specifically hired to do so, but more often they drifted into the working area during the right season and hunted up jobs. Loggers' work depended on seasonal demands in the building trades, especially in the yellow pine forests of the Carolinas and in the big timber areas of California, Oregon, and Washington. Some farm laborers followed the combines northward in the Midwest, California, and the Palouse country in eastern Washington, working as shockers and loaders of grain sacks; some worked as fruit, vegetable, and nut pickers around the Great Lakes, in California, in Washington's Yakima Valley, and in other agricultural areas. In the South much of the cotton crop was planted, cared for, and harvested by tenant farmers and sharecroppers. For miners the work could be relatively continuous as long as the lodes held out: coal in Kentucky, West Virginia, and Pennsylvania; silver in Nevada and Colorado; iron in Minnesota; copper in Montana and Arizona; and oil in Pennsylvania, Texas, California, and Oklahoma. Kentucky miners, for example, had some relatively good times during most of the

1920s: $4 per shift of ten hours had been an attainable wage, but by 1931 the rate fell to between $1.50 and $2. And instead of five- or six-day weeks, the best weeks meant two or three days of work.[13]

The working class usually got their first jobs when they were young. Some factories and mines employed seven- or eight-year-olds. Family businesses and farms started children working as soon as they could. "I started washing dishes in the restaurant about five," recalled Robin Langston, who grew up in Hot Springs, Arkansas. "I'd get up on a Coca-Cola box to bend over the dish trough." Textile mills, particularly in the South, used the children to duck in and out of the small spaces between the whirring and whirling machines. Some states required that workers in heavy and dangerous industries be at least eighteen years old, but children often lied about their age to get a job. Tom Luketich had worked on farms and on road gangs for forty cents per hour, ten hours per day, three days per week until he was sixteen. Then he landed a place in a steel mill by claiming he was two years older. In 1929 Florence Nesko got her first job in a baseball cap factory when she was thirteen, and was paid $4 weekly. She soon quit and went to work for three times the money labeling metal polish bottles. Ray Czachowski's brother and sister both went to work when they were fifteen, his sister as an aide in a hospital and his brother as a laborer for a gardener.[14]

GETTING TO WORK

Most blue-collar workers walked or, if it was available, took mass transit to work. A 1934 survey of Pittsburgh workers revealed that 28 percent walked to work, 48.8 percent rode streetcars, 1.7 percent rode the commuter railways, and 20.3 percent drove cars to their jobs.[15] In most cities and suburbs public transportation was accessible to the working and middle classes, although in the mid-1930s as many as one-third of the working class lived near enough to the job to walk, or were so poor they had to do so.[16] Commuter railroads linked some suburbs to center cities, often stretching forty or fifty miles out from the city limits. Middle-class commuters who chose not to drive were the mainstay of the commuter rail lines. These rail lines continued to be popular until after 1945, when a combination of taxation and federal support for auto roadways and airports signaled a precipitous decline to near disappearance for the commuter rails. For intercity transit, the passenger railroad was still the most common form of transportation, and the most dependable. The majority of the African-Americans who made the great migration northward in the 1915–1945 period did so on the train, although Jim Crow practices confined them to the noisiest and most polluted cars (at the front), did not permit them to purchase food in transit, and prevented them from securing sleeper cars even if they had the money.

Approximately 40 percent of the eastern urban working class in the mid-1930s took the streetcar to work. But even as they were getting accustomed to or continuing a family tradition of getting up, dressing, grabbing breakfast, and hotfooting it to the streetcar, the routine was changing before their eyes, although they probably did not know it until word leaked out that the line was closing. One day the cars simply stopped coming, sometimes with no warning. In the 1920s and 1930s, many of the streetcar lines were going into bankruptcy or were being bought up by auto manufacturers, who closed them. Fare hikes were usually met with hostility and sometimes boycotts, and the rights to a line or to build a new one cost too much in graft and investment for the enterprise to be profitable for many businesspeople. The number of miles of streetcar track peaked at nearly 73,000 in 1917, but declined steadily until 1948, when 18,000 miles remained in service. General Motors bought up bankrupt streetcar lines, tore up the tracks, and replaced the streetcars with rubber-tired vehicles, much to the discomfiture of many of the riders. City planners viewed streetcars as old-fashioned and applauded such moves. The number of streetcar riders plummeted from an apex of 15.7 billion riders in 1923 to 8.3 billion riders in 1940. Electricity as a power source for transportation was being replaced—and with great speed in the 1920s—by the power of the gasoline engine. Rather than the transportation of people, electricity assumed a central role as illuminator (replacing oil-based kerosene) and communication medium.

AFRICAN-AMERICANS

Black workers were able to obtain some of the benefits of the industrial expansion and economic growth of the 1920s, especially when the United States entered World War I. Segregation in the Armed Forces discouraged black enlistment. At the outset of U.S. involvement most black leaders urged their followers to pull together with the white majority in hopes that the battlefield experience might alleviate the racism that was everywhere. But the military was as racist as the rest of society, and African-Americans were at first denied the opportunity to serve in battle. Their lot was to act as servants and mess boys, performing menial tasks. The Marines refused to induct African-Americans altogether. Only after pressure from the NAACP and other groups did the Army form black fighting regiments.[17]

The many working-class white men who joined in the crusade reduced the available pool of workers in many heavy industries. Chief among the industries affected was automobile manufacturing. Automakers were in a particularly difficult position because there had been an explosion in demand. In 1905 8,000 cars were registered, or about one for every 1,100 people. In ten years *2.3 million* autos were registered. By 1925 the number of registered cars had exploded to 17.5 million, and the curve continued upward, albeit at a much slower rate: 22.5 million in 1935, 25.7 million by 1945.[18]

Faced with this boom in demand and a depleted white male labor pool, automakers recruited black workers, especially in the South. Sometimes manufacturers worked deals with the railroads to provide free or discounted transportation northward. Throughout the South, black railroad porters left copies of black-owned newspapers that advocated migration to the north, such as the Pittsburgh *Courier* and the Chicago *Defender*. Although the tasks they were assigned in the factories and mills were predictably the hardest and lowest paying, and the unions often refused them membership, the pay was better. (Some union resentment was based on feelings in addition to or other than racial antagonism. African-Americans were sometimes brought in as strikebreakers, although they were not always aware of what they were walking into when they arrived at the job on the first day.) Black workers (primarily men) found work in the auto, steel, meat-packing, and garment industries, as well as in domestic service, teaching, and racial and neighborhood service industries such as newspapers, funeral homes, moving companies, barber and beauty shops, restaurants, and entertainment.[19]

In urban ethnic and racial enclaves, small businesses—greengrocers, butchers, barbers, shoemakers, and small general stores—provided special ethnic supplies and credit to neighborhoods, and spoke the language of the district. In the towns and villages scattered throughout the rural countryside the general store functioned as post office and supply depot for the necessities and niceties of life: They were small versions of the department stores that were beginning to take command of urban shopping. These operations taxed the owners with long hours, bookkeeping chores, unpaid bills and debts, and an assortment of physically demanding tasks, especially if they sold heavy goods such as furniture and agricultural supplies.

THE WORKPLACE EXPERIENCE

Members of ethnic and racial groups stuck together in the workplace. Stanley Brozek, born in 1910 of Polish immigrant parents, recalled that "the Irish had, when I was a youngster in the open hearth [steel mills], the first helper, second helpers, and most of the slaggers. . . . The Irish also predominated in the machine shop, and the Scotch, Irish, and English were roll turners." Similarly, Louis Smolinski remembered that "at the Edgar Thomson [steel] mill the maintenance department was mostly Irish people. . . . The Polish people dominated the foundry. And in the finishing department there was Polish, Slavish [sic], and colored, not too many colored."[20]

Life in the workplace for the industrial blue-collar worker was dangerous. There was virtually no regulation, no insurance, and no company fear of a lawsuit when someone was injured or killed. Louis Heim "got a job over [at the foundry]. They put me on chipping. But after two weeks the dust was so bad that my lungs were polluted. When I coughed, black dirt would come out." Blue Jenkins, an African-American man working as a grinder, recalled that "you'd have goggles on, naturally, because of the sparks flying, but when you'd take off your goggles, you'd just see the part where your goggles were and the rest of your face would be black and your lungs. You'd just spit up big clots of dirt." Amelia Brown (a pseudonym) just missed meeting her maker. After the Remington Arms plant where she worked closed down at the end of World War I, she tried to find work at another factory, but was unsuccessful because "they wasn't hiring any 'colored.' . . . And then about a month later someone made the mistake of lighting a cigarette and the place blew up and hundreds of people were killed."[21] *Survey* magazine reported in 1917 that 80 percent of New York City's street cleaners eventually suffered from some sort of job-related disability. Most of the maladies were either of lung diseases from the dust raised or bacterial infections from the offal in the streets.[22]

Unsafe working conditions and layoffs and terminations with little or no warning were not the only threats to the security and certainty of wage earners. Although strikes had been a prominent part of the American working scene since at least the last quarter of the nineteenth century, there was relative peace between capital and labor after World War I began. In large part this wartime domestic peace had been a result of the governmental controls imposed for the war effort. The White House had created the National War Labor Board, which heard more than 1,000 cases and issued decisions by which both labor and capital agreed to abide. President Woodrow Wilson had recognized the American Federation of Labor as a legitimate negotiating body, and for its part the conservative union distanced itself from the more militant International Workers of the World. The "Wobblies" were powerful, however, and gathered support all over the country and especially in the northwest. The AFL grew too, from 2.7 million members in 1916 to 4 million in 1919.

Struggles and Bias

POSTWAR STRIKES

One-eighth of the labor force had won the forty-eight hour week in 1915; one-half did by 1920. Real income rose for manufacturing workers and miners by 20 percent in the war years, and farm prices skyrocketed. But food prices more than doubled and clothing prices more than tripled. After the armistice, businessmen tried to roll back the concessions made to labor during the war, and workers strove to press their gains further. The Amalgamated Clothing Workers struck on November 22, four days after the armistice, seeking a 15 percent wage hike and a forty-four-hour week. They won. In January 1919 a general strike froze Seattle. The biggest strike in American history—365,000 steel workers—stopped that industry: miners, policemen, textile workers, and others also walked out.

Market fishers struck the industry in southern California in 1919; sardine fishermen stayed out and blocked the docks in sympathy. Woolen-mill workers struck the forty-nine American Woolen Company mills in New England in the same year, demanding a work week reduction from 54 to 48 hours with no reduction in pay. The company finally agreed to a work reduction but not the pay demand, and reserved the right to require overtime at one and one half the regular hourly rate. In Monessen, Pennsylvania, John Czelen remembered the "strikebreakers wearing guns . . . if you walked with another person, the coal and iron police would club you." That 1919 strike was lost; workers got their jobs back only when a priest or friend of management interceded for them. Many went back rather than lose the only equity they had—their house. Those in company-owned housing were not so fortunate. "We lived in Company houses which Pittsburgh Steel owned," Rose Popovich remembered. "We moved up on Walnut Street in 1919 when there was a steel strike. We had to move because they tore down the houses and built barracks for the scabs." Joe Rudiak's family was also "thrown out of the company house . . . after the steel strike came along."[23] By the end of the year more than 3,500 strikes, idling 4 million workers, had occurred. Unskilled workers lost most of their battles; the more conservative and smaller unions representing skilled workers succeeded more often, but not as completely as they had expected.

The tendency to blame "outside agitators," in this case social-ists and Communists, for internal problems is as old as the settle-ment of the United States. Puritan New Englanders simply ran troublemakers out of town, and many Americans began their ideological commitment to the nation with the assumption that the land and the people were virtuous, and thus internal divi-sion was the work of aliens. In the twentieth century, the gov-ernment, and in particular the newly formed General Intelli-gence Division of the attorney general's office (headed by young J. Edgar Hoover), exacerbated tensions already gripping the middle class and the wealthy by blaming the left for nearly every problem between labor and management. When Com-munist revolts toppled governments in Eastern Europe in 1919, it seemed to many that the United States was next.

Seeming proof of the imminent struggle on American soil came from both the Russians and a few American radicals. The Bolsheviks, after establishing the Third International in March 1919, called for worldwide revolution and working-class revolt. But that call was dwarfed in its effect by the May Day plot. Postal investigators discovered twenty bombs in the mails, in-tended for prominent capitalists such as John D. Rockefeller and federal officials such as Supreme Court Justice Oliver Wen-dell Holmes. Soon afterward eight devices were detonated in different cities across the United States. The witch hunt was on, not only for anarchists, but also for Communists and socialists.

Wobblies were beaten up and murdered. Their killers were routinely acquitted in 1919 and 1920, but the IWW partisans seldom got off. Federal agents arrested more than 1,000 Wob-blies, and many leaders got sentences of up to twenty-five years. The House of Representatives refused to seat Victor Berger in 1919 and 1920, after the Milwaukee socialist won both the general election and the subsequent special election. Only in 1922 did Berger, victorious again, get his seat.

THE PALMER RAIDS

In November 1919 Attorney General A. Mitchell Palmer began his move for the presidential nomination and the eradication of radicals. In twelve cities federal agents arrested 250 people. In a characterization of the radical "type," Palmer synthesized much of the American public's confusion of medicine, psychology, phrenology, and racial nationalism of the hate groups of the era. "Out of the sly and crafty eyes of many of them leap cupidity, cruelty, insanity, and crime; from their lopsided faces, sloping brows, and misshapen features may be recognized the unmistakable criminal types."[24] The equation of criminal behavior with appearance was also rooted in the nineteenth century, in the work of Italian penologist Cesare Lombroso, who claimed to have done enough research on criminals to identify a discernible "criminal type." Lombroso had many followers in late nineteenth- and early twentieth-century America, particularly after the nation's police and penal bureaucracies discovered a "crime wave" in the immediate post–World War I era. Many critics characterized crime and political militancy as equally dangerous to the social fabric, and discovered the attributes of the criminal and the radical among the immigrant working class, African-Americans, or, less commonly, the rural poor.[25]

The 1919 Palmer raids were a preface to the big roundup. On January 2, 1920, Palmer's agents arrested more than 4,000 people, and hauled in another 2,000 during the next six weeks. A banner headline in the Berkshire, Massachusetts, *Eagle* reported, "MORE THAN 450 ARRESTED IN 'RED RAIDS'; OVER HALF THE NUMBER WILL BE DEPORTED." The article described the raids and listed the number arrested in Massachusetts, New Hampshire, Rhode Island, and selected major cities across the country. The headline referred only to New England for its 450; New York and Brooklyn together accounted for that many "reds." Newspapers and average Americans applauded the raids, convinced that a massive conspiracy to overthrow the government was afoot. Half of the captured were not deported; 600 aliens were sent off and nearly all of the rest were freed in a few weeks.[26]

For immigrants, Jews, Catholics, and African-Americans, the Red Scare and other nativist outbursts also meant job discrimination and limited access to public and private facilities throughout the country. Joe Rudiak remembered that "craftsmen . . . had the good jobs. . . . There were no ethnic people working in these places, although they were craftsmen too. These people were even able to build violins and build furniture." He also recalled that "we only had a few blacks. They gave them the worst jobs, which paid little money. . . . It was sandblasting. If they sandblasted for six months then you had silicosis for the rest of your life." "When I first went into the mill," recalled Orville Rice, "they had them [African-Americans] down in the sewers. . . . They were never given . . . any opportunity . . . to rise above the level of laborer."[27]

Ray Czachowski had the discrimination shoved in his face. "I remember once going for a job at Pittsburgh Railways. . . . I put in an application, but as soon as they saw the 'ski' on the back, they tore it right up in front of me." Ethnic groups were biased against other outsiders as well as the WASP (White Anglo-Saxon Protestant) power structure that kept them out. During a big strike in Cokeburg, Pennsylvania, in the late 1920s, one union official characterized strikebreakers as "the colored people, and all them hillbillies . . . them Dagos [who] would fight."[28]

THE KU KLUX KLAN IS REBORN

The Palmer raids did not bring the attorney general the presidential nomination, but they lent an aura of legitimacy to some of the darker elements of the American psyche. In the midst of the Red Scare one of America's most renowned indigenous hate groups, the Ku Klux Klan, was reborn. The Klan was not simply racist, although that was a strong part of its appeal to many Americans. It was also vehemently and violently anti-union, anti-Semitic, anti-Catholic, anti-prostitution, anti-smoking, anti-dancing, anti-"petting," and anti-liquor. Some elements of the Klan opposed teaching evolution in the schools as well as women's suffrage. In 1918, for example, a strike at the shipbuilding yards in Mobile, Alabama, was broken up by Klansmen, and the strike's leader was abducted; in Birmingham the steelworkers' head man mysteriously "disappeared" shortly before a threatened strike.

The Klan grew slowly between 1915 and 1920. But as the Red Scare hysteria took hold, organized labor flexed its muscles, and African-Americans migrated north, the KKK gained a foothold in the countryside and in cities such as New York; Chicago; Omaha; Youngstown; Dallas; Los Angeles; Portland, Oregon; Portland, Maine; and Rochester, New York. Up to 4 million Americans donned the white robes and hoods and paid $10 and homage to local and regional officials of the "Invisible Empire." There were chapters at Harvard and Princeton as well as at colleges in the South. The Klan was weak in most of the rural Great Plains but powerful in the region's cities and throughout most of Ohio, Indiana, Illinois, the South, Oregon, and Colorado. After a spurt of growth in the early 1920s, the Klan began to decline after 1925. Although it was still a force to be reckoned with through the 1930s, the lynchings, floggings, and tar-and-featherings declined by World War II.

Other exclusionary groups, such as the Royal Riders of the Red Robe, "a real patriotic organization to all Canadians, Englishmen, and other White, Gentile Protestants," and the Junior Order of United American Mechanics (a group with nineteenth-century roots), also gathered followers in the early 1920s. The climate of opinion that made the Klan and other nativist groups so popular—and made D. W. Griffith's *The Birth of a Nation* a long-running hit for years after its initial release in 1915—also brought about the immigration restriction acts of the early 1920s. These laws set up quotas for immigrants, at first allowing no more than 3 percent of any nationality that had resided in the United States in 1910 to enter in any year. The 1921 law was altered in 1924, reducing the percentage to 2 percent of any nationality residing in the United States in 1890. Since immigration patterns began to change dramatically after 1890, the acts were clearly designed to keep out more of the "new immigrants" from southern Europe and eastern Europe.[29]

For African-Americans, the Klan and segregation meant an almost constant threat to their lives and livelihood. The Klan

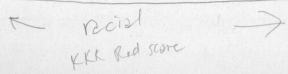

racial
KKK Red scare

had established an irrational vision of the purity of white womanhood, and the slightest insult to or innocent contact with a white woman could result in flogging, tarring, or lynching, the latter sometimes complete with genital mutilation and burning. Jews were harassed as Christ-killing duplicitous merchants and shysters; often their Friday night services were disrupted by roving bands of Klansmen shouting insults and occasionally breaking windows. Catholics were depicted as evil Popish conspirators, and were blamed for the assassination of three presidents. "Loose" women were warned out of town or flogged.

Consequently many African-Americans took off for the north and the relative safety of their own urban enclaves, as well as the protection of the Urban League and the National Association for the Advancement of Colored People. Jews banded together in urban residential areas and in their temples and organizations such as the Anti-Defamation League. Catholics kept a tight hold on group solidarity in their churches, their schools, and in groups such as the Knights of Columbus. Because of the immigration restriction acts, it was more difficult for newcomers to the United States to get the rest of their families to the New World, even if they had the money. Some families, separated because of war or with funds only to send part of the family over, never got back together.

HARD TIMES AND UNION POWER

Black farm workers struck in Arkansas in 1922. Tried for "conspiracy," they were acquitted. In general, the 1920s were hard times for laborers, organized and unorganized. Oil workers struck the Long Beach, California, depot (then the largest in the world) several times in the early 1920s. The sardine fishermen's union went on strike in 1923 to force the canneries to buy exclusively from union fishermen after post–World War I deflation cut dockside prices from $12 to $5 per ton. They failed, but the actions of both sides established a pattern of strikes and conflicts throughout the next two decades. Many strikes throughout the 1920s ended with workers going back to work (if at all) for nothing more—and sometimes less—than they had when they went out.[30]

Union membership declined from 5 million in 1921 to 3.5 million in 1929, and it bottomed out at 2.7 million workers in 1933. But by 1937 there were 4.5 million union members, many of them in the newly organized and powerful Congress of Industrial Organizations, which had rejected the older American Federation of Labor's craft and skilled worker orientation. Unemployment in the Depression motivated workers to take chances and join the unions, although not all the strikes were the fruit of national union organization. Grass-roots organization and consolidation often spurred action because when organizers showed up or employees revealed their intent to organize, they were usually fired and blacklisted, which meant they could not get work in other companies in the region. When Harlan County, Kentucky, coal miners struck in 1931 after their wages had been cut, mine owners blew up strikers' soup kitchens, kidnapped leaders of the strike, and killed organizers or ran them out of town. Left to starve while working or on strike, many found themselves "eating wild greens . . . such as . . . violet tops, wild onions, forget me not, wild lettuce and such weeds as cows eat, as a cow wont [sic] eat poison weeds."[31]

The first of the sit-down strikes—a new tactic—began in November 1935 at Goodyear Tire and Rubber in Akron, Ohio. In these confrontations workers reported to their jobs, and at a prearranged time simply stopped work and "sat down," refusing to leave the factory. By 1936 the sit-downs had spread to the other major rubber companies, and in 1937 almost 500,000 workers in the auto, shipbuilding, baking, and steel industries occupied plants. By May 1937 Detroit auto manufacturers had experienced 300 sit-down strikes, and there had been more than 900 since the first such action against them had occurred in November 1935. Writing in *Harper's* magazine in May 1937, Edward Levinson noted that "a news service recently counted up the twenty-four strikes of a single day and found that sixteen of them were of the sit-down variety. . . . The sit-down striker, like Ghandi, has a righteous feeling—the idea that he is the most peaceful of all strikers."[32] Gallup polls in 1937 found that 76 percent of the population favored the existence of unions, but a vast majority opposed the sit-down strike. In early 1937

67 percent of those polled thought that states should prohibit sit-downs; 57 percent thought the militia should be called out to end them; 67 percent thought that General Motors was correct in its refusal to negotiate with the sit-downers.

Strikes of all kinds often turned violent. Workers were killed throughout the country during the strike year of 1937. So obsessed with keeping out the United Auto Workers was Henry Ford that Richard Frankensteen and Walter Reuther, the union's two most important organizers, were savagely beaten by Ford's private police for distributing union literature on an overpass in front of the entrance to the River Rouge plant. Gallup's 1937 polls found that two-thirds of the surveyed thought Ford was within his rights and responsibilities to bar labor organization.[33]

Working-class Americans therefore faced difficult choices in their workday worlds. In dangerous environments with little or no insurance or security they nonetheless faced great obstacles from employers should they try organizing. After the Wagner Act (1935) made labor organizing somewhat safer and outlawed certain management practices and public opinion had come to support the principle of unionization and collective bargaining, there was still no guarantee that staying out of the workplace on strike would gain much. Workers at Pittsburgh Plate Glass stayed out fourteen weeks in 1937 for three cents an hour. (The company had offered a five-cent hourly raise initially, and the strikers finally took eight cents.)

Farming

NOSTALGIA AND REALITY

As risky and sometimes as unproductive as strikes were, industrial workers at least had their organizations to provide solidarity. Farmers and farm laborers had less than that. Agriculture occupied a precarious economic position and an exalted cultural position in the United States between 1915 and 1945. In film, on the radio, and in elite and mass literature the farm and farming continued to be a formulaic topic of reverence. City folk might ridicule the dirt farmer and the hayseed, but the movies and literature offered another message. Early thirties films such as *State Fair, The Life of Jimmy Dolan, Stranger's Return,* and *Our Daily Bread* celebrated the farm as it was beginning to blow away in the Midwest and farmers continued to suffer in their decade-long depression. Magazines such as Bernarr MacFadden's cheesecake and health-nut *Physical Culture,* as well as the more mainstream *Liberty* and *New York Evening Graphic,* pitched the healthful and otherwise salubrious countryside, without concentrating much on the labor of the farm. Elite culture had its rural proponents too. Twelve southern intellectuals, including Allen Tate, Robert Penn Warren, John Crowe Ransom, and Frank Owsley, made the case for their white conservative brand of agrarianism in a highbrow book of 1930, *I'll Take My Stand: The South and the Agrarian Tradition.*

But for almost all farmers and rural folk, reality was a somewhat different matter. Agriculture and agricultural life had undergone enormous changes by 1915. Owners of giant commercial farms, heavily capitalized and heavily indebted, banded together for promotional purposes with the aid of state agricultural departments. More rapid and more technologically sophisticated transportation systems promised and delivered fresh fruits all over the country all through the year if one had the money to pay the increased prices for California fruit in the midwinter East or Midwest. The attachment of the relatively small internal combustion engine to tractors transformed cultivation for the farmers who could afford the new machines. New, more compact machinery—midget combines, for example—harvested crops in relatively tiny forty-inch swaths, thereby opening up smaller parcels for production. At the same time the agribusiness farms of the Midwest and other parts of the country might be worked by large tractors and combines that swept up the grain in twenty-foot swaths. As one California wheat grower put it in the early 1940s: "We no longer raise wheat here, we manufacture it. . . . We are not husbandmen, we are not farmers. We are producing a product to sell."[34]

Science and technology also revolutionized the crops grown.

Hybridization had been a laboratory success in agriculture schools and seed company research and development departments for decades, but the first commercial raising of hybrid corn (more for fodder than as food on the grocery shelves) began in the 1920s. The new varieties were available in quantity by the early 1930s, and between 1935 and 1939 there was a fivefold increase in the number of acres of the newer varieties under cultivation. Twenty-five percent of all corn grown in 1939 was hybrid; 77 percent of the corn acreage in Iowa was hybrid in 1940.[35]

With its long growing season and plentiful fuel supplies, California became the most mechanized and productive agricultural area in the country. Irrigation projects doubled the acreage under cultivation in the Sacramento Valley between 1910 and 1920. Livestock production was altered and in some cases enhanced by the increasing use of artificial insemination for larger animals and incubation and scientifically mixed feeds for chickens. Fish meal feeds, a by-product of the California fishing industry, were 20 percent cheaper than meat scrap and grain feeds, and fowl grew faster on the protein-rich product. California chicken production reached 21 million annually by 1930, or roughly twice what it had been in 1920. In 1918, 20 percent of the baby chicks produced annually were hatched in incubators; by 1944, 85 percent came into the world under heat lamps. Ten thousand chick factories produced 1.6 billion chicks that, from 1918, could be sent to farmers through the mail.

A TALE OF WOE

The economics of farming, for all the enthusiasm in some quarters about hybrids, machinery, and artificial insemination, were for most farmers a tale of woe. There had been a brief flurry of farm prosperity during and immediately after World War I, but by the mid-1920s prices had collapsed, particularly for cotton and wheat. This deflation was not economy-wide, however. Wages increased for most of the middle and working classes, and prices for many manufactured goods increased. (Automobiles were the great exception. Ford cut the price of the Model T nearly every year.)

Farmers were unprepared for the sudden collapse in the early 1920s. Many had borrowed to expand land under cultivation to take advantage of the high prices, and, as in past agricultural expansions, some of the land was marginally productive. Editor Carey McWilliams's father was "a prosperous cattleman in northwest Colorado. In 1919, in the wake of World War I, the cattle market fell apart. From 1914 to 1918 western cattlemen had experienced a bonanza. They continued to expand. They thought it was going on forever. It didn't. They all went to the wall, including my father."[36] Truck farmers dealing in vegetables and fruits and who were near markets for their produce survived better and longer, but eventually everyone in the trade—even some of the big businesses—was hurt. The stock market crash and the ensuing Depression only made things worse.

ROLES AND CHORES

Work roles on smaller, family-held farms had similar patterns of responsibility, whether the household was a Wisconsin dairy farm, upstate New York fruit-belt operation, Iowa corn producer, or Texas cotton farm. Women generally cared for smaller domestic animals, the family garden, and the younger children; preserved foods; and did housework and some field work. Poorer farm women took in laundry to make ends meet. Men usually handled the large animals, fixed the farm machinery when it broke down, and did the plowing and planting. Everyone helped with the hoeing (weeding) and harvesting. Building and fence maintenance were usually male jobs.

Poorer farm men took part-time seasonal jobs in slow summer months. Southern tenant farmers and sharecroppers, for example, often went to cities such as Memphis, Birmingham, and Savannah for work, leaving women and children to handle all aspects of the farm. Many families made do only when one or occasionally both parents worked at other jobs. Herman Green worked at an industrial job full-time while he tried to make his poultry farm work in the late 1930s and early 1940s, and Maria Kresic remembered that she worked in the fields "just like a man" on her butcher father's farm near Steelton, Pennsylvania.

During his entire working life at Lebanon Valley Iron and Steel and later Bethlehem Steel, Jacob Light also ran his father's farm near Lebanon, Pennsylvania.[37]

The typical day for most farmers began as the sun came up (or before then in winter months). Before breakfast men and boys went out to the barns and stables to feed stock, and in some cases milk cows and collect eggs if the chickens were laying. Large animals were turned out to pasture in warmer months and in winter if the weather was not too severe. Meanwhile, women and girls set about making breakfast, which, if the family could afford it, usually consisted of eggs, meats—bacon, sausage, ham, or beefsteak—and some form of bread and coffee. After morning chores and breakfast, some farmers went off to their daytime jobs, while others began the daily routines of mucking out stables and barns or cleaning the droppings from fowl raised on wire (as opposed to free-running birds). Usually boys got stuck with cleaning stables, pig pens, and chicken coops as soon as they were old enough, although if the Y chromosome missed a family for a while or altogether, girls did their share of mucking. Dairy farmers had to move milk to cooling areas or take it to collection points for processing and packaging. A few had pasteurization units on the farm.

Many farmers grew much of the fodder for their stock, and therefore their year was punctuated by the annual rhythm of loading spreaders and manuring fields in late winter, plowing, disking, and planting in spring, cultivating in summer, and harvesting in the autumn, as well as haying whenever the fields were ready. Many farmers planted fields with alfalfa, timothy, or other feed grasses, so haying often required much of the work of a cash or fodder crop. In the evening, cows had to be brought back from pastures or let into barns if they knew enough to come home, and milking and cooling chores again were done, as was the egg collecting. Watching and ministering to sick animals was a critically important task, since one bad break or lapse could condemn a whole herd or flock. Sheep ranchers had additional annual tasks. Ewes had to be midwifed or both the mother and the lamb would perish. Shearing—

difficult, hot work—relieved the sheep of their wool, but not always without protest from the animal.

Farm life was different on the fruit farms of the East and West Coast states and the big cattle ranches of the middle and far West. Fruit farmers began the season in late winter when they had to prune their trees. Most of the summer's vertical growth, in part stimulated by the previous year's pruning, had to be removed, since most trees will not bear fruit on new growth. Weeding around trunks kept unwanted plants from taking precious moisture and soil nutrients and was a never-ending chore. Dusting the trees commenced with the first breaks of spring, and had to be done in ten- to fourteen-day intervals (except when the trees were in bloom) thereafter. Too much rain forced the conscientious fruit grower to spray more often, however, since it would wash away the insecticides before they did in the insects and molds. Harvesting brought out the entire family, machines if they were available, and a migrant work force. Packing, shipping, storing, and in some cases processing occupied many fruit growers. (Apple cider was one product that sometimes came from the home press, although most processing occurred at plants.)

The greatest change in the daily lives of workers in the beef cattle-raising industry had occurred before 1915, when the rail lines and the packers transformed the business. Railroads transported cattle to central slaughtering houses in the Midwest, and refrigerated railway cars made it possible to ship sides of beef to cities and towns all over the country. Railway shipping ended the cattle drives to Nebraska and other depots; as they disappeared and more of the range was fenced, most of the cow punchers who worked the herds vanished. A few men and fewer women were still needed to ride and mend fences and to brand and feed the animals at big spreads such as Wyoming's King Ranch, but scientific agriculture and better feeds required less open-range pasturage. The demands of the huge meatpacking firms and the new agriculture relegated the cowboy to a marginal role, akin to that of a farmhand, part-time carpenter, occasional blacksmith or farrier, and stable man.

ROVERS AND ROAMERS

Orb Gossett, born in Texas in about 1888, recalled those idealized times for reporter Kenneth Allsop in the 1960s:

> I've been a roving cowboy all my life. My father was a rancher in
> Throckmorton, Texas, and I began riding when I was eight. I worked
> for dozens of ranches, through Texas, Wyoming, South Dakota, and
> New Mexico, always moving on. The ranges were bigger then. They
> didn't have no corrals. You just rounded up the longhorns and roped
> 'em down by the fire for the summer branding. We'd brand 30,000
> calves a year. I thought I was tough and didn't wear a slicker.... I just
> toughed it out, sleeping in wet bedding and riding all night. . . . I
> carried a six-shooter, everyone did.[38]

Gossett and other cowboys like him were not migrant workers
in the sense that the pickers and harvesters who followed the
crops were. But many did move along on an annual basis, following a well-worked path up-country in the summers and back
down south as winter set in.

Those agricultural laborers who followed the harvests could
be found all over the country, and in increasing numbers as the
economic collapse of the 1930s dragged on. Wheat and corn
workers followed the combines northward from Texas in the
summer. They worked a swath 300 miles wide and 1,000 miles
long, from north Texas to the Canadian border. Max Naiman,
who eventually became a lawyer, "was a restless youth. In 1918,
at the tender age of fourteen, I shocked and thrashed grain. I
made three treks to the Western States. I worked the harvest
fields of the Dakotas, Montana, and so on. I used to ride the rods
and the blinds. . . . I met the Wobblies. I lived in [hobo] jungles."[39] Gangs of migrant harvesters followed the crop's ripen-
ing, moving by boxcar from area to area. Until 1925 combines
had not completely dominated the harvest, so there was still
much handwork in the collection of the grain. But workers
were being displaced by the machine: 33,000 fewer men were
needed in 1926 than in 1920, 150,000 fewer in 1933. Sleeping
in mobile vans and eating basic foods prepared by kitchen wagons, their days were long and difficult. Shockers gathered and

stacked the straw behind the combine as it cut and stripped the grain. The dust was thick and the work hot and unending. Workers had to keep up with the machines, becoming, like their analogs on the automobile or other assembly lines, part of the machine. Two hundred thousand men spent months without changing their clothes much or avoiding lice. Some left their families and small farms to earn the extra cash that they hoped would make the difference between holding on to and losing the family farm. Others just kept moving and hoped to get work in mines in Montana or the other Rocky Mountain states. In the 1920s and 1930s approximately 35,000 workers, some of them veterans of the season's wheat harvest, annually appeared in the Yakima Valley to pick Washington apples, cherries, and hops in the late autumn. Mexicans and Mexican-Americans picked beets in Colorado, cotton in Arizona, and fruits and vegetables in California, Oregon, and Washington. White and African-American migrants picked fruit and hops in New York and other Great Lakes states. When the harvest was complete, some turned southward toward home, and others just drifted.

CRISIS

In the 1930s, faced with a massive migration of down-and-out families and single people looking for work, food, and shelter, the Farm Security Administration built camps for migrant workers. In California these consisted of a wooden platform on which workers pitched a tent. (Tents could be rented for ten cents per day.) Most camps filled to their 300-family capacity in a short time. In Robertson, Texas, the FSA built a long low barracks with a shed roof for migrant workers. Each unit was two rooms deep with a small four-pane window on each side of the front door. All had electricity. On farms where migrant laborers had been employed for years, owners usually erected simple wooden structures to temporarily house the workers. Most of these sheds were devoid of electricity and plumbing, and as many as two dozen workers commonly crowded into buildings twelve feet square.

In a 1939 article on migrant labor conditions, journalist Frank

Taylor described the situation of Mexican fruit pickers in California. "The Mexicans pitched their tents in orchards or made camp in the rude summertime shelters. They picked the fruit, collected their wages, and faded over the horizon to the next crop."[40] Asian workers had been pickers in California in the early twentieth century, preceding the Mexicans, but many growers thought the Mexicans were better laborers. Undoubtedly long-standing race hatred of Asians influenced the growers' opinions, although bias against Hispanic workers was also intense.

Migrant laborers generally fared poorly in the eyes of their employers and local citizens. A 1939 Works Progress Administration report on cotton pickers in Arizona noted the conflict between the need for the laborers and the general public's distaste for them. "Arizona residents . . . dislike the cotton workers because of their poverty characteristics for which Arizona itself is at least partly responsible. Though Arizona's most valuable crop cannot be harvested without them, the migratory cotton pickers are everywhere regarded as pariahs."[41]

These attitudes helped make some migrant workers willing recruits for one of the few organizations that spoke for them— the International Workers of the World, or "Wobblies." Beginning their organizational work in about 1915, the IWW had enrolled more than 50,000 workers by 1918. Unabashedly sympathetic to socialism, they were hated and harassed throughout the nation, and especially where they were most powerful, in the Midwest and Northwest. "Pick-handle brigades" of residents in the Dakotas went after the "Wobbly menace" during the latter's campaign for better working conditions and pay for wheat shockers in 1917. So threatening were the Wobblies that the South Dakota *Morning Republican* urged "every member of the vigilante committee over twenty-one [to] supply himself with a reliable firearm. . . ."[42] The IWW did not shun violence either, and its attempt to organize farm workers and its embracing of Marxism were to many farmers a threat to their land, their investments, and their livelihood.

SHARECROPPERS AND TENANTS

Migrant laborers were less commonly employed in the Deep South. There tenancy and sharecropping were the most common means landowners used to control their property and have it worked with minimal investment. Each year landowners advanced their tenants money for seeds and other supplies. The tenant or sharecropper had to raise a crop, harvest it, and bring it in for weighing or other measuring in order to repay the debt and pay the rent for the land, house, and sometimes for farm equipment. The cycle usually kept the renter in debt, creating a virtual serfdom that bound families to the land. Because many black and white sharecroppers were illiterate, and landowners kept the books and had all the legal advantages, it was difficult to break out of the cycle. The tenants' small farmsteads often did not provide enough income for a family to survive, so many worked at other jobs—either as laborers on other farms or in local industry. If on the coast or near a waterway, some worked harvesting fish and shellfish for themselves and for market. Sharecropper Quincy Cusic worked a small farm in rural Maryland and the inlets and shores near his home, bringing in enough oysters, fish, and crabs to eventually buy his own land.[43]

In 1915 nearly two-thirds of the 5 million African-Americans in the United States lived in the rural South. In southern Maryland in 1910, only about one-fourth of the African-American heads of households owned land. In the South as a whole the figure was about the same. Land ownership among African-Americans had been increasing slowly in the region, from 179,418 in 1900 to 211,087 in 1910, but leveled off between 1910 and 1920, in part because many of the more than 1 million black people who moved northward between 1915 and 1928 had gone by 1920.[44]

Entire families worked the farms, almost always with horse- and mule-drawn equipment. In late winter or early spring, depending on weather conditions and regional folk wisdom, the crop was planted. All through the spring and early summer cotton had to be weeded and thinned, and insects warded off. Fieldwork eased off until the harvest in September, a cycle that afforded many men and women the opportunity to ply other trades. But picking was hard handwork, and backbreaking. Once gathered, the cotton bolls—full of seed—were taken to a gin, where the seeds were removed. Sometimes the gin owner or operator took some of the payment for the service in the form of seeds, which could be pressed into oil or used as a landscape base on the miniature golf courses that proliferated for a time after 1930.

Throughout the year women on these farms had to cook, clean, raise the children, and find other work, such as laundry and cleaning, to make money. Children gathered wood from the surrounding area, and no piece was too small to put aside for the wood pile. Bigger pieces had to be cut and split with axes and saws. Both boys and girls were required to tend the family garden and fruit trees, if there were any, and feed the family's livestock, which usually meant chickens and hogs. Chickens had to be penned each night or foxes, weasels, hawks, and skunks made short work of the birds or the eggs.

The harvest brought the duties of food preservation—drying and canning—and after that, butchering the hogs. After the first few frosts in the upper South, and by November in any case, neighbors assembled for the slaughter and cutting of the animals. Help was essential because hogs were heavy and awkward to handle, and they had no interest in becoming hams, roasts, chops, and bacon. This was to be the family's main source of meat for winter. Hams, sides, and shoulders were "salted down," or rubbed with a mixture of salt, black pepper, and sometimes cayenne pepper. If molasses or sugar were added, the meat was "sugar cured." Treated meats were laid on planks in a meat- or smokehouse for four to six weeks, and then hung to let the salt drip off. Then they were ready for the smoking process—several days over a slow-embered fire that had to be carefully and constantly tended. Children had to make certain there was enough of the right wood to smoke the meats, and sometimes were entrusted with keeping the fire at the proper smoking level. Once finished to the family's taste, the meat was hung from rafters in the house or in a "cooler" in the yard. As soon as they were old enough, boys fished and girls took over housework and child care.[45] Winters were occupied with house and farm repairs, other paid labor when it could be obtained, and staying warm.

But almost no sharecroppers and tenant farmers benefited when the price of wheat more than doubled between 1914 and 1917. The expansion of cultivation of the southern Great Plains began almost from the start of the European hostilities, and within five years acreage under plow had doubled from Kansas south. Much of the land was marginally productive, but the prices were high—and so was debt for machinery and land. Hoping to keep on making money to get out of debt, farmers kept the land in production even after the prices crashed in 1920 and 1921.

CLOUDS OF DUST

Rainfall was sporadic and geographically uneven between 1915 and 1929, but 1930 was an unusually dry year nearly everywhere in the Midwest. A wet summer came in 1931, good for production, if not for prices. But the drought came again in 1932. Sod that had been broken up after eons of existence as grassland, its root systems sliced and useless as a binder, became dust in 1933, 1934, and 1936. In early 1934 the wind began to pick up velocity and the soil. In April the first of the really big blows occurred—darkening the skies as the dust clouds passed. When it was over, drifts of soil had been rammed up against anything that would stop them. It killed chickens, wild birds, just about anything small that could not get away from it or hide. Dust was inside the tightest houses, on dishes, in cabinets, and inside drawers. "Before my husband was laid off we lived in a good home. It wasn't a brick house, but it wouldn't have made any difference. These storms, when they would hit, you had to clean house from attic to ground. Everything was covered in sand."[46] In mid-May the next blow occurred, but unlike the previous month's catastrophe the wind did not blow south from Colorado and Kansas; it went due east, all the way to and out into the Atlantic. The plains had come to New York, after a stop in Chicago that by most estimates had left about ten million or twelve million tons of dust on the city. Cattle developed lung conditions as if they had been West Virginia or Pennsylvania coal miners. A wet handkerchief tied over the mouth and nose was the required costume accessory during the storms. Between 1932 and 1940—when the rains finally returned in sufficient quantity to ameliorate the drought—parts of Kansas, Colorado, Oklahoma, Nebraska, and Texas simply blew away in what is probably the greatest ecological disaster the United States has yet experienced.

The drought and winds attacked the southern plains in 1933, but the northern plains suffered a different sort of catastrophe in that summer—grasshoppers. "One time we were driving up to Aberdeen [South Dakota]," recalled Ruth Loriks of Arlington, South Dakota. "It was during the grasshopper days in 1933. The sun was shining brightly when we left home. When we were about half way, it just turned dark. It was the grasshoppers that covered the sun."[47] In the Sacramento Valley in 1937 and 1938, the opposite ecological catastrophe bedeviled farmers: Huge floods washed out farms and displaced nearly 1,000 families, some of them escapees from the Oklahoma drought and dust.

The Dust Bowl launched thousands of families onto the road, heading for wherever they thought they could find work. California seemed like a good choice—the weather was warm and there was still dirt in which seed might grow. Called "Okies" and "Arkies" because Oklahoma and Arkansas were the origin of many of the down-and-outers, they were scorned by Californians. Editor Carey McWilliams relates, "Once I went into the foyer of this third-rate motion picture house in Bakersfield and I saw a sign: Negroes and Okies upstairs."[48] Eventually California and Los Angeles police (among others) stopped the migrants on the roads heading into the state, which had no idea how to handle such a massive migration. As one journalist put it, "It is as if the entire population of Cincinnati were to visit Cleveland and, once there, decide to remain indefinitely."[49] They competed for the migrant farm labor jobs that had previously gone to Mexican, Japanese, Chinese, African-American, and local white workers. There was resentment and violence on both sides.

Lumbering, Fishing, Mining

LOGGING

In the other major extractive industries—lumbering, mining, and fishing—weather played a much less prominent role, although storms and rough seas endangered fishermen, and hard rains could make life difficult and dangerous for loggers. Mud eased the sliding of logs but made footing treacherous and bogged down heavy equipment. Similarly, snow and ice in the northern forests could make the woods impassable but also could provide a smooth run to sledge the logs out of the forest.

In the South winter was less of a problem for loggers, and much of the work was done by African-American laborers. Life in the camps could be brutal and vicious, since owners or overseers did not adhere to labor contracts, which usually included some form of temporary housing and food. Louis Heim left Pennsylvania for North Carolina in 1913, when he was eighteen years old. There his uncle asked him to run a logging camp. "There were mostly colored fellows there. . . . I relied on these big colored fellows, who knew what to do. And I found out they were getting rotten meat to eat because the old overseer was getting a kickback. . . . I found a good butcher and got them good meat. And I didn't carry a gun and a bull whip."[50]

Logging was dangerous, hard physical labor. Stihl's gas powered chain saws were not mass-produced until the 1930s, and not used widely until after 1945, so axes and one- and two-man felling saws were the common tools. A falling tree sometimes went where it was inclined to go, regardless of sawing angles and driven wedges. The benign and peaceful tree trunk became a projectile of huge weight and momentum when it snapped off its cutting hinge. Sawn trees hung up on those still standing were called "widow-makers" for good reason.

During good times many loggers who were married spent their working days far away from their families, who lived in the small towns and hamlets that encircled and only occasionally penetrated the deep woods. Logging camps tended to be rough places with few women, with the exception of those who worked in saloons selling liquor or themselves.

MINING

This isolation was less common for married miners, even in the intermountain West. Because the veins of ore were not quickly mined out, towns grew up near the pits and shafts. Butte, Carson City, and other mining towns endured and prospered, sometimes wildly so for a time. Liquor and other diversions proliferated, and mining towns, like settlements around logging areas, were on the borders of civilization.

Mining had its own set of horrors, even if it was relatively unaffected by the weather. Working conditions were usually difficult beyond the comprehension of modern observers. Beneath the earth's surface it was always damp, sometimes wet, and always dangerous. Cave-ins were commonplace, in spite of massive support timbers. There was continuous pressure to produce more ore, and this often led to careless drilling, hammering, and blasting techniques. Air deficiencies, ventilation problems, and the threat of explosions were constant, especially since mining techniques produced dust that could easily ignite from the kerosene lamps that were used in most mines until well into the 1930s. Miners also faced the danger of gas explosions, since even the best geologists of the era could not be certain of the location or existence of pockets of natural gas. Miner Joe Sudol (born in 1905) remembered "walking over the hill and all those people who were killed were laid out. What a smell from the explosion that burned them people."[51]

Nearly all miners suffered from lung impairment, whether they were mining lead, copper, coal, silver, or other minerals. Stacia Treski's father lost four fingers in an accident in a coal mine, disabling him for the rest of his life. By 1931 he also had the dreaded black lung—a condition brought about by years of inhaling the coal dust that the mine company's power drills blasted out when face masks were unknown. "He had black lung so bad he could only walk up the stairs once a day to go to bed." Her husband also tried the mines, "but he would come home so wet, so black, coughing and everything, we looked for something else." Helen Serafim lost her father when "both he and his laborer were killed because of the falling in of the

Threshing machine, wheat truck, straw wagons and five men, Jackson, Michigan, Autumn 1940. (Arthur Siegel. *Courtesy Library of Congress.*)

Pouring a test mold while a blast furnace is being tapped, Pittsburgh, Pennsylvania, July 1938. (Arthur Rothstein. *Courtesy Library of Congress.*)

Migrant bean pickers, Seabrook farm, Bridgeton, New Jersey, July 1942. (John Collier. *Courtesy Library of Congress.*)

Mexican-American workers recruited and brought to Arkansas Valley, Colorado, to harvest sugar beets, ca. 1940. (*Courtesy Library of Congress.*)

Dust storm approaching, Lubbock, Texas, May 1939. (Russell Lee. *Courtesy Library of Congress.*)

Indian cowboys, Loomis, Washington, ca. 1915. (Herbert Gregg. *Courtesy Library of Congress.*)

Sawing down a tree, Grant County, Oregon, July 1942. (Russell Lee. *Courtesy Library of Congress.*)

Unloading salmon, Astoria, Oregon, September 1941. (Russell Lee. *Courtesy Library of Congress.*)

Renick and Gladski drilling to set a blast, Shenandoah, Pennsylvania, ca. 1938. (Sheldon Dick. *Courtesy Library of Congress.*)

Strikers guarding a window entrance to the Fisher Body plant, factory number three, Flint, Michigan, January or February 1937. (Sheldon Dick. *Courtesy Library of Congress.*)

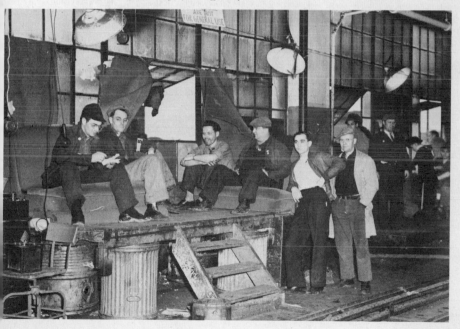

Road signs, Ducktown, Tennessee, September 1939. (Marion P. Wolcott. *Courtesy Library of Congress.*)

Ku Klux Klan parade, Springfield, Ohio, September 8, 1923. (*Courtesy Library of Congress*.)

Drinking fountain, Halifax, North Carolina, April 1938. (John Vachon. *Courtesy Library of Congress*.)

Scraping and softening a hide in an Indian fishing village, probably western Oregon, October 1939. (Dorothea Lange. *Courtesy Library of Congress.*)

Women aircraft workers finishing transparent bomber noses for fighter and reconnaissance planes at the Douglas Aircraft Company plant, Long Beach, California, 1942. (*Courtesy Library of Congress.*)

[mine] roof. . . . They brought him home in a black buggy with two black mules." In 1935 in Gauley Bridge, West Virginia, called the "village of the living dead," 476 of 2,000 miners had died of silicosis, and the air was thick with silica dust. Miners in the tunnel claimed that they could not see more than ten feet in front of them, so much silica dust was in the air.[52]

Miners commonly lived in company-owned housing and were expected to make their household purchases at the company-owned store, where prices were generally higher than the retail competition. In one Kentucky town in the 1930s, the houses were described as "dreary rows of dilapidated shacks, lacking even the most rudimentary sanitation; mud and scanty brown grass where gardens and streets might have been." Moreover, if purchases at the company store declined, miners usually got a note asking them what was wrong. "All the camp folks know that failure to increase purchases after receiving such a note may be punished by dismissal."[53]

FISHING

East Coast, Gulf of Mexico, and Great Lakes fisheries began to get strong competition from those on the Pacific coast in the early twentieth century. Before 1910 only 2 percent of the national harvest of fish was landed in the Pacific. The ocean had been considered too rough for the small wind-powered craft that hauled in most of the fish in the United States. Large motorized fishing craft altered the calculus of the fishing industry so that by 1915 Pacific fleets landing salmon, sardines, and tuna were beginning to change American fish-eating habits as well as livestock-feeding practices.

The Pacific was rich. One observer from Santa Cruz remembered that the schools of sardines offshore were so dense that the seabirds feeding on them formed an impenetrable black cloud just above the surface of the water.[54] Harvesting open-seas sardines, tuna, and salmon off California's huge coast soon enabled the state's fisheries to outproduce all other states. On any body of water, but especially on Pacific swells, landing nets loaded with fish (a grueling job by any account) was just the beginning of the labor of commercial fishing. Processing plants for canning food fish or transforming sardines and fish by-products into chicken feed employed thousands of workers yearly. By 1915 Californian A. P. Halfhill had developed the process of baking tuna in steam, then canning it. He toured the United States periodically into the 1920s promoting his "chicken of the sea" to Americans, who for a time preferred canned salmon to the newer canned tuna.[55] By 1925 Long Beach, San Diego, and Monterey dominated the California packing industry; Boston and its environs the Northeast; Baltimore the mid-Atlantic states; and Seattle and Portland the Northwest.

Portuguese immigrants were an important part of the New England fishing industry, plying the waters for cod, bluefish, and tuna. West Coast Azorean men abandoned the whaling industry for the abalone camps that Chinese fisherman had left, and trolled for albacore as soon as motorized fishing vessels made the practice reasonably safe. They were joined by Japanese-American fishermen in the tuna hunt: By 1920, two-thirds of the licensed fishers in San Pedro were Japanese. Japanese owned 50 percent of the 400 boats in the port, and landed 80 percent of the fish.[56]

Between 1915 and 1925, typical southern California fishing boats were big enough to hold but one day's catch, three crewmen, and a fifteen- to twenty-five-horsepower engine. Their catches went to the canneries in San Pedro and San Diego, where they were processed into the canned tuna and salmon Americans had begun to integrate into their diets by 1915. Many of the cannery workers lived in tuna or salmon company housing that, like company housing in most industries, was barely more than shelter: Absent from most were running water, electricity, and much space.

By the late 1920s Halfhill had made his point, and large-scale tuna fishing dominated the industry. Long boats between 95 and 125 feet long, powered by large diesel engines and with enough fuel storage area on board to enable the boats to travel up to 5,000 miles or thirty days without returning to port, revolutionized both the fishing industry and the lives of the crews. Refrigerated holds held up to 150 tons of tuna, and crew members increasingly found the cycles of their lives altered, from day-to-day trips (often long days in the summer) to sojourns at sea more akin to the great whaling voyages of the previous century. Like agricultural workers, some fishermen had been migrating annually for several years before the advent of the big tuna boats. Monterey fishermen had moved north to fish sardines in the summer or farther south to hunt tuna or mackerel, thereby spending weeks and even months away from home and family.

American fish processors, like their analogs in the wheat business, initially benefited from the outbreak of World War I. The hostilities in Europe effectively closed the North Sea to fishing, thereby eliminating one of the world's great sources of sardines, herring, and other food fish. The western hemisphere and parts of Europe not blockaded became markets for American fish and fish products. But after the war ended the market collapsed, especially for sardines. Prices returned to 1914 levels and canneries up and down the American coasts closed. A moderate recovery in the industry occurred after the recession in 1920 and 1921, and the Depression had less disastrous consequences for the fishermen and canners than it had for many other American workers. In part this was because the postwar crash was so severe, and in part the diversification of canners into fish meal livestock feed enabled them to make use of much of the 75 or 80 percent of the fish that had been wasted previously, particularly in the tuna industry. Total landings declined on the West Coast in 1930–1931, but increased for tuna and sardines (by 7 percent and 25 percent, respectively). Landings for the twelve other leading fish declined by an average of 19 percent.[57]

Working Women

IN FACTORIES AND MILLS

Men constituted the vast majority of American wage earners between 1915 and 1945. Nonetheless, between one-third and one-fourth of married working-class women worked outside the home, primarily in factories or as domestic servants. In *Middle-*

town, Robert and Helen Lynd's study of Muncie, Indiana, 55 of 124 working-class wives worked outside the home at some time between 1920 and 1924. In Cooperstown, New York, the International Cheese plant employed women for most of the packaging and the operation of the cheese presses, while men handled the unloading and managerial duties. Maria Kresic, a Slovenian butcher's daughter from Steelton, Pennsylvania, left school to work peeling potatoes for a neighbor for $1 weekly. One African-American woman, who preferred to use the pseudonym Amelia Brown, married in 1915 and almost immediately saw her husband go off to the north to get better-paying work. He had been making $1 per day at a "railroad shop" in Waycross, Georgia, but "people had started coming up North. They heard about how much money the people were making and they started the influx up there." In 1917 Brown followed her husband to the Sun Ship Company, where he worked in the boiler room. She got a job as a "water boy" that paid $4 per day.[58] Some women also found employment as salespeople in department stores, as well as in secretarial, clerical, and other "lace-collar" jobs. The number of women in clerical jobs surpassed the number of women in factory jobs by 1930.[59]

World War II opened, if only for four or five years, millions of jobs for women. Thousands entered the military: 140,000 in the Women's Army Corps (WACs); 100,000 in the Navy (WAVEs); 23,000 in the Marines; 14,000 in the Navy Nurse Corps; and 13,000 in the Coast Guard. They did not see combat, but replaced many men in noncombat jobs and performed traditional women's roles such as nursing. And they received equal pay for the jobs men had held.

More than 16 million men left for military service in World War II. Their disappearance from the work force and the simultaneous need for more production opened doors for women as never before. Nine million women were gainfully employed in 1940. Estimates of the total number of working women in the war years vary from 15 million to 19 million, depending on the way the labor force was measured and whether the total includes women who worked for only part of the time or for all of the time. Whatever the measure, for the first time in American history the number of married women in the work force outnumbered the number of single women bringing home wages. On a day-to-day basis this meant that more and more children had to be cared for by grandmothers, aunts, uncles, retirees, schools, churches, movie houses, or the streets. It thrust mothering responsibilities on older daughters among the white working class of modest means in a fashion previously known only to African-American and poorer working-class families. It was an economic hardship for many, since nonmilitary working women's wages in the early 1940s were 55 percent of men's in similar jobs. In 1939 women had done slightly better, getting 62 percent of men's pay for the same jobs.[60]

IN DOMESTIC SERVICE

The domestic service occupations were populated almost entirely by women, and after 1915 the number and percentage of domestic servants at work in American households declined steadily. Between 1910 and 1920 the ratio of servants per family in five northeastern cities was more than halved, from 79 per 1,000 families to 35 per 1,000 families. The ratio of domestic servants per family was even lower in rural areas. By 1930 the census revealed that 39 percent of "other domestic and personal service" workers were African-American and 18 percent were foreign-born. The trend during the 1930s was toward the servant force becoming increasingly African-American. By 1940, 46 percent of the force were black women. Immigrant women had abandoned domestic service for better-paying factory jobs or in-home work for which they could enlist their children or at least watch over them.[61]

The typical day of a servant was ten to twelve hours long, beginning at six A.M. Thus a woman without daughters who were old enough or a parent living in her home had to get out of bed at four or five A.M., prepare breakfast for her spouse and children, do someone else's housework for the rest of the day, come home, prepare food, clean her own rooms, and collapse. This earned her about $1 per day, in addition to transportation expenses that many but not all employers paid. It is no wonder that students of domestic service have found substantial evidence of tension existing between servants and those they served. Women were exhausted and the work was humiliating. Lone unemployed women often drifted, and some worked as prostitutes, staying away from what little poor relief there was (through private church organizations or settlement houses), both because of the humiliation they felt about their condition and because their would-be helpers often tied moral strings to relief.

HOUSEWORK AND HOUSEHOLD TECHNOLOGY

For the working class and most of the middle class, the unpaid labor of the household fell to women and children. Middle-class women were increasingly doing more of their own work, since the number of servants had declined and the cost of hiring them had increased, thereby taking many middle-class families out of the market for service. Even those women who worked full-time jobs outside of the home and those who did piecework in their homes still had nearly all the household chores left to them.

Historian Ruth Cowan estimates that between 1920 and 1940 the average middle-class woman at home worked between approximately forty-eight and sixty hours weekly. Her estimates are based in part on two comprehensive surveys conducted by the U.S. Agriculture Department in 1924–1925 and 1930–1931 of 1,500 rural and urban households.[62] The lengthy work week, in spite of the new electrically powered vacuum cleaners, washing machines, refrigerators, and, less commonly, dishwashers or garbage disposals, demonstrates the expansion of work expectations for middle-class women. More complex meals became fashionable status symbols, clothes were laundered more often, and increasing social pressure to wear more white clothing transformed the laundry process nearly as much as the electrically powered washing machine. The 1920s vogue for larger houses that reached the middle class just as domestic servants were getting rarer also meant more work.

Part of the calculus of household technological innovation and everyday working life for American houseworkers were the ideological constructs that altered the image of housework.

After World War I, the chore aspect of the job drew less attention than did the weight of responsibility for the family's well-being. Family health maintenance had been an important part of nineteenth-century prescriptive literature, but after World War I, housework became a measure—perhaps the most important measure—of a woman's personality, her affection for her family, and her responsibility to the nation. Love for the husband and children could be proven in the degree of whiteness in clothes and strength and stamina of the family. So important were these responsibilities that women were cautioned not to leave them to servants. Thus emerged the idea of housework as "different" work, labor that did not require any financial reward because of the returns of emotional fulfillment it brought. The long hours, unending repetition, difficult and unpleasant tasks, and the loneliness of the job were subsumed under the rubric of responsible motherhood.

The tasks could be made easier, however. That was the tactic of the appliance advertisers and dealers, especially those implying they could bring the houseworker a "mechanical servant." This enabled the literati of household advice in magazines and books to evade the central ironies of the servantless household for the expanding middle class. By 1920 what had been work for servants and the "lower orders" was endowed with a special new importance, like that of a craft and a profession. Institutes like that of *Good Housekeeping* magazine promoted this image. The actual physical labor of the home, at least for the middle class and the wealthy, was separated from the idea of the tasks, enabling these women to escape identification with a class of women they wished to avoid and many had hoped to supervise. By 1945 the common complaint in the mass media was not that the tasks were work, since machines allegedly took care of that, but that the job was a lonely one. "It is the isolation that hurts," wrote Mary Roche in the *New York Times Magazine* of June 10, 1945. "Why must this be done in solitary confinement?"[63]

Whatever the cultural and social meanings of housework, it was not machines alone that fundamentally altered the actual tasks. The compact electric motor—and the rapid expansion of the availability of electric power to consumers—were the agents of change for the houseworker. Only 8 percent of all American households were wired in 1907, but within five years that figure had doubled. By 1920 it had more than doubled again: 35 percent of all American homes had the new power. By 1941 the U.S. Bureau of Labor Statistics estimated that 80 percent of all American residences were wired.[64]

THE ELECTRICAL REVOLUTION

At first most homes were wired only for lights. In 1912 16 percent of the population lived in houses with electric lights; 63 percent did so in 1927. Electric lights replaced the dimmer, smelly, dirty, and dangerous open flame of kerosene lights, and appealed to Americans ever fearful of fire. They also eliminated cleaning lamp parts and snipping wicks, and cleaning the soot left by the lamps. By 1920, technological breakthroughs in the development of resistance coils for toasters, hot water pots, and hair-curling tools, as well as in the improvement of small electric motors for vacuum cleaners, washing machines, and refrigerators, spurred many homeowners to have additional wiring installed.

Between 1910 and 1920 one-piece electric-motor-driven vacuum cleaners, sewing machines, and clothes washers were on the market, and the price of electricity was falling. Electric mixers (essentially eggbeaters with motors) and food grinders could be had by the end of World War I. After 1915, refrigerators powered by a small electric motor integrated into the food storage component were popular. Only electric ranges were slow to take hold of middle-class consumers' imagination and wallets. Where natural gas was available, gas ranges remained far more popular than their electrical counterparts because they had been available with oven thermostats since 1915, when the American Stove Company introduced them. In the 1930s, when the reliable inexpensive electrostatic thermostat made electric cooking and baking more easily controlled, electric ranges captured a larger part of the market.

The middle and wealthy classes constituted almost the entire market for these appliances before World War II. Their enthusiasm for these machines relegated the eggbeater, the washboard, the wringer, the gas light, the kerosene light, the cast-iron pressing iron, the carpet beater, and the coal and wood cookstove to the attic, basement, secondhand store, summer cabin, hunting camp, or junk pile. For the working class these were still the tools of housework, and would remain so for most until after 1945.

Early twentieth-century appliances were expensive and designed for use by servants. They looked like smaller versions of the large industrial machines that performed similar functions. But by 1915, as the servant population dwindled, appliances took on a more furniturelike appearance, albeit with the streamlining associated with science, technology, and the "future." Advertisements stressed that the new machines were "mechanical servants," doing the work almost by themselves. Of course they were nothing like the automata the ads implied them to be: The myth of the mechanical servant was an effective strategy for those who never had servants or could not afford them. The wealthy still employed servants after World War I and the hired help used the machines.[65]

By 1920 running water was a standard convenience for most middle-class urban and suburban homes. On farms the hand pump in the kitchen and outside provided the water, because many rural homes had no electricity to run pumps until the mid-1930s. By 1930 hot and cold running water and self-fired hot water heaters were the norm for the urban middle class and wealthy.

Poorer Americans in cities and the country still did most of their housework the old way until after World War II. Washday meant heating a boiler full of water on a coal or wood range, rubbing clothes on a washboard, turning a hand wringer, and hanging clothes on a drying rack or clothesline. Rose Popovich, who did the laundry of twelve boarders, recalled that her family "didn't have no washing machines. We did it by hand. I used to stand on a box to reach the washboard so that I could do some socks. I was only six years old. . . . A woman in those days never thought of having laundry done without boiling it. You had these stoves with four plates on them and you burned wood and coal here. Then you heated your boiler up on top of the stove and you boiled those clothes."[66] The clutter and confusion and danger of washing in cramped working-class homes was captured by Margaret Byington in her 1910 study of Homestead, Pennsylvania. "The kitchen, perhaps fifteen by twelve feet, was steaming with vapor from a big wash tub set on a chair in the middle of the room. The mother was trying to wash and at the same time to keep the older of her two babies from tumbling into the tub of scalding water that was standing on the floor."[67]

The poor, who had little or no access to running water and very limited heating facilities, used commercial laundries when they could scrape the money together. These laundries provided a range of cleaning services, from "wet wash," which was picked up wet, carried home, and dried and ironed, to "finished," which included ironing and folding. Commercial launderers enjoyed their best days in the 1920s: Gross receipts in 1929 were twice those of 1919. The electric washer and iron, as well as the Depression, brought the laundry back to the house until a brief renascence of commercial laundering occurred during the economic boom that followed World War II.

Technology also altered the final step in laundry—ironing. Westinghouse began to promote its electric irons as early as 1909, stressing the relative ease of continuous ironing with an instrument far lighter than the cast-iron pressing gear of the past. Gone was the constant reheating of heavy irons on a hot stove or range; gone was the imprecise switching of irons to keep the temperature hot enough to press but cool enough to avoid scorching, since now thermostatic controls kept the heat at a more or less constant level. By the early 1940s the continuous rotation ironer, or "mangle" (perhaps so named because of what it might do to one's hands if caught), was on the market for those who wanted to be seated while pressing large linens, a task that may have been less common before the machine was mass-produced and inexpensive.

Keeping floors and carpets clean was a constant battle. Since most roads and driveways were dirt or stone, dust was continually blowing around from the action of the wind or vehicles. Horses remained an important source of transportation for many people until the end of the Depression, and therefore horse manure (which dried quickly and became dustlike because of the normal incomplete digestion of the animals) was an additional problem.

As in other appliances for the home, the compact electric motor created a new machine—the vacuum cleaner—out of an old form, the carpet sweeper. In 1915 the American Hoover Suction Sweeper Company began production of a machine that changed little in appearance for twenty years. An upright apparatus with a small motor mounted directly over the sweeping brushes, the Hoover looked industrial and was marketed as a tool that did a better job cleaning, but did not necessarily save time. Montgomery Ward introduced a cheap ($19.45) portable machine in 1917 in the company's catalog. By the mid-1930s manufacturers had hired industrial designers to repackage the essential machine in a shell that sent the signal of "new," "more efficient," and "better," although there were no technological alterations. Henry Dreyfuss redesigned the Hoover 150 in 1936, and the Hotpoint 500 was repackaged in 1937.

FOOD PREPARATION AND STORAGE

The machine and design revolutions of the era also transformed the kitchen and cooking. The triangle floor plan—in which the sink, range, and refrigerator were located on the points of a compact triangle—was popular in kitchen design by the 1920s and promised to save steps and work for those working in the kitchen. It had been promoted by, among others, reformer Christine Frederick in *The New Housekeeping* (1913) and *Household Engineering* (1920). The combination of base cabinets, wall cabinets, stainless steel or enameled steel surfaces, built in sinks, and, for the well-to-do, garbage disposals and dishwashers became a standard by which new kitchens were measured by 1940.

Gas and electric ranges helped change and lighten the labor of cooking, eliminating the tasks of hauling wood, tending a fire that was uneven and temperamental, removing ash, and cleaning up the mess that ash removal inevitably caused. But the poor and many rural Americans could not avoid these chores. Only 35 percent of the rural dwellers had electricity by 1940, and gas was still relatively scarce in the countryside. Although 14 million homes cooked with gas in 1930, 7.7 million still used coal or wood for fuel. Oil users numbered 6.4 million, and slightly less than 1 million used electricity.[68]

Cutting and chopping the raw materials and tending the cooking remained part of the cooking chores, unless the family used prepared foods. Commercially canned foods of all sorts, from the familiar fruits and vegetables to exotic tinned meats and shellfish, could be found on many grocers' shelves. Factory-made biscuits and quick cereals were boxed and available by 1915, as were the products of the "cereal barons" of Battle Creek, Michigan. Commercially baked bread was readily available in most of the country by 1930 and popular among the middle and upper classes, who had no inclination or time to bake. For those in the baking trade, the market for commercial bread meant a routine that got them out to work at about three or four in the morning, so that the first loaves would be ready for the shoppers, who expected fresh bread by seven. Middle-class, elite, and some working-class consumers demanded whiter and blander bread that was easier to store and more consistent in texture than "immigrant" fare. Like whiteness in clothing, whiteness in bread was a status symbol, a sign by which the middle class and the well-to-do distinguished themselves from the working class and to which many workers and their children aspired.

But not everyone who could buy the new goods wanted to, or thought that they were signs of high status or technological sophistication. Many immigrants sneered at those who bought the white stuff or the tin cans. A Croatian immigrant living in Iowa recalled in 1914:

> Foreign-born people used to make disparaging remarks about the native American women sitting in the shade fanning themselves while the foreign-born women sweated in their kitchens putting up hundreds of jars of beans, tomatoes, preserves, jellies, pickles, beets, fruits of all kinds. Instead of putting up vegetables, meats, etc. for the winter, the native Americans bought canned goods from the store. None of the foreign-born women would be caught dead with store bread on the table.[69]

Many Russian-born Jewish immigrants called white bread *"kvatch,"* a disparaging term for its gooey consistency. They preferred homemade or small bakery-made rye or dark pumpernickel. Maria Kresic "canned all my stuff," even though she worked full-time in a coat factory near Steelton, Pennsylvania. "Sometimes there was as high as 900 jars in the cellar. We even had peach trees and I canned my own fruit," as well as the vegetables from their garden.[70] Many farm families also preferred to process their own foods even if they could afford commercially canned goods. Home canning increased in volume among farmers after 1917, and the farm price crash of the immediate postwar era reinforced this tendency. A Maryland Agricultural Extension Department Survey in 1933 found that more than one-half of the farm population prepared all their canned goods. New Deal relief workers encouraged home canning as a way to better provide for the family during the Depression, much to the discomfort of commercial canners.

For the urban and suburban middle class and the wealthy, and for the poor who could not afford the time or the investment in canning jars and boilers, the food processing giants provided a cornucopia of products, often promoted as more convenient and safer than homemade goods. Technological and organizational revolutions made it possible for giant meat-packers such as Armour, Swift, and Wilson to dominate the tinned meat market; Washburn-Crosby and Pillsbury to reign over the flour world; Heinz, Campbell, and the California packers to take over the canned fruit and vegetable market; C. W. Post and W. K. Kellogg to climb to the top of the cereal pyramid; and Kraft and Borden to rope in huge segments of the dairy products industry.

The canners had a receptive audience in American households because storing fresh produce and meats was a vexing problem. In rural areas with no access to ice or no storage facilities, vegetable kilns (usually underground) or cellars were used for root crops, and cabbage pens protected it and other, similar vegetables from the ravages of frost. Vegetable cellars were either dug under a house or consisted of a hole into which the vegetables were put in layers separated by straw. If a spring was nearby, it provided storage for dairy products packaged in

crocks and in wooden boxes. In any case, the chances for contamination by bacteria were good, and many rural Americans
caught periodic diseases that affected their digestion and
drained their stamina when they most needed it.

For most urban Americans iceboxes were still the norm until
the end of World War II. Ice delivery men were still part of the
city scene, and struggling with blocks of ice and the water that
remained once it had done its work continued to be a part of
the day's routine. The smaller capacity of the icebox also required more daily shopping and the purchase of smaller quantities of perishables, thus denying the poor the economies of
quantity buying. Those without refrigerators often stored butter, cheese, and meats in basements, and thus sometimes ate
food that the modern palate would find unappealing and
spoiled.

But Americans with some money were able to take advantage of a revolution in home food storage that began in 1913
with the advent of the "Kelvinator"—refrigeration. Gustavus
Swift had been involved in the development of the refrigerated
railway car in the late nineteenth century, but the technology
of that era was that of large machines that worked well in
boxcars but took up too much room in the home. (The early
household behemoths were usually comprised of two units—
the food storage locker and a large compressor.) In 1916 the
Frigidaire Company was established, and within three years it
was bought by General Motors. In 1923 General Electric commissioned A. R. Stevenson to survey the competition in the
home refrigeration industry, and he found fifty-six different
companies selling machines for about $450. Since most Ameri-
cans earned less than $2,000 annually, refrigerators were still a
luxury item. Moreover, the early units were so unreliable—
leaky tubes, malfunctioning compressors, and broken thermostats and motors were the most common complaints—that electric companies figured that service calls for each unit occurred
about four times annually.

By 1930, however, General Electric and General Motors developed the "monitor top" models, which had a smaller motor in
a cylindrical cabinet atop the food storage cabinet. The GE

monitor top sold 50,000 units in 1929, and Henry Ford was presented with the one millionth produced in 1931. By 1941, 3.5 million refrigerators were produced, and prices had dropped to less than $200. Like the automobile, the refrigerator was one of the most popular and successful machines in American history, in spite of its high cost when compared to other large durable consumer goods. 1930 production figures were double those of 1929; production doubled again in 1931, and nearly doubled again in 1935.[71]

Technology altered Americans' activity in all areas of work—home, office, factory, forest, farm, mill, and mine—but it did little to ease uncertainty, and may have even exacerbated it. Housework chores and expectations expanded and women faced louder clamoring from critics in the popular media, the church, and government about their responsibilities for their families' success as breadwinners or students. Manufacturing and extractive industry workers confronted more powerful machines that were often more dangerous than older tools, not only because of their size and power but also because management swelled production demands to meet the potential of the tools, to pay off debt incurred acquiring them, and to garner more of the market. Office machinery made it possible to complete some clerical jobs more quickly, but the tools did not alleviate the work loads of secretaries, clerks, and stenographers. Salesmen and managers had telephones and automobiles at their disposal in order to pursue clients more vigorously, but also faced pressure to expand the geographic area in which they competed. New technology, moreover, could do nothing to prevent economic collapse.

The opportunity to work that drew working-class women out of the home had little appeal for the middle class and the wealthy. The newly available jobs were usually factory blue-collar work, and constituted a decline in status for women of means. The military did draw some women from the middle and wealthy classes, but volunteer work for nursing groups was more attractive to them, as it had been in World War I. Wartime job opportunities also stimulated a demographic shift of considerable proportions. Approximately 20 million Americans left home to find work somewhere else. The wartime need for massive production created jobs, but primarily in heavy manufacturing districts. Seven million left farms for cities; 2.5 million went in the other direction. Thirty-five states lost population during the war, but California grew by 2 million; 500,000 of the newcomers went to Los Angeles.

Two hundred thousand people moved to Detroit during the war. After considerable pressure from the federal government (and guaranteed high profits), the automobile industry converted to the manufacture of tanks and other armaments. Conversion of auto plants to tank and other military production slowed the rate of increase of car registration during World War II, but the onset of peace after 1945 shifted consumption into overdrive again. Car registrations had declined 10 percent immediately after the 1929 crash, but rebounded by 1937 to 89 percent of what they had been in 1929.[72] Prosperity returned in a wave of government spending and war production. Per capita income nearly tripled between 1940 and 1945. Stimulated by price supports and guarantees, good weather, new fertilizers, and more efficient mechanization, farm production shot up and farmers' cash income nearly quadrupled between 1940 and 1945. This bonanza did not help the small farmers much. Still hounded by Depression debts, with little capital to invest in new machines and fertilizers, most of the profits went to the big operators, who often bought up small farms as the residents took off for jobs in the cities.

2

CRASH

THE GREAT DEPRESSION—the longest and most severe economic crisis in American history—began with the collapse of the stock market in 1929. The immediate effects were felt by the relatively few individuals who had all their assets in stocks and who were heavily in debt to finance their gamble for big money. There were well-publicized suicides and much despair, but for the majority of Americans the crash was a distant event—at least in late 1929. Most had no money in the market; most had little or no excess cash to invest. Their day-to-day lives changed, to be sure—at first slowly, and within a year with increasing speed. For farmers and workers in some industries who had experienced hard times before the stock market plunge, life became more difficult. Many in the middle class, riding high on the expansion of the white-collar sector that occurred in the 1920s, had their egos and their dreams bruised or shattered. They lost their jobs, their newly won status, and their pride. In the end, the Depression left, as historian Caroline Bird put it, an "invisible scar" of shame and fear on millions.

Some of the wealthy not only weathered the Depression but profited from it if they had been conservative investors. William Benton, a prominent business executive and senator from Connecticut, described a graph of his firm's fortunes and that of the stock market as "A cross. As the stock market plummeted into oblivion, Benton and Bowles went up into stardom. When I sold the agency in 1935, it was the single biggest office in the world."[1]

71

The Crash

CAUSES

There was no single cause of the Depression or explanation for its magnitude. It came about and stayed around because of a confluence of powerful currents. Throughout the 1920s, and in particular in the early years of the decade, the agriculture, manufacturing, and construction sectors of the economy were growing, but in many cases they did so in part to keep up with the debt payments many had incurred during the boom years of World War I. As manufacturing and agriculture continued to generate ever-growing supplies of foods and consumer goods, overproduction—a great fear of some economic prognosticators—began to encounter underconsumption in both the export and domestic marketplaces. Between 1915 and 1929 wages increased for the working population as a whole, but did so unevenly and more slowly than did production. The wealthiest 1 percent of the American populace enjoyed a 75 percent increase in their incomes in the 1920s, a jump that accounted for much of the 9 percent across-the-board increase in wages during the decade. As a result of this selective prosperity, workers were increasingly unable to purchase many of the goods they produced and had been counted upon to consume.

The business sector had, like the distribution of wealth in the country, become economically top-heavy. The 200 richest corporations (excluding finance operations) controlled nearly 50 percent of the corporate wealth of the United States. Moreover, their positions were often built upon enormous debt; when the financial crisis came in October 1929, it tore out the underpinnings of many of these enterprises. The unregulated operation of the stock market tempted many large and small companies and investors to try to increase their assets by making a quick "killing" on Wall Street. Since it was possible to buy stocks with virtually no money other than loans, many buyers borrowed heavily to cover the purchase price of stocks, and then succeeded in using the stocks as collateral to buy more, or, in some cases, to finance the original loan. When stocks began to decline, banks, finance companies, and broker-age houses collapsed. Americans who had trusted banks with their savings "ran" to collect their cash, only to find that there was no money—some or all of their savings had simply van-ished forever.

The severity of the crisis in the United States was exacerbated by the instability of the European economy, as well as American tariff policies. In the early 1920s, American investment in Europe helped stimulate recovery from the depredations of World War I. European demand for American goods, especially nonagricultural products, was strong after the war, and there-fore deflected concern about overproduction. But American investment declined as the decade wore on, as many corpora-tions and investors began to favor the stock market as a vehicle to increase their wealth. Moreover, European demand slack-ened as manufacturing in England and on the Continent righted itself after the war, and American tariffs limited the sales of European goods. Unable to sell their goods in the United States, European nations found it increasingly difficult to raise the money to repay their war debts. The European economy began to crumble in the late 1920s, but it was the American collapse in October 1929 that ultimately ensured a long and painful worldwide depression.

MAGNITUDE

The economic free-fall that occurred in the United States was overwhelming in its magnitude and in its breadth. In Septem-ber 1929, a single share of Montgomery Ward stock sold for $138; within three years $4 could buy it. The *New York Times* industrial average of selected stocks fell from 452 to 58. The nation's gross national product, the total value of all goods and services produced, fell from $104.4 billion in 1929 to $74.2 billion in 1932. The former figure equaled $857 for every Amer-ican; the latter $590 for each person. Within three years of the crash, 75 percent of the value of all securities—$90 billion—had vanished.

Wages were slashed—20 percent in manufacturing and 23 percent in mining within three years—but prices fell only 16 percent. In 1929 the average annual wage in industrial labor was slightly less than $1,550; by 1933 it had dropped by one-third. In the same year, construction workers took home half what they had made in 1929. Orville Rice recalled that "when the depression come in, they reduced our wages without tellin' us any reason why. No negotiation at all. They just knocked us down to thirty-five cents an hour."[2] Millions were fired or laid off. News that the United States was no longer the land of opportunity spread quickly, and with dramatic effect. For each immigrant entering the United States in 1932, three went back to the old country.

Prices and demand for products of the extractive industries nose-dived. West Coast sardine fishermen had gotten a steady $11 per ton of fish through the 1920s; by 1932 they could command only $6 per ton.[3] As the Depression in the agricultural sector worsened, demand for fish-meal fertilizers and livestock foods—a major revenue source for sardine processors—dried up. Prices for farm products were so low that farmers lost money by raising livestock, crops, or producing eggs and milk. In 1932 and 1933 many organized and dumped milk and slaughtered livestock to raise prices. Oscar Heline, a farmer from Marcus, Iowa, remembered that "people were determined to withhold produce from the market. . . . If they would dump the produce they would force the market to a higher level. The farmers would man the highways, and cream cans were emptied in ditches and eggs dumped out. They burned the trestle bridge, so trains wouldn't be able to haul grain." Carey McWilliams, editor of *The Nation,* traveled through California and "saw all kinds of crops being destroyed. . . . They would throw citrus fruits [in dumps] and spray them with tar and chemicals."[4] Mines closed down all through Pennsylvania's coal regions, Minnesota's iron areas, and the ore-rich Rocky Mountains.

Federal Department of Labor statistics reveal that in 1929 3.1 percent (1.5 million) were unemployed. The number rose to 4.25 million (8.8 percent) in the next year, and moved upward to 8 million (16.1 percent) in 1931. In 1932, an election year and an almost certain loss for the Republican Herbert

Hoover, the spiral continued its rise: 12 million (24 percent) were out of work and millions more became unwilling part-time employees. There were conflicting estimates of the number of unemployed, but it is safe to assume that between one-quarter and one-third of the work force was without any work. Another one-quarter to one-third were part-time workers who wanted full-time work or were employed at jobs below their skill level and below levels at which they had formerly worked. Black skilled workers were unemployed at twice the rate of their white counterparts; women were laid off before white men.

In 1936, even after "recovery" measures had been adopted, 9 million were still out of work. By 1939 about 8 million were unemployed, representing 17 percent of the work force. Government service and management jobs had actually increased by 1 million between 1929 and 1939, but there were 1.3 million fewer construction jobs than there had been when the crash occurred. In 1932, 64 percent of all New York City construction workers were out of work. In October 1933, 1.25 million of the city's inhabitants were on relief, and an estimated 1 million others were eligible.

As the construction industry collapsed, so too did the lumber industry. Louisiana, which had led the southern states in lumber production in the 1920s, produced less than 1 billion board feet of lumber in 1935; at its zenith in the mid 1920s, the state's lumbermen were producing more than 4 billion board feet annually. The other Deep South states had been consistently turning out approximately 2 billion board feet of lumber yearly in the 1920s; they too produced less than 1 billion board feet in 1935. In the Pacific Northwest states—California, Oregon, and Washington—lumber production declined by two-thirds between 1925 and 1932. Production in Washington fell from 7.5 billion board feet in the mid-1920s to slightly more than 2 billion board feet in 1931 and 1932.[5] Demand for pulp also fell, as magazines and newspapers folded, both from the impact of the radio and the general economic crisis.

Thousands spent the nights under bridges and overpasses, in culverts if they were dry, and anywhere else they could get away from the weather. In 1938, 17,000 slept in church and government shelters on an average night. Others, primarily single men but also some women and families, lived in shacks, sheds, or dugouts built of anything they could find—cardboard boxes, tar paper, scrap metal. Groups of these abodes were derisively called "Hoovervilles," indicating where much of the blame for the Depression was placed. In the basement rubble of a section of buildings razed for a proposed new freight terminal for the New York Central Railroad, writer Jeannette Griffith in 1931 encountered "a mammoth packing box and carefully stepping feet . . . walking toward me. . . . The box bounced to earth near a partly open cellar work. A man quietly set to work to dig-in his box. The lot at first glance looked empty . . . but here and there thin columns of smoke rose from pipes sticking through the uneven ground. I had to watch my step not to walk on ground-level roofs." Oklahoman Peggy Terry remembered "all these people living in old, rusted out car bodies. . . . There were people living in shacks made of orange crates. One family with a whole lot of kids were living in a piano box. This wasn't just a little section, this was maybe ten-miles wide and ten-miles long."[6]

Residential construction declined precipitously. In 1925, 937,000 units were built or begun; in 1933, that number was 93,000. Between 1928 and 1933 new building starts dropped 95 percent and home repair expenditures fell 90 percent. In 1926, 68,000 foreclosures had occurred, many of them in the rural areas hardest hit by the economic downturn in agriculture. In 1930, 150,000 lost their homes; in 1931, 200,000 did so; and in 1932, one-quarter of a million foreclosures occurred. In the spring of 1933 banks foreclosed on more than 1,000 home mortgages daily. Ray Czachowski's father lost his house right after the crash; his mortgage from the "Polish Falcons on the South Side" of Pittsburgh was called in. He did not have the cash to pay off the remaining principal, and he could not find another lender.

After the crash, banks foreclosed on farmers' loans with increasing frequency throughout the country. Iowan Harry Terrell's uncle lost his 320-acre farm " 'Cause they foreclosed the

mortgage." They held auctions of a family's equipment, livestock, land, farm buildings, and house to generate cash to pay off
the debt, but after a few years neighbors sometimes banded
together to fight off the banks. Farmers "got the idea of spending
twenty-five cents for a horse . . . ten cents for a plow. And when
it was all over, they'd all give it back to him [the indebted farm-
er]. It was legal and anybody that bid against that thing . . . they
would be dealt with seriously, as it were."[7] More than one
banker changed his mind about foreclosure when shown a
noose hanging from a barn rafter or a bucket of tar. Bonnie
Parker and Clyde Barrow probably escaped the police as long
as they did because they allegedly destroyed mortgage docu-
ments when they relieved banks of their cash.

One-half of all home mortgages in America were in default
by the end of 1933. The value of real estate plummeted: A
$5,000 house in 1926 cost about $3,300 in 1932.[8] Out West a few
enterprising families without homes but with a car discovered
that for $2 they could secure a season-long camping pass in a
national park. In Yosemite, Yellowstone, and other parks, rangers encountered families trying to make the best of a forced
"vacation."

In cities and other industrial areas the Depression crushed
many of the working class, especially those who constantly lived
on the edge of insolvency. Entire factories closed down. In
Muncie, Indiana, sociologists Robert and Helen Lynd found
that 25 of the city's 106 factories operating in 1929 were closed
in 1933, and others were open only sporadically. Joe Rudiak,
who worked in Lyndora, Pennsylvania, building flatcars, was
making good money in 1929 more than $4 per day until
"about two, three weeks after that [the crash] the place closed
down. Everybody lost their jobs. So there was no work. I didn't
get back to work up at the plant again up till about 1936—'35
maybe." Thirty canneries were processing California sardines
in 1929; twenty were left in 1932.[9]

HOME LIFE; HOBOES

Such conditions—poverty, hopelessness, uncertainty—had far-
reaching effects on Americans' day-to-day lives. The marriage

rate declined steadily: by 5.9 percent in 1930–1931; by 7.5 percent in 1931–1932. Joe Rudiak played in a band that made the wedding circuit, and he found that "even the weddings had slowed up. The churches were falling apart, the social activities and everything. So we went hungry with the rest of them." He and his fellow musicians had counted on the food at the weddings to supplement their diet.[10] Those who had children had fewer of them. In 1915 the birth rate per 1,000 Americans was 25; in 1933 it was 6.5.

Consumer spending patterns reflected the hard times. In 1933, jewelry sales in Muncie had declined 85 percent from those of 1926. The volume of business in grocery stores declined by 50 percent; dime stores lost 33 percent of their sales volume, retail men's clothing sales declined by two-thirds, and women's retail clothing sales fell by 50 percent. All retail trade declined 39 percent.[11] Spending for food decreased dramatically, and the acquisition of food was a major struggle for the poor. Many scraped by on stale bread and whatever they could forage or grow. George Treski, who like many other workers was getting at most two days of work weekly, worked the family farm. "We would kill hogs, calves. You raised your own potatoes and cabbage."[12] Others were not so fortunate. Many city dwellers were reduced to ransacking garbage cans. Children especially suffered. Sixty-five percent of the African-American children in Harlem suffered from malnutrition during the 1930s, and the American Friends Service Committee reported that in one school in a mining region that straddled Kentucky, West Virginia, and southern Illinois, 99 percent of the children were underweight.

Those who did manage to fend off the bankers and other lenders, and who found some sort of food, faced another trial—fuel for warmth and for cooking. Most foraged firewood from forests if they were nearby. Many workers around Steelton, Pennsylvania, did so in the early Depression years until "people got greedy and even took the planks from a bridge on the [company's] property." Unemployed coal miners dug coal in abandoned mines, hauled it out, and distributed it first to widows and then to those who dug it, in alphabetical order.[13]

Domestic violence and child abuse increased as men found it difficult to cope with worklessness and families scrapped over money. Men and boys (and some women and girls) ran away from home in ever-increasing numbers. Labor organizer Larry Van Dusen admitted, "My father led a rough life: he drank. During the Depression, he drank more. There was more conflict in the home. A lot of fathers—mine among them—had a habit of taking off. . . . And there was always the Saturday night ordeal as to whether or not the old man would get home with his paycheck." More than 25,000 "whole entire families disappeared . . . just drifted," not only to another place as the "Okies" did when they headed for California, but continually.[14] Hundreds of thousands of single men and women, young and old, married and single, rode the rails, trying to find work, swiping a meal, doing odd jobs here and there, sleeping where they could. Many children and young adults left home because they could not get food or work there. Joe Morrison, a coal miner and steelworker from southwestern Indiana, recalled that "In '30 and '31, you'd see freight trains, you'd see hundreds of kids, young kids, lots of 'em, just wandering all over the country. . . . The one thing that was unique was to see women riding freight trains. . . . Dressed in slacks or dressed like men, you could hardly tell 'em." In Los Angeles, one of the hobo and hitchhiker meccas because of the climate, 200,000 adolescents were housed in free flophouses and midnight missions in 1932. In the same year, in selected city shelters in Phoenix; El Paso; Oklahoma City; Washington, D.C.; Ogden, Utah; and Memphis, 15 to 27 percent of the hobos were under twenty one. Two hundred thousand people rode the rails of the Missouri Pacific alone in 1931. Thirteen thousand had done so in 1929.[15]

Most of the hobo "jungles"—encampments near rail lines and water in which fires could be built without harassment from the local police—were populated by single men. During the Depression some in California and Oregon were as much as a mile long. Those women who rode the rails alone or with other women were constantly threatened with rape or the demand of sex for food and shelter in hobo culture. Few ventured into the "jungles."

Not everyone who left home took to the trains. Many of the families that left the Midwest did so in automobiles loaded with all that they had or could attach to the vehicle. Others walked. But when they got to their destination they were not necessarily welcome. Los Angeles police stopped migrants with roadblocks and turned them back. One hundred twenty-five policemen in sixteen border patrols stopped every "suspicious" car. Still, despite all these efforts, 13 percent of all transients in the United States in 1935 ended up in California.

RELIEF; HOOVER

Relief efforts were scattered and uncoordinated, especially during Herbert Hoover's administration. A staunch Republican, the former secretary of commerce had ironically planned much of the European recovery aid the United States had offered to the Continent. But he was a captive of his own economic ideology and the illusion that the economic chaos was short-lived. In that misperception he was a comrade with all sorts of ordinary Americans who also were certain that recovery was just around the corner and that the United States would not fall into the mire that was Europe or the Soviet Union. Hoover favored private voluntary efforts, and some of them aided the desperately poor, but often with a surprising result for recipients. Orville Rice remembered that "those that went on welfare— that is before they had public welfare—the plant, that is, the corporation, issued welfare vouchers to the employees that were laid off. And they would go every week and get a basket. And then, when it was all over, the company demanded that they pay back in dollars and cents the value of all the items they had received in their baskets . . . when you started back at work the company took so much from your pay." Widow Maria Kresic obtained $40 monthly in public assistance for her four children and herself, but in 1934 she was notified that she would have to pay it back. Eventually she got a Works Progress Administration job cutting material for seamstresses. When her eldest child finished school and went to work to help the family, a neighbor informed on her and she had to quit her job.[16]

Some of Hoover's advisors asserted that a hands-off policy

would most quickly right the foundering ship. The suffering and even death that would occur would be convulsive, to be certain, but according to the most conservative of Hoover's Cabinet, the end would be a healthier economy. Applying aspects of Charles Darwin's theories of natural selection to the American economy, these advisors thought that those who survived would be the "fittest," and overall the nation would be better off. That extreme did not suit the president, but neither did massive state intervention.

By 1932, with the Depression a long-term reality, Hoover was in deep political trouble. He did little to demonstrate the leadership and compassion Americans wanted, and was responsible for an action that in the eyes of many marked him as hostile and uncaring. In the summer of 1932 World War I veterans demanded immediate payment of the bonuses promised them for their service in the war. Though the bonuses were originally scheduled for payment in 1945, the House of Representatives had acted to grant them in 1932. Hoover aggressively fought against the bill, and won a narrow victory in the Senate. From all over the country incensed veterans made their way to Washington to protest. The Bonus Expeditionary Force, as they were called, camped out all over the capital and demanded to meet with the president. Hoover not only refused, he called out the Army to disperse the bonus marchers. Under the command of Douglas MacArthur, Dwight D. Eisenhower, and George Patton, the Army, in full battle dress, used bayonets, water cannons, and tear gas to rout the protesting veterans, who were armed with stones and clubs. Oklahoman Mary Owsley's husband "went to Washington. To march with that group . . . the bonus boys. He was a machine gunner in the war. He'd say them damn Germans gassed him in Germany. And he come home and his own Government stooges gassed him and run him off the country up there with the water hose, half drowned him." Chicagoan Jim Sheridan recalled how "a big colored soldier, about six feet tall . . . one of the bonus marchers" was injured when "a [government] soldier hit him on the side of the legs with a bayonet."[17]

Hoover left the presidency a ridiculed and despised man,

soundly defeated by Franklin D. Roosevelt. In the end he failed
to recognize either the enormity of the problem or the need for
new thinking and massive action. Moreover, his relief measures, limited as they were, did not reach those who needed it.
Joe Rudiak complained that "government relief . . . wasn't publicized among the ethnic community." He and his fellow Poles
had no "connections" with the politicians. "They were all
Anglo-Saxons . . . and the one that did represent the district was
more or less in favor of the company and the Republican strong-
hold . . . [then] Roosevelt got elected and then things started
moving."[18]

Roosevelt Triumphant

THE NEW DEAL PROGRAMS

New York patrician Franklin D. Roosevelt has been vilified by
Republicans and conservatives for decades because they
thought his New Deal programs smacked of socialism. In fact
Roosevelt's actions probably saved capitalism for the United
States and may have short-circuited the potential for the political upheaval that permeated Europe. He was aware of the
rewards of wealth and position, and was not about to give up
either.

When he took office in 1933, the nation was in a banking
panic. Banks had begun to fail before the crash, especially in
primarily agricultural areas, but after the stock market collapse
there seemed to be no stopping the tailspin: 659 failed in 1929;
1,350 in 1930; 2,293 in 1931; 1,453 in 1932. "Solvent" banks
closed for inauguration day, but many had been closed for
days—"bank holidays," they were called—to prevent further
depletion of their revenues. Depositors could not get money
out or put it in. A special session of Congress, called for March
9, met and enacted the Emergency Banking Act. Drafted by 2
A.M. and introduced when Congress met at noon, it was signed
by 9 P.M. The strongest banks were allowed to reopen for business after inspection by the Reconstruction Finance Corporation, a federal agency created (with reluctance) by Hoover in

1932. The weakest and insolvent banks were forced to reorganize under government supervision before they could reopen. Then on March 12, over national radio, Roosevelt explained the banking crisis and what the government was doing about it in the first of his "fireside chats" to the nation. These broadcasts utilized Roosevelt's gift for oratory and personalization—qualities perfectly suited for the medium—to at least calm and reassure Americans who had concluded that the government was paralyzed by the Depression. The next day the bank "run" was over. Depositors lined up at banks. Roosevelt's impact on the urban working class was both real and mythic: "The New Deal was a blessing," according to Tom Luketich. "You better be a Democrat if you are a laborer working for a living. . . . Roosevelt gave the people the right to work."[19]

Roosevelt promised a "new deal" to the American people in his acceptance speech at the Democratic convention in 1932. Early in his administration Roosevelt and his "brain trust"—a group of lawyers and university faculty brought in to counsel the president—began to work with Congress to create a series of agencies to relieve the financial suffering of many of the hardest hit of the public. The Civilian Conservation Corps, created in March 1933, put to work at reforestation and conservation projects 250,000 young men from families eligible for relief. Two million additional men served in the CCC by 1940, when the agency went out of existence. Called "Roosevelt Roosts" by many of the recruits, work for the CCC meant army discipline and thirty bucks a week, twenty-five of which went home to their families. But the CCC failed to reach some of the neediest of the nation's young. Eighteen was the minimum age for work, and as many as 50 percent of the wandering youth were younger. Many of the others could not or would not meet other requirements for CCC work—a home address, families or dependents whose identities they would divulge, and references. Still, by 1935 half a million young men were at work, 50,000 of them African-American.

The National Industrial Recovery Act, created in May 1933, and its offspring, the National Recovery Administration, or NRA, set about to plan the industrial economy for the longer-term goal of economic stability. By establishing codes agreed upon by manufacturers, consumer representatives, and labor, the NRA sought to regulate production and set prices. It also guaranteed labor the right to bargain collectively. But ultimately the Supreme Court disagreed with the administration's method, and probably the intent of the law: In 1935 it found that the act was unconstitutional.

Two offshoots of the NRA helped working-class and lower-middle-class Americans get back to work, if only for a while. The Public Works Administration and the Civil Works Administration, both created in 1933, embarked on a program of road and park maintenance and building, government building construction, and giant projects such as the Tennessee Valley Authority power plants and dams. The CWA put 4 million people to work in its brief existence (about one year), and PWA employees put in 4 million man-hours. The Works Progress Administration succeeded both agencies, and in its six-year existence beginning in 1935 it employed 8 million different people, including construction laborers, writers, engineers, artists, foresters, and musicians.

The Federal Emergency Relief Administration, created in May 1933, provided direct assistance to the neediest, and the Agricultural Adjustment Act, passed in March 1933, set up a system whereby farmers could get higher prices for their products and relief from bankruptcy and foreclosure proceedings. The aim of the AAA was to retrieve the ratio of farm prices to industrial goods' prices that had existed between 1909 and 1914, when farming was still profitable, if not exorbitantly so. In some cases these agricultural policies backfired, however. Landlords in the cotton-growing South sometimes used the federal payments for land left fallow to buy machinery and then force tenant and sharecropping farmers off the land. The president's first months in office did not necessarily show a politically or economically consistent approach to the crisis, but they did manifest action and some attempt to bring the country back from what seemed to be the edge of a precipice.

THE SHAME OF WORKLESSNESS

For many, the reality of losing a job meant the shame of relief and the hopelessness and bewilderment of fruitless job hunting. Orville Rice was "laid off, off and on from 1930 until 1936. At one time we were unemployed for as long as six months without getting a day's work. You might report for work every day of the week for seven days and not get a day's work. Then you might get a day, a day and a half, two days. This was going on through the years [until] it come down to the point where you didn't have anything and most everybody was living on welfare flour. . . ." Those who went on relief often did so reluctantly, as a last resort. Rose Popovich finally "had to go on relief" after her grocery debt reached $50. She and her family borrowed and even begged to make interest payments on their house. "I just paid interests. I couldn't pay on the principal." She recalled standing in line at the Red Cross all day in all sorts of weather to try to get cloth she could sew or food, only to have the agency close before she made it to the window. Stacia Treski "finally went on relief. Everybody needed it. My parents didn't realize though, that when they took it you had to have a lien on your house. First they gave us $7.50 per week, but then an investigator came and practically told you how to live."[20]

The number of people in major cities on relief or working in government project jobs was staggering: one in six in Pittsburgh; one in five in Chicago; one in four in Akron and Detroit; one in three in Cleveland; one in two in Flint. Some Americans ridiculed and condemned those on relief as freeloaders and bums, and there were probably some who might have been accurately characterized as such. But what the critics missed was the shame of relief for the vast majority of the populace. "Some of the people applied for public assistance," Joe Rudiak recalled, "but they were very much in shame." Louis Heim tried his hand at all sorts of work before finally going to Associated Charities for help. "I went down there and walked around the block three times before I got nerve enough to go in."[21]

The middle class responded to unemployment and relief

much as working-class Americans did, but many broke down more quickly when their world—their jobs—fell apart. The white-collar world had its daily stresses, but the job was almost always there; unlike in the mines and mills, offices did not shut down sporadically during the year. Sporadic and chronic unemployment was thought to be a working-class problem. Promotions might be competitive and might not come along as quickly as advice books and magazine articles promised if one "fit in," but the opportunity was supposed to be there. Journal editor Frank Moorhead's job vaporized in 1931. His "egotism" was "an anaesthetic allaying the first pains," he wrote in an article in *The Nation*. Like others of his class, he took great pains to maintain appearances after he became unemployed. "I had opened up an office in one of the bedrooms at home and was typing 'Now is the time for all good men to come to the aid of their party' hour after hour, in order to make the neighbors think I was still working—for a living. . . . Now that I am broke I always carry a few silver dollars, so that I can jingle them and not feel downcast."[22] Unlike most of the working class, he at least had a few silver dollars to jingle.

The ethos of personal responsibility for all of life's good and bad occurrences that had dominated American culture in the late nineteenth and early twentieth centuries exacted a heavy toll on Americans of all classes in the Depression. Those who were failing or who had failed reasoned that even if one-third of the work force was unemployed, there were still two-thirds working, albeit at reduced wages or lower-level jobs than those to which they were accustomed or for which they were trained. The shame of the unemployed was visible, according to Frank Moorhead. "I should like to find out at what stage of your poverty other people realize or sense it. . . . I guess, after all, it's in the droop of the shoulders, the look in your eyes—furtive, expectant, resentful."[23]

At first there were some who considered the hard times a retribution of sorts, a readjustment after the "fools' paradise" of the 1920s. The greed of capitalists large and small and the corruption of politicians at the public trough made many Americans cynical. Gerald W. Johnson, in a 1932 article in the magazine *Current History* entitled "The Average American and the Depression," noted that "the Depression came to our street in 1931. . . . Frankly, we are scared." And bitter: "We are somewhat resentful because we think the Depression has been made worse than it need have been because of the stupidity of our rulers. . . . We have discovered the dismal and faith-shattering truth that in times like these such men as Henry Ford, Charles M. Schwab, and J. P. Morgan have trouble enough solving their own problems."[24]

Robert S. and Helen M. Lynd returned to Muncie in the mid-1930s to continue their study of "Middletown," and *Middletown in Transition* was published in 1937. The Depression certainly was the most important fact of life for the residents of that typical American town. At first—and for five or six years after the crash—the residents of Muncie denied the seriousness of the problem and seemed to rely on boosterism and bravado to cope with the chaos. Businessmen large and small hated Roosevelt and the New Deal. Workers had the opposite opinion of the president, and were not attracted to the radicalism that drew some working people and intellectuals toward socialism and Communism. "If a man doesn't make good," the prevailing ideology held, "it's his own fault."[25]

This pervasive sense of self-blame resulted in responses of shame and guilt to the reality of worklessness. Louis Banks, whose family left cotton growing in Arkansas for Chicago like many other black farmers, recalled "the shame I was feeling. I walked out [on my family] because I didn't have a job. . . . I wouldn't let them see me dirty and ragged and I hadn't shaved. I wouldn't send 'em no picture." Louis Heim remembered that "then this Public Works Project came along. . . . I think Roosevelt's program saved the self-respect and sanity of a lot of men. It did mine. It bothered me that I had no work." Those women who had not worked outside the home experienced many of the same feelings of shame, as if the entire family had failed in a land where anybody was supposed to be able to "make it" if they worked at it. Many of all classes tried to fool their friends as long as possible; families "doubled up" in already overcrowded apartments or houses to avoid relief and the shame of applying. Sociologist Mirra Komarovsky, in *The Unemployed Man and His Family* (1940), found a high incidence of impotence in unemployed and underemployed men. Komarovsky also discovered deep feelings of shame if wives and children worked when the father was out of work. "The feeling of disturbance and humiliation apparently exists irrespective of the intellectual convictions of the man . . . in his own estimation he fails to fulfill . . . the very touchstone of his manhood—the role of family provider."[26]

If a person's worth was measured by money and goods, as it had come to be by the 1920s, then poverty was tantamount to worthlessness, and the descent from an established position was devastating. Some Americans who had resented the public high living of the era between the armistice and the crash took a bizarre comfort in the hard times, much like those nineteenth-century ministers who celebrated financial panics as evidence of God's retribution for human wickedness and a recruitment opportunity for the church. Those 1.5 million Americans who had invested in the stock market and lost most if not all of their money were considered greedy and deserving of the embarrassment, shame, and, in extreme cases, death they suffered. This was a hard-nosed logic because so many Americans—not just the Wall Streeters—suffered.

The fear and uncertainty wrought by the Depression was a boon to advertisers already attuned to the idea of using scare tactics to sell products. The Gillette Razor Company made it clear that a bad shave could be a contributing factor in job loss or a blown interview. As Roland Marchand has demonstrated, the painterly, "cultured" ads of the 1920s were replaced by the rougher "clenched fist," grim determination ads of the 1930s. "Gee, Pop—They're All Passing You" screamed an Ethyl gasoline ad in the February 1933 issue of *Fortune*. A small boy leans forward in the front seat, clenching his fist and looking as if his life depended on not being passed, and his father, neatly dressed and hatted, looks ahead with the blank humiliated look of a beaten man. The ad copy speaks of the "lost youth and power [that will] come back" to the car with Ethyl, but the subtext is clear from the visual message: It is the father who is being passed by. "You still don't like to be left behind," the ad warned.[27] These tough-it-out ads were signs of hostility to the alleged overconsumption and the pressure to perform that had characterized much of the advertising ethos of the previous decade.

Stung by an economic system over which they had little or no control and a political system that seemed unresponsive and distant, both working-class and middle-class Americans turned toward the politics of Franklin D. Roosevelt. The privations of the one-third who were out of work and the one-third who were underemployed were constant and severe. The uncertainty that the Depression brought on these people never completely left many of them, and as a result job security became a preeminent concern for labor negotiators after World War II. Pensions and the promise of retirement stability became the most important elements of employment contracts and benefit packages for many employees. Many workers had uneven and unpredictable incomes before 1929; but with the stock market's collapse and the economic chaos that followed went much of the optimism—albeit a fragile one—that had driven the middle class and provided a model for the working class.

T HE OPPORTUNITY for Americans to own a house and some ground to cultivate is one of the most potent and enduring elements of American ideology. The image of a small frame house, a fence, and a garden is common enough in the visual arts to be a cliché. The idealized house is small, corresponding to the size of the middle-class family of the twentieth century. The (presumed) larger families of the urban immigrant working class could not fit in these structures, given the recommended and widely held belief that it was necessary to have separate bedrooms for parents and male and female children. There are no boarders in this house, and in the idealized landscape no big-city buildings are in sight. The image is a sign—of suburban or country living, apart from the world of work. It is a place in which women take in no laundry or piecework and from which the male of the household departs by automobile or, less commonly, by public transportation to work in some undisclosed and vague white-collar job. The image signifies the values of democracy rather than those of privilege and deference.

It is important that the building material is wood. Brick and stone buildings can be too imposing for this visual and ideological ideal: Those materials connote wealth, industry, and, perhaps unconsciously for some, even institutions of containment. Some churches and many of the country's shrines to political, military, and cultural heroes, such as Mount Vernon and Monticello, are frame buildings, and usually white, which places them in a middle ground between the home and the institutions of government and religion. They are expressive of their power because of their scale, yet their materials are comforting, conservative, and nostalgic.

Apartments, tenements, grand homes of the rich, and other city residences—dwellings in which most Americans actually lived—are not part of this ideal, at least in mainstream popular culture. For many urban dwellers, therefore, the image was an unrealizable aspiration; for some it was irrelevant and undesirable. The latter saw the freestanding house as isolated, apart from the activity and opportunity of the city and town. Many European immigrants who had lived in cities all their lives could not imagine life away from streets and a multitude of other people. To them the country and the farm represented the peasant and the backward. They wanted no part of either.

This enthusiasm for the city was counterbalanced by a powerful set of yeoman and agrarian myths that had been promulgated by Jefferson and others since at least the beginning of the nineteenth century. Proponents of this synthesis equated all sorts of virtues—honesty, political wisdom, honor—with working the land and raising livestock, and most if not all of the vices of the human race—greed, duplicity, crime, sexual license—with cities. But the Jeffersonian ideal did not endure a century of American history unchanged. By 1915 the laboring aspect of country living had disappeared from this image, leaving the house and garden alone in (presumably) the suburbs.

Housing, Ideal and Real

OWNING A HOME

The white frame single-family house ideal reveals the powerful position of Anglo-Americans, but by 1945 this image was a goal that transcended class, ethnicity, and race. The freestanding suburban house was a reality for many Americans, but it was beyond the reach of most because of the vagaries of the economy in the thirty years after 1915 and because of legal and other impediments, such as high down payment requirements, the practice of granting mortgages for only a short duration before renegotiation, and race and class discrimination by mortgage lenders. The 1920 federal census revealed that 46 percent of the American population owned their own homes, and most of those lived in the country. Urbanites were predominantly renters: 73 percent of the residents of New Orleans rented, 75 percent of all Atlantans, 82 percent of all Bostonians, and 88 percent of all New Yorkers. There were exceptions to this pattern in small cities: in Zanesville, Ohio, in 1926, 70 percent of the families had annual incomes below $2,000, but 80 percent owned their homes. New home construction surged between 1920 and 1929, but it crashed when the stock market did. Mortgage foreclosures in the Depression turned the dream of owning a house into a nightmare of uncertainty and desperation. In a 1931 census of the Lower East Side of Manhattan, 15,000 men and women were without a home, living in religious missions, in flophouses, in subway tunnels and on subway platforms, at the Salvation Army missions, and in city-supported lodging houses.[1]

Both immigrants and natives bought houses in the early twentieth century, but immigrants seemed to have sacrificed or saved for the purchase in greater numbers than their incomes might have suggested. By the late 1920s, 40 percent of all first-generation immigrants, including nearly 50 percent of all Poles, 40 percent of all Italians, 54 percent of all Czechs, and 45 percent of all Lithuanians, were homeowners, but 29 percent of all second-generation immigrants and only 19 percent of all native-born Americans owned houses. In Cleveland approximately 60 percent of the Italian and Slovak immigrants had purchased homes by 1930, and of those moving into the middle class (at least in financial terms), 69 percent of all Italian and 80 percent of all Slovak immigrants owned houses.[2]

FINANCING A HOME

Financing a house often required sacrifice and some fancy footwork. Jews often formed their own construction and finance companies, and they tended to build and live in urban apartments, rather than in single-family homes. Perhaps because of their encounters with discrimination in Europe and the United

States, many valued investment in businesses more highly than in real estate, since the former was more easily liquidated than the latter. Other immigrant groups opted for single-family or occasionally multiple-family residences, often financing them by having the entire family working to meet the demands of the mortgaging system of the era.

The typical mortgage available between 1915 and 1935 was for between five and seven years and for 50 to 60 percent of the cost of the house. The principal was not usually paid off in this period, and borrowers had to negotiate another loan with the original or a new bank when the first loan term had elapsed. At this time a bank could refuse a borrower a new loan and demand cash payment of the rest of the principal. Borrowers could try to find a new lender, but what usually occurred was that the next loan was offered at a new and generally higher interest rate—often as high as 18 percent—payable in three years. Borrowers who agreed to the terms of a loan could not be slow in making payments: Missing two monthly payments usually meant the bank foreclosed and all was lost. Ethnic groups often felt the sting of discrimination in their negotiations, and even if they didn't, they usually had to contend with bankers who were unfamiliar with their language and customs. Many ethnic groups formed their own loan associations to try to gain some measure of control or at least comfort with the process. By 1916 there were, for example, seventy-four Polish-American associations lending money to others of Polish descent.

The Depression stimulated a radical change in traditional housing financing. Roosevelt created the Home Owners Loan Corporation and the Emergency Farm Mortgage Act in 1933 to protect people from foreclosure. Forty percent of all eligible Americans applied for assistance, with great regional variation: 99 percent of those Mississippians eligible applied, but only 18 percent of eligible Maine residents did so. Between 1933 and 1935 the HOLC lent more than $3 billion for more than 1 million mortgages. The HOLC also introduced a new mortgage form—the self-amortizing, twenty-year mortgage with uniform payments.

The Federal Housing Administration (FHA) became law on June 27, 1934. The FHA did not lend money, but insured loans so that banks could make more of them. It also set up new guidelines for mortgages, allowing up to 93 percent of the principal to be borrowed, to be paid back at a fixed interest rate for twenty years or longer, amortized over the entire period. It established minimum standards for construction of new houses and the condition of older houses, and required objective inspection of properties to be financed. The results of the legislation were astonishing. Housing starts and sales, at 93,000 in 1933, leapt to 332,000 in 1937; 399,000 in 1938; 458,000 in 1939; 530,000 in 1940; and 619,000 in 1941.[3]

The federal government also backed housing projects for low- and middle-income families in the 1930s. In 1933 the Housing Division of the Public Works Administration began construction of 21,000 units in forty-nine projects in cities throughout the nation. In 1939, FHA-sponsored Edgemoor Terrace, a 400-unit, six-room housing development, was completed north of Wilmington, Delaware. At $5,150 the houses were not cheap, but the down payment was only $550, and the monthly payment of $29.61 was less than the rents many in the area were paying. Lenders required a guarantee of steady work, and that was a problem for many potential borrowers.

Even if the cash for a down payment was available and work was steady, buying a house was still risky. Zoning and uniform building codes were uncommon in most of the country in 1915, so the owner of a dream house could one day find a rendering plant or some other disagreeable operation being built next door. The first zoning ordinances, designed to separate industrial from residential areas and, in some cases, to keep workers from moving into some middle-class neighborhoods, were instituted in Los Angeles in 1909. By 1930 they were in effect in nearly 1,000 cities and villages, affecting more than 46 million inhabitants.[4]

As secretary of commerce under both Harding and Coolidge, Herbert Hoover was a leader in housing reform and in efforts to aid families in more efficiently managing their homes. In addition to the Advisory Committee on Building Codes (1921) and the Division of Building and Housing (1921), he set up the Bureau of Home Economics and Homemaking Information Centers (1923), and published a multitude of pamphlets on building codes, building materials, and household products. After the Smith-Hughes Act was passed in 1917, the Agricultural Extension Service joined the Grange in sponsoring classes in homemaking for rural women. National Better Homes Week (usually the last week in April) was established in the 1920s to provide models of household efficiency and sanitation for consumers. By 1930, 682 model single-family homes had been opened.

FHA standards and administrators' attitudes sometimes impeded efforts of the working class and the poor to borrow for housing in inner cities. Appraisal techniques and standards favored white suburbs and discouraged renovation of older homes in established neighborhoods, especially row houses that were deemed too crowded and too close to the street. Those who lived in tenement apartments in cities, in decaying frame or row houses, in company houses, in cabins and other small rural buildings, or, for the most destitute, in cardboard or scrap wood and metal shacks were left out of FHA benefits.

WORKING-CLASS HOUSING

With larger families than their middle-class and wealthy counterparts, as well as boarders, newcomers, and relatives looking for work, home life for the working class was characterized by little space and few conveniences. In a 1913 article in the *Journal of Home Economics*, Mabel Kittridge identified a typical working-class family and described their living situation. Eight family members and one boarder occupied a four-room flat that cost $19 monthly. The father and two of the children worked in a local factory (the father earned $12 weekly), and the mother made artificial flowers at home. All slept in the same room and each child shared a bed with two or three siblings. In 1936 the St. Louis City Planning Commission surveyed forty-four areas surrounding the business district of the city (8,447 houses) and found that conditions had not improved much. Only 40 percent of the immigrant population had indoor toilets and the tuberculosis rate was three times that of the rest of the city. Margaret Byington's 1910 study of workers near Pittsburgh revealed that only fifteen of ninety (17 percent) had indoor toilets.[5]

Crowded living conditions were common among the working class because boarders were both a financial necessity and a neighborhood service. Newly arrived immigrants expected lodging with people from their home village until they could get on their feet; so too did relatives. But most households brought in boarders for the income they generated. Joe Rudiak, of Lyndora, Pennsylvania, "lived in company houses owned by the Standard Steel Company, and each . . . were all frame and painted red. . . . They had, lined up for let's say half a mile and about five hundred feet deep, rows of these shanties. . . . As high as five, six, seven boarders would come in. . . . There was nine of us and as high as four boarders. Mostly it was all relatives and folks from home."[6]

A Chicago survey of Polish and Lithuanian families conducted in 1914 revealed that the average family had slightly more than four boarders living in its home. Rose Popovich's mother started a boardinghouse in Monessen, Pennsylvania, immediately after arriving in the United States in 1912. She had hoped to pack the beds with boarders each night, and she succeeded. Renters were "so in need of housing that they were willing to sleep even three on one bed." The real entrepreneurs took in people working different shifts to maximize the number of bodies that could be sleeping on a few beds. Five dollars each month got a boarder laundry and room; the weekly food bill was divided among the boarders, which meant that the proprietors' food costs were met by the boarders. Rose shined the boarders' shoes on Saturday nights for twenty-five cents for each pair. Some got her presents at Christmas and Easter.[7]

Most working-class apartments and housing had minimal storage and few rooms. Kitchen cabinets and closets were virtually nonexistent: They were too expensive and there was usually no room for them even if there was enough money. Typical rooms had open shelves, pegs, boxes and trunks that doubled as seats, an occasional chest of drawers, a table, a cookstove, a washtub, a few chairs, beds and mattresses, an inexpensive record player (by the 1920s), and a used sewing machine. Few of these homes had running water, and almost none had running hot water. John Parracini, from near Scranton, lived in a boardinghouse with few comforts. There were "no carpets. There was no rocking chair. There was no couch. Just common wooden chairs. I remember there was a great big table, and benches on each side of the table, and a great big kitchen."[8] With little storage and often no icebox until the 1930s (when the advent of refrigerators made them outmoded and cheap), working-class women relied on street vendors and small grocery stores to supply food for daily cooking.

For the working class, kitchens served many functions in addition to cooking. It was a social area: Courting couples could spend time and friends could sit around a table and talk, play cards, or otherwise socialize. Margaret Byington described a typical working-class kitchen in Homestead, Pennsylvania, in 1910: "On one side of the room was a huge puffy bed, with one feather tick to sleep on and another for covering; near the window stood a sewing machine; in the corner an organ—all these besides the inevitable cook stove upon which in the place of honor was simmering the evening's soup. Upstairs in the second room were one boarder and the man of the house asleep. Two more boarders were at work."[9]

AFRICAN-AMERICAN HOUSING

Black Americans in urban areas almost always had to live in segregated neighborhoods in the most dilapidated structures and with the fewest municipal services. Many of these houses were in the alleys that connected the streets with the interior spaces of city blocks where once stables and carriage sheds had stood. As automobiles replaced horses, these buildings were converted into or replaced by two- and three-story multiple-family residences.[10] The small open spaces between the buildings and alleys were often full of debris, since hard-pressed families often sent children and adults to scavenge the city for metal to be resold, as well as for wood and coal for heating and cooking. Most apartments in alley buildings resembled southern "shotgun" houses in plan—one room wide, and two or three rooms deep. In the back room, or just outside in warmer climates, was a hand pump for water. For many African-Americans, the urban alley apartment or house had one or two more rooms but less yard space than the former slave cabins or other houses in the country that many had left.

Black families with enough money to live in better housing had difficulty doing so because of racial prejudice. Segregated accommodations were the norm all over the country. Rebecca Taylor, in a 1980 interview, noted that "when I came to Plainfield [New Jersey] I discovered that Plainfield was as segregated as the South. . . . I didn't see any difference, because the theatres were segregated, the hospitals were segregated, the churches of course." The manager of the Commercial Theatre in Chicago confirmed that Taylor's experience was as true for the Midwest as it was for the East Coast. "White people don't like to sit next to the colored or Mexicans. . . . We used to have trouble about the first four months, but not now. They go by themselves to their place [the balcony]." The family of Amelia Brown (a pseudonym) "couldn't move where we would like to live. . . . The whites wouldn't rent to us." The Federal Housing Authority, organized to protect homeowners and make mortgages easier to obtain, used an appraisal system that discriminated against black loan applicants and against borrowers seeking mortgages for houses in integrated neighborhoods. The 1939 *Underwriting Manual* succinctly stated its prejudicial position: "If a neighborhood is to retain its stability, it is necessary that properties continue to be occupied by the same social and racial classes."[11]

The interior condition of these houses varied from the barely tolerable hovel to the immaculate abode of Washington, D.C.'s famous "Aunt Jane," whose youngest daughter began each school year with twenty-six clean, pressed dresses. Used furniture and appliances, recycled fruit and milk crates, and inexpensive or free secular and religious prints—especially calendars—decorated many of these homes. In a 1946 publication examining Washington, D.C., alley apartments, sociologist Marion Ratigan found many homes and apartments furnished "with only a mattress on the floor, a kerosene burner and a small pan . . . no table, no dishes, not even a cup," and a few appointed with "Biedermeyer and Hepplewhite chairs, a pier-glass table and a Governor Winthrop desk, filled with such treasures as a Cappi della Monte [sic] plate, a Meissen group, odd pieces of Wedgwood and Sèvres china, hobnail and milk glass, and innumerable figurines and dolls."[12]

COMPANY HOUSING, TENEMENTS

Some companies offered inexpensive rental housing to attract workers in boom times and to keep them from moving around, thereby saving the firm unproductive training time for new workers. "Sociological departments" of some firms investigated the home lives of their renters, and urged families to live up to standards of behavior and cleanliness the company established and publicized by means of classes, prizes, and threats of dismissal. In 1917 the U.S. Bureau of Labor Statistics estimated that at least 1,000 companies provided rental housing for workers. *Homes for Workmen,* a 1919 publication of the Southern Pine Association, asserted that workers were 25 to 33 percent more efficient if they lived in company housing. Monthly rent was usually one week's salary. In 1920, the average company town consisted of enough units to house one-third of the work force, with more highly skilled workers having first choice of the units. The percentage of workers that could be accommodated in company towns was higher in southern textile and western mining and logging towns, since these were usually more isolated than the industrial centers of the Northeast and Midwest.[13]

The architecture of many of these and other working-class freestanding houses was plain and boxy, usually two rooms wide and two rooms deep, with little usable second-story space except for storage. In urban areas, where land was often very expensive, workers' housing often had only two rooms on the ground floor, but had full or at least habitable second floors and a crawl-space attic. In the use of interior spaces, both types of four-room houses were akin to the hall-and-parlor houses of seventeenth- and eighteenth-century America. Kitchen and dining areas were in the same room, with a parlor, or "best room," and two bedrooms. Easy to build and move, many were constructed en masse of precut structural members and sheathing. Few were airtight, and cellars were a rarity.

Those who lived in tenement apartments often had only a kitchen and bedrooms surrounding it. In the kitchen was usually the apartment's only heat source—the kitchen range—and family members and boarders crowded into the room for heat, food, and socializing. In most of these buildings only one-half the bedrooms had windows; the others were on the inside of the building and shared a wall with the interior bedrooms on the other side of the tenement. A top-floor flat with skylights cost more to rent and was the most desirable to live in if the extra work of climbing stairs was worth the extra light and expense. Bathrooms were in the hallways and sometimes thirty or forty people shared but one facility. Often water pressure was weak—a drawback on the upper floors—or nonexistent.[14]

Electricity was relatively common in the small, predominantly white cities of the Midwest: 73.7 percent of all Zanesville, Ohio, houses were wired for electricity, 90 percent had running water, 60 percent had an indoor bathroom with toilet and tub, 96 percent had piped-in gas, 89.6 percent had a gas range, 69 percent had a telephone, and 48 percent owned a car.[15] But electricity was rare in much of rural America until the New Deal Rural Electrification Program brought power to about 35 percent of those areas by the 1940s. Middle-class farmers who had survived the hard times of the 1920s and 1930s often had advanced indoor plumbing if they were close enough to electric lines so that they could power a pump. The Department of Agriculture's 1934 *Farm Housing Survey* found some regional differences in the number of houses equipped with modern plumbing, but for the most part it was absent. Twenty percent of Missouri farmhouses had a kitchen sink with a drain; 7 percent of Kentucky farmhouses had an indoor bathroom; 25 percent of Washington state farmhouses had a flush toilet. The survey also discovered that only 17 percent of Ohio farmhouses had electric service. The Rural Electrification Program of the New Deal brought electric power to some, but most rural

example of survey

Americans would have to wait until after 1945 to catch up with their urban counterparts in accessibility to electricity.[16]

Farmers' Housing

TENANTS AND SHARECROPPERS

White and black tenant farmers and sharecroppers faced a more severely deprived living situation in more cramped quarters. In 1939 Martha Haygood's *Mothers of the South: Portraiture of White Tenant Farm Women* revealed that only 8 of 200 Tennessee tenant farm households could have afforded electricity if it had been available, and none had running water. The architecture of these houses was a variant of vernacular building forms that had been constructed by rural Americans for centuries. One-room cabins, two-room "shotgun" houses, two-room "saddlebag" houses (side-by-side rooms with a small hall between and an open space between the rooms), and two-room "dogtrot" houses (rooms on a horizontal axis to the road—as in the saddlebag house—with an open space between the rooms, all under one roof) constituted the major forms. Porches and yards surrounding these structures served not only as grazing and pecking grounds for livestock, but also as gardens, work spaces, and socializing areas. (Trash and garbage were fed to hogs and dumped at the extremities of the uncultivated land.) Many were built of logs with mud chinking; some were of sawn lumber. Roofs of corrugated metal, horizontally laid tar paper, or shake shingles were most common, in some cases having replaced the straw or march grass thatch that had been brought to North America by African and Caribbean immigrants during the slavery era.[17]

Like their early American hall-and-parlor counterparts, the largest of the two rooms on the first floor served as kitchen, playroom, workroom, washroom, and sometimes bedroom. By the early twentieth century the packed mud floors of many of these cabins were covered with wooden planking. Ceilings were usually left unadorned and second-floor joists were often left exposed. Walls were occasionally plastered and white-

life in south - more that text

washed, but most were covered with a combination of newspaper and tar paper coverings, and sometimes wallpaper. "For years," remembers Diana Morgan, a North Carolina–born social worker in the 1930s, "I never questioned the fact that Caroline's [a former cook and laundress for Morgan's family] house was papered with newspapers. . . . She was always gracious and would invite me in. She never apologized for the way anything looked."[18] Religious artifacts—prints, crosses, and Bibles—and photographs of the family were common decorations and accoutrements, and many poor folk had a prized firearm—usually a shotgun—hanging on the wall near the door. On the wall near the kitchen stove hung the pots, pans, and other cooking utensils, as well as washing and drying cloths. Clothing was also hung from nails and hooks.

Most tenant farmers and sharecroppers filled their houses with a combination of homemade, used, and mail-order furniture. As in urban homes of the poor, lightweight chairs that served social and work purposes were common, as well as food storage "safes," which were ventilated yet secure enough to keep out mice, rats, raccoons, and opossums. On the second floor were beds and storage spaces for the family's possessions, and the smoked meats that they hung from rafters.

Nearly all of the rural poor hauled water from a nearby stream or pond, and a few from dug wells. Front yards in the South were usually deliberately grassless. All shrubs and other greenery were pulled out and the yard swept with a dogwood branch broom every dry day. The open dirt yard was both a firebreak and a no-critters land in which snakes and vermin could not hide and approach the house unseen during the day. Flower beds were the exceptions to this ban, and the roses, chrysanthemums, holly trees, and cedars tenants typically grew provided cut flowers and greens to decorate the interior. Most of these farmsteads also included a variety of outbuildings, including a summer kitchen (in hot climates), a chicken coop, a vegetable kiln, an outhouse, a meat house (for storage), and sometimes a smokehouse and a corn crib. Small fenced areas might contain pigs or a vegetable garden. Usually the house stood between the road and the fields the family worked, with the backyard blending directly into the field crops.

If they could afford it, many tenants and sharecroppers moved up to larger houses, or expanded the smaller building they lived in if they could manage to buy it. By building out the back or, less commonly, up, the pattern of the next-generation house became two rooms over two rooms. These newer houses or additions usually used more up-to-date construction technology, substituting balloon framing for post-and-beam framing, sawn lumber for logs, and nailed joints for notches, mortises and tenons, and treenails.

Marylanders Nora and Quincy Cusic, for example, moved into their one-room rural log cabin in 1916 as tenants, and within four years moved out to a four-room house. As George McDaniel discovered in the research for his book *Hearth and Home,* the Cusics never considered the tenant house "home," but did think of their next house in that way. The Abraham Medley family, black tenant farmers who moved into the house in 1921 and lived there until 1978, thought differently about the house. They divided the nineteen-by-sixteen cabin into four rooms—two rooms downstairs and two rooms upstairs under the rafters. Unlike the Cusics, who all slept downstairs in one big room and stored goods upstairs, the Medleys slept upstairs—parents in one room and children in the other—on corn-shuck mattresses on iron bedsteads, unless it was so hot that pallets on the floor were more comfortable.[19]

MIDDLING FARMERS

Homesteads of more well-off rural whites and blacks included the same outbuildings as their poorer counterparts, as well as barns, stables, carriage houses, and specialized structures such as tobacco barns. Post-and-rail or board fences enclosed pastures and pens, fields, and sometimes the house. These middling farmers purchased furniture and furnishings when they could, since these were signs of success and modernity, while the old homemade goods were emblematic of the "old days." Pressed-back chairs, clocks, mirrors, and bureaus like those offered in Sears Roebuck catalogs, rattan and cane-backed rockers, and overstuffed sofas of the Sears type were the furniture of choice.

A bookcase with glass doors and a china cabinet graced the parlors of the upwardly mobile, providing storage space for books, finer china, and decorative pieces. The better china and flatware of modestly successful rural people were new, if inexpensive, goods—thin-bodied, floral-decorated earthenwares often embellished with a fine gold band on the plates' edge so that they resembled more expensive porcelain. These goods replaced the old heavier-bodied earthenware and enameled tinwares (called "graniteware") that the family had used, or added a "special occasion" china service to the household. Silver-plated flatwares in traditional American or French rococo styles replaced plain steel or other older eating utensils or became the "company" goods. Flashy urban art deco or older art nouveau styles found few enthusiasts among rural people.

The Suburbs and the City

SUBURBAN GROWTH

Between the rural house or cabin and the urban house and tenement was the middle ground of the middle class—the suburb. Real estate development, especially tract housing, expanded as entrepreneurs in the 1920s began to more effectively use the technology of mass production in home building, and the demand for middle income housing grew as the middle class increased in number. Moreover, the expansion of public transportation and the advent of the cheap automobile opened up large and hitherto impractical sites for housing.

For decades the wealthy had maintained homes in both the city—the seat of business and high culture—and the country or the seashore. But with the opening of the vast landscape around the cities to the streetcar and the automobile, the best of both could be had by those in the middle of the socioeconomic spectrum. In the late nineteenth century, the streetcar had opened up lands along its lines; by the 1920s the automobile opened up the spaces in between the streetcar tracks for development. Between 1920 and 1930 the suburbs grew twice as fast as the cities. Shaker Heights, outside of Cleveland, increased its population 1,000 percent; fueled by the expansion of the motion picture industry, Beverly Hills grew 2,500 percent; Elmwood Park, near Chicago, grew by 717 percent. Less expensive suburbs mushroomed as well, although not as quickly, since the automobile was essential to their growth and many members of the poorer segments of the middle class bought cars later in the 1920s than did their more wealthy counterparts. Still, in Illinois and Michigan alone, seventy-one new municipalities were incorporated in the 1920s, two-thirds of them around Chicago, St. Louis, and Detroit.[20]

Lot sizes in new developments were generous by urban standards—averaging approximately 3,000 square feet in older streetcar suburbs and 5,000 square feet in automobile suburbs. The suburbs also offered the middle class exclusivity; restrictive covenants were often attached to deeds to shut out those few Jews, African-Americans, Mexican-Americans, Irish, Italians, Asians, and other immigrants who had the money and desire to move out of the city to the suburbs. The suburban ideal was white, Anglo-Saxon, and northern European, and sometimes only Protestant.

Urban conditions also stimulated this transformation. Cities had become more congested as automobile use increased. Traffic jams were a commonplace; the average speed on Manhattan's Fifth Avenue in the late afternoon in the 1920s was less than three miles per hour. There was little or no space to park all those cars, and merchants and municipal governments were unwilling to spend much money for parking lots on urban real estate that was escalating in value. The advent of the auto also made some urban streets into a battleground. In residential neighborhoods people often pelted strangers in cars with rocks and other projectiles, and drivers often hurtled through the streets at high speeds. As in European cities, the street had been a social area for many residents, and a playground for children. The cars disrupted the pace and the pattern of the residential street. New York City planners opened a new era with the installation of a block signal stoplight system in 1923; in 1924 General Electric began production of timed electric stoplights. To ease congestion and stimulate economic growth, some cities built massive highways to convey traffic, such as Detroit's eight-lane Woodward Avenue, which connected Detroit with Pontiac. Chicago completed the Elevated Drive north of the "Loop" by 1929; Boston built arteries north and south of the center of the city; and at the time of the stock market crash plans were on the drawing board in Philadelphia to build seven routes to bypass the center city. The Delaware River Bridge connected Philadelphia and Camden in 1926 and the George Washington Bridge spanned the Hudson River between New York and New Jersey in 1933. Parkways, traffic circles, timed traffic lights, bridges, and tunnels were constructed with what seemed to be dizzying speed. A few limited-access parkways, such as New York's Long Island Motor (1911), Bronx River (1923), Hutchinson River (1928), Saw Mill River (1929), Cross County (1931), and Los Angeles' Arroyo Seco (1940) were built to accommodate the new clientele of commuters and suburban dwellers. In the end these projects did speed traffic flow and decrease congestion for a while. But they also helped hasten white middle-class flight to the suburbs in the 1920s, thereby forming concentric rings of metropolitan settlement, with the poorest people living near the center.[21]

Middle-class settlement patterns, improved roads, and the pervasiveness of the automobile brought about the growth of suburban shopping centers between the world wars. The first such set of stores was the Country Club Plaza, outside of Kansas City. Begun in 1923 and opened in 1925, the Moorish, red-tile-roofed extravaganza was landscaped with greenery and artificial waterfalls and fountains. Only eight shopping centers were built by 1945, a result of the Depression and World War II's tightening of money for such projects. All were built in affluent suburbs: Upper Darby Center, in Ardmore, Pennsylvania (1927 and 1928); Highland Park Village, near Dallas (1931); River Oaks, in Houston (1937); Hampton Village, in St. Louis (1941); Colony, near Toledo (1944); and Shirlington, in Arlington, Virginia (1944). Merchants figured that the suburban middle class was a more profitable market, and that suburban land was still cheap enough to build both stores and free parking lots. The suburban shopping center could also be pitched as safer and more exclusive than the city store, a message that resonated with middle-class uncertainties about immigrants and African-Americans who were populating cities in ever-increasing numbers after World War I.

Especially in the suburbs, but wherever it was located, the middle-class home was supposed to be a place of refuge from the commercial world. In the nineteenth century this conception of the home was refined and codified in popular literature, architectural form, and home furnishings. In these "secular sanctuaries," as writers referred to them, beauty, religion, learning, and other high-culture pursuits were preserved, encountered, and appreciated, and here they exercised their alleged influence upon the characters of men hardened by the Darwinian world of capitalism. In this protected environment women were given the roles of civilizer and softener, nurturer and helpful companion, roles that granted them influence but little real power.

In the early twentieth century slightly different visions of the home and of family roles emerged. The Progressive ideal of efficiency and the newly energized middle-class and elite commitment to the preservation of health and fitness helped alter the older ideology and the look and function of the home. The kitchen and bathroom became focal points for advice and criticism, superseding the previous era's concentration on the parlor and dining room.[22]

CITY HOUSING

In 1915, typical middle-class housing in towns and cities was large and multistoried. Three floors and 3,000 square feet of living and storage space (not including a basement) were realistic expectations for the growing class of mid- and upper-level managers and bureaucrats and their families. Ornamented neoclassical and American colonial–style buildings with expansive windows and generous residential lots (60 or 80 feet wide by 150 or more feet deep) were grander than previous generations could have hoped for. Mass-produced machine-made decorative devices, from carved interior paneling to stained glass by the running foot, made it possible for many middle-class Americans to build and buy what had once been available only to the top end of the merchant class.

Most people living in these residences were white, Anglo-Saxon or northern European, and Protestant. With smaller families (three, four, or five children, according to the census tabulations of 1900–1940) and a commitment to more space for each child, the typical middle-class home consisted of a downstairs parlor, a living room, a library or den, a dining room, a kitchen, storage closets, and a small lavatory. Upstairs were bedrooms and a full bath, and for a small and declining number, servants' quarters (if they were not on the third floor). The attic was the primary storage area. Basements were for the heating system, coal storage if necessary, tools, and some food storage. For the middle class, who profited most by the building boom of the 1920s, oil-fired, forced-air central heating was common. (The rest of the population could not afford central heating until after World War II.) Most middle-class homes were equipped with interior bathrooms, running water, and gas hookups for ranges. Nearly all were electrified throughout, and electric household tools and appliances—fans, vacuum cleaners, irons, lights, and some clothes washers—were commonplace.

There were some regional distinctions in the architecture of middle-class housing. In the Southwest and southern California, revivals of Monterey ranches and stucco-and-beam buildings were popular. Tudor half-timbering and colonial revival houses found favor in the East, and stone "farms" and "rambling" country houses appeared in Pennsylvania and the upper Midwest. But while the decoration and historical style of these houses differed, the arrangement of spaces was in most cases that of the middle-class form described earlier.[23]

THE BUNGALOW

The exception to the trends of spatial organization and historic architectural style was the bungalow, a form that probably originated in California in the first decade of the century. By the 1920s it had spread all over the country. In its 1927 survey *Zanesville, Ohio and Thirty Six Other American Communities,* the R. O. Eastman Company, Inc., discovered that the typical working-class house of that midwestern city was a four-room, one-story bungalow. The bungalow offered a new, smaller, and stripped-down form of architecture and interior space. Typically, it was a one- or one-and-one-half story building with a low pitched roof, wide eaves, and a front porch. The porch was usually supported by massive short pillars of stone or brick, enhancing the low profile of a house that was designed to look as if it were one with the earth. Clever interior arrangement of spaces eliminated most of the halls and passages between rooms that characterized more formal Georgian or other European-influenced floor plans of the era. Low ceilings, plain or simply curved stained oak or pine moldings, and stained or clear-finished wooden floors conveyed a sense of simplicity that had begun to gain adherents as the "mission" and "arts and crafts" furnishing styles became popular in the early twentieth century. Built-in seats, bureaus, buffets, tables, and other accoutrements provided more open space but restricted options in furnishing arrangements.

Bungalows were also popular because they were cheaper to build and buy than were grander homes. They were smaller—usually approximately 1,500 square feet, but as small as 800 square feet—yet the larger bungalows still provided two, three, or sometimes four bedrooms as well as the kitchen, dining room, living room, and two baths. Plans and renderings could be had from popular magazines such as the *Ladies' Home Journal* for as little as $1. Considered by many as a "starter house," bungalows provided younger members of the middle class and others with limited incomes the chance to live the suburban dream.

The bungalow also succeeded as a popular style because its visual cues resonated with the Progressive efficiency ethos and the health concerns of the early twentieth century. The front porch and restrained interior ornamentation of the house signaled fresh air, sanitation, and the outdoorsy, sunshine-and-suntan culture of California. By 1915, southern California had become a symbol of youthfulness and energy, a combination of Mediterranean and tropical visions that were at once healthful, sensuous, and relaxed. More efficient houses that could be kept spotless with allegedly less effort left families, and particularly women, with more time for outdoor life with the children.

RUSSEL WRIGHT AND "EASIER LIVING"

The celebration of youth that occurred in the 1920s and the popularity of California life-styles and architecture also showed itself in dramatic changes in the everyday life and artifacts of the household. Important in this context was the designer Russel Wright. Wright, an aesthetic product of the "mission" style of furnishings of the early twentieth century, and a passionate believer in the democratic possibilities of both the bungalow and the arts and crafts movement, developed line after line of popular tablewares and furnishings for the informal life-style advocated and reinforced by the bungalow and California youth culture.

Born in the Midwest and educated in art and design at Princeton, Wright entered the home furnishings market in 1932–1933 with his spun aluminum tablewares. They sold well because their form and appearance were strongly influenced by the art deco style that glorified the machine and celebrated speed, and because aluminum—one of industry's cheap new materials—was cheap. They also may have appealed to some consumers' sense of history because they looked like they were made of a traditional American material—pewter. Treasured by many Americans, pewter was expensive and difficult to manipulate by complex mass-production machinery.

Wright promoted what he termed "informal serving accessories" and "stove to table" wares for the easygoing entertaining he advocated. He encouraged Americans to celebrate their own foods and traditions with his "corn sets," which consisted of matched salt and pepper shakers and a rounded matching pot for holding melted butter. Spaghetti sets, pretzel baskets, and serving dishes for informal cocktail parties (a new entertainment form popular after prohibition was repealed in 1933) were important parts of Wright's lines of goods.

Wright also designed ceramic goods for the home in the 1930s. Mass-produced in simple and elegant forms that were neither streamlined nor otherwise extreme in their modernity, the forms of "American modern" pottery were commercial successes that endured for decades. The colors he selected were restrained—coral, sea-foam green, brown, and gray, for example—and they seemed both organic and yet slightly unnatural, a restrained combination of messages for a culture that both celebrated the machine and worried about losing the bucolic farm and the parklike woods. Wright's colors and marketing also stressed the acceptability and even desirability of mixing colors in a family's furnishings—another blow to formality and a suggestion of the impulse to "personalize" the home. This idea was best expressed by social advisor Emily Post in her 1930 book *The Personality of a House*, in which she lectured that the house's personality "should reflect your personality, just as every gesture you make—or fail to make—expresses . . . whatever characteristics are typically yours." Wright offered consumers a chance to buy mass-produced goods and still define themselves as somehow different from the "crowd." With several colors and several forms of tablewares, the permutations were almost endless.[24]

Other important innovations in home furnishings of the 1930s were Fiesta Ware and inexpensive glasswares now termed "Depression glass." Heavier and bulkier than Wright's wares, Fiesta Ware also suggested a democracy of the dinner table. It was inexpensive—sometimes "given away" as a premium by movie houses—and came in a variety of colors that could be mixed as well. It was a lower-quality earthenware than Wright's and it broke easily. Its flurry of popularity may also have been due to its coloration. The bright reds, blues, greens, and some of the pastels in which Fiesta Ware came were aggressively unnatural, the result of the triumphs of chemistry. Depression glass was also available in a multitude of colors and designs. It too was mixed by many homeowners in their decorative schemes, but like Fiesta Ware, its popularity waned by the 1940s.

THE KITCHEN AND THE BATH

Wright's products, Fiesta Ware, and Depression glass allowed Americans to be stylish, but they also were furnishings that could be marketed to respond to another of the era's domestic concerns—sanitation. The scientific sanitation movement that permeated American culture after World War I focused Americans' attention on the kitchen and bath. These rooms and this imperative provided the most receptive environments for the modern streamlined design of the 1920s and 1930s. Sears, Roebuck and Company hired industrial designer Raymond Loewy in 1935 to modernize the design of the "Coldspot" refrigerator. Loewy transformed the Coldspot from a boxy and bulky machine with a barely concealed motor to a white enameled unit with rounded corners, no visible legs, and a concealed and integrated motor. The smooth gleaming surfaces offered no hiding place for dirt: the Coldspot was a signal of science, modernity, and health, just as the older forms had been signals of the old and the unsanitary. It worked. Sales rocketed from 65,000 to 275,000 in one year.

Kitchen designers embraced the new styles and materials, adding glass doors and shelves to kitchen cabinets, and successfully promoting chrome-plated tubular steel chairs for the kitchen eating areas in the 1940s. Glass manufacturing giant Libby-Owens-Ford's "Day After Tomorrow Kitchen"—a takeoff on the 1939 New York World's Fair's motto "The World of Tomorrow"—was almost entirely made of glass, and featured an appliance-filled area that resembled an innovation in fastfood service popular in the era, the Automat. So popular was the all-glass kitchen that the firm produced three of the models and moved them to department stores all over the United States for fifteen months in 1944–1945. Like the glazed, stainless steel, and enameled surfaces of other kitchens, the glass kitchen signified "sanitary" and "scientific."

The bathroom was similarly changed by the cultural demands of sanitation and science. By 1915 the bathtub was transformed from the footed cast-iron heavyweight to the molded and recessed (but still heavy) double-shelled enameled tub. With a standard length of five feet, house designers developed the compact bathroom, often only five feet wide. In it were the tub (set across the wall farthest from the door), a small enameled sink, and a toilet. The whole room was in some cases covered with white or, later, pastel tiles. The bath as appendage to the bedroom—certainly a desired architectural device from the bath fixture manufacturers' point of view—was recommended if not necessarily adhered to by builders and homeowners since about 1915. Well-heeled Americans installed baths with bedrooms as a matter of course by the 1920s, perhaps reflecting the influence of hotel layouts and small but posh urban apartments.

By 1940 mail-order merchants offered a complete set of bathroom fixtures for $70, well within the reach of the steadily employed working class. The middle class, searching for ways to distinguish itself from the less affluent working class, had since the late 1920s turned from pure white to colors and color coordination in the bath. This was the obverse of Russel Wright's argument for mixed colors for personalization, but the seeming contradiction is explained by understanding that matched sets of tablewares—Wright's most numerous products—had been common in all grades of tablewares for over a century, and thus his support of mixed colors represented an affirmation of individuality that was a break with the usual practice. The color-coordinated ensembles of bathroom fixtures, bed and bath linens, kitchen cabinets and utensils, appliances, and even automobiles and auto interiors were, if not new ideas, new applications of an old idea, to be used to assert class distinction.

In the early 1920s the choices in bath linens were limited to white with the occasional red or blue piping. Cannon began marketing matching colors and different styles of linens (at a premium) in 1924. Martex introduced its fashion lines in 1926, including patterned towels as well as colors. By the late 1920s the "ensemble" idea had been picked up by manufacturers of other household goods for the bath and kitchen. Standard Plumbing Fixtures introduced ten shades in its line, including red, gray, avocado, orange, black, pink, and blue. Crane, Kohler, American Sanitary Manufacturing, and C. F. Church broadened their palettes. Church offered toilet seats in "nine pastel shades and nine sea-pearl tints."

What is to be made of this apparent disregard for what only shortly before had been the signal of sanitation? White had meant clean and orderly, as in laboratories, hospitals, and clinics. But the pressures of class aspiration and exclusivity had helped devalue the meaning of whiteness, at least in the bath, and to a lesser extent the kitchen. Colors meant money beyond the necessity for buying the goods. Colors also meant fashionability and "smartness," that irreverent snobbery that insisted (perhaps with the nervousness of class uncertainty) that one was above the common worker or petit bourgeoisie. The "smart" could ignore the overkill of whiteness; they assumed cleanliness for themselves and did not have to prove it.

For most Americans, art deco and art moderne—the avantgarde styles of the era—were unacceptable in home furnishings, other than for appliances and accessories such as lamps, and art objects such as "dancing lady" statuettes and cosmetic cases. The majority of the population was most comfortable with the forms, styles, and designs that were derived from English, French, arts and crafts, and American colonial styles. Academic and voguish critics winced at "colonial," "French," or "Tudor" style pieces that resembled nothing ever imagined in those cultures, but to their owners these variations and combinations represented "culture," civilization, economic success, and the pleasure of the new. Mail-order catalogs and retail outlets abounded for the willing consumer, loaded with new factory-made goods for the home.

It was in the graphic and visual arts of the era, and in advertisements and product packaging in particular, that nearly all Americans were likely to encounter line and form denoting speed and industry. Here products were pitched as new or modern, and chic. Art deco and art moderne also appeared as decoration on or in large-scale commercial buildings from St. Paul to San Antonio and from Seattle to Savannah. Interior decoration on federal post offices (commissioned in the Depression years to put artists to work), railroad trains (by 1934), and automobiles (by 1932) all took on the curvilinear look of streamlining and the angular and attenuated look of art moderne.

The home of the middle class living in the suburbs was, on the surface, very different from everyday life at the turn of the century. Indoor plumbing, electricity, motorized appliances, new appliances, automobiles, and for many a smaller, plainer, and, some argued, healthier home was the norm. More room, and allegedly more time for the family and the children on lawns or on porches, indicated at least an architectural change.

APARTMENTS

For those in the middle class who stayed in the city, the apartment building or the apartment hotel offered some of the amenities of private suburban living, albeit without the grass, but with the benefits of urban living. In 1919 the expensive Manoir Frontenac opened in Kansas City. Its 103 units contained electric grills in the kitchenette (for breakfast preparation) and an electrically driven dumbwaiter that transported hot meals upstairs from one of the hotel's three restaurants. Because of their urban proximity to large power houses, even apartments built for those of modest means often offered residents conveniences such as centralized vacuum cleaning and central laundries.

Urban apartment buildings offered residents proximity to the city's cultural offerings that many middle-class and wealthy Americans treasured. Apartment living also did not tie the dweller to the place for more than a year or, in some cases, a few months. There were no banks involved and no assets tied up. Interior space may have been less grand or extensive than that of the suburban homeowner, but for many, more space meant more worry. The threat of crime that many associated with the city was eased for some by the security guards and doormen many apartment owners hired to buffer the inhabitants from street life. And there was no grass to mow and often no automobile to maintain.

Whatever their class and whatever their immediate surroundings, there were certain commonalities in the everyday lives of Americans in their houses, whether they were suburban bungalows, urban apartments, rural cabins, or older, more stately houses in urban residential areas or the agricultural countryside. In most cases, technological innovations such as central heating and indoor plumbing separated the classes, although that distinction between working class and middle class began to break down by World War II. Technological changes tell something of the altered ways of getting things done— cleaning, ironing, cooking, and washing, for example—but new technology and new materials do not necessarily change basic behaviors. A new electric iron might be easier to use, but the gender of the worker remained the same. The old patterns— birth, growth, courtship, marriage, middle age, and death— remained, not exactly the same as before, but fundamentally so.

"Jersey Meadows"—squatters' houses in a city dump, Newark, New Jersey, April 1939. (Arthur Rothstein. *Courtesy Library of Congress.*)

Bread line beside approach to the Brooklyn Bridge, New York, New York, ca. 1935. (*Courtesy Library of Congress.*)

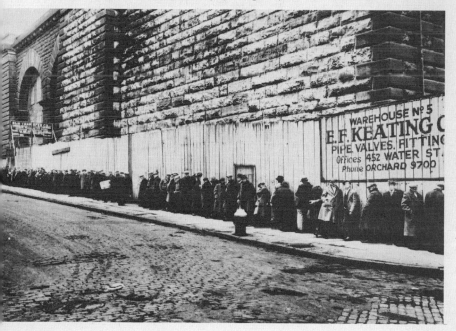

Hoboes hitchhiking out of California after police chased them out, Los Angeles County, California, ca. 1935. (Dorothea Lange. *Courtesy Library of Congress.*)

Two families from Chickasaw, Oklahoma, heading for the pea harvest, but unable to find work because they have no money for a trailer license, Santa Maria, California, ca. 1935. (Dorothea Lange. *Courtesy Library of Congress.*)

Living room of Enos Royer, Lancaster County, Pennsylvania, ca. 1938. (Sheldon Dick. *Courtesy Library of Congress.*)

"The Hill," Pittsburgh, Pennsylvania, July 1938. (Arthur Rothstein. *Courtesy Library of Congress.*)

Creole family cabin, Jenning, Louisiana, ca. 1920. (*Courtesy Library of Congress.*)

Indian tenant farm couple, McIntosh County, Oklahoma, June 1939. (Russell Lee. *Courtesy Library of Congress.*)

Baptismal service of the Primitive Baptist Church, Morehead, Kentucky, August 1940. (Marion P. Wolcott. *Courtesy Library of Congress.*)

Lois Slinker teaching the fifth grade in a one-room schoolhouse, Grundy County, Iowa, October 1939. (Arthur Rothstein. *Courtesy Library of Congress.*)

Students' recreation room, Holy Cross College, Worcester, Massachusetts, ca. 1920. (*Courtesy Library of Congress.*)

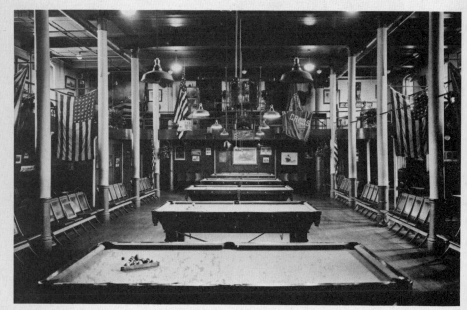

Mrs. Elizabeth Almoney in her living room with photographs of her three sons in uniform, November 1942. (Marjory Collins. *Courtesy Library of Congress.*)

Japanese-American evacuees arriving at the Santa Anita Reception Center, Los Angeles, California, March 1942. (Russell Lee. *Courtesy Library of Congress.*)

Eight Mexican-American children eating lunch—tortillas wrapped around chilis, June 1941. (Russell Lee. *Courtesy Library of Congress.*)

Davis Drug Store, Fort Smith, Arkansas, ca. 1920. (*Courtesy Library of Congress.*)

4

GROWING UP, GOING OUT, GETTING OLD

I N 1945 the intimate family world of 1915 seemed—and was—gone forever. The Great War, the middle-class expansion of the 1920s, the crises of the Depression, technological innovations in consumer goods, and World War II seemed to have altered family relationships, challenged traditional gender roles, and offered new social and economic expectations for many Americans. Many World War I soldiers returned with knowledge and experience of a more open (or at least less straightlaced) attitude toward sex and marriage. In the 1920s young people with access to automobiles took advantage of the mobility and the privacy the car offered to escape parents and chaperons while courting, and therby undermined the Victorian codes of conduct their parents had experienced. The economic and social dislocation wrought by the Depression disrupted family roles when fathers could not find work and men, women, and children lost their homes and drifted. World War II, which from the outset of American participation was seen as a long and deadly fight, was the catalyst for many marriages, "good-bye babies," and the expansion of employment possibilities for many women.

Yet certain images—and to a greater extent roles—of the sexes remained powerful, and were sustained. Men were to be responsible breadwinners—and physically strong and dominant. Women were supposed to be nurturing and emotional, physically weaker but bedrocks of familial stability. Boosted by their victory in the Great War in 1918, reinforced by the business boom bravado of the 1920s, men's self-image—defined in large part by their ability to earn an ever-increasing amount of money—took a severe beating in the Depression. Physical strength and grit were insufficient as the world stumbled and lurched toward chaos. Frank Merriwell, the still-popular fictional hero of numerous boys' books of the turn of the century, won football games by sheer strength and will, carrying the bulk of the other team's defense over the goal line as time ran out. But Merriwell, Flash Gordon, Superman, and all sorts of other fictional heroes did not work in the corridors of Washington or in the offices of businesses sending men home with no work.

Women were responsible for cushioning the uncertainties of war and economic dislocation, and were the arbiters of the new rules of courtship and child-rearing of the era. These were roles of complexity and contradiction because the mass media often portrayed women as weak, even frivolous. The "Mom" who was the foundation of the family was the roundish figure of comfort and steadfastness brilliantly limned by Norman Rockwell in his rendition of "Freedom from Want" in 1943 or the women portrayed on the soap operas introduced after 1930. But she had competition: the elongated lithe figure of advertising's "smart" set. The latter offered little comfort in the Depression: In fact, "smart," stylish women were implicitly humiliating to those men who had lost their jobs after the crash.

The archetypical family structure of popular culture—husband and wife and children in one household—was predominant enough to maintain the stereotype, but there were many variants. Working-class Americans, whether immigrant or native-born, often packed the family lodgings with boarders to make ends meet. Their parents sometimes moved in during difficult times or as their health declined. Although many families valued education highly, children often went to work as early as they could to increase family income.

Black family structure in the city and in the countryside was most often that of the two-parent household. In the alleys and residential streets to which they were confined by poverty and racism, extended kinship and community care were provided by the neighborhood. While in some cases there may have been little participation in the white rituals of formal marriage and therefore the "legitimacy" of births in legal wedlock, extensive kinship networks remained strong over substantial distances. Throngs of relatives of three and four generations reconvened for births, annual "homecomings," and funerals. There was considerable housing turnover among poor farmers and tenants, but, as George McDaniel has shown in his study of rural Maryland, those who moved in were often kin to the departed.[1]

Bearing and Raising Children

BIRTH

The number of American children born in hospitals increased steadily between 1915 and 1945: By 1938 more than 50 percent of all infants were delivered in hospitals. In part this change was due to an alteration in Americans' image of the institution from that of a building full of sick, infectious, and dying people to that of a center of sanitary science. Other important factors in the increased number of hospital-born children included a growing trust of physicians and the successful marketing techniques of the baby food industry. All created strong pressures on parents to allow professionals to supervise the birth and direct the feeding of infants. In rural areas home births with midwives or male physicians in attendance were more common than they were in cities, but were declining in frequency. The automobile made it possible for physicians to get to a bedside faster and for patients to travel to hospitals with more ease than either could previously. New drugs, new diagnostic tools, and new treatments offered the promise of decreasing infant mortality, but not for all. Infant mortality among urban black Americans was twice that of urban whites in this era. Medicine's bright promise was as white as the inside of a hospital.

NURSING AND "FORMULA"

Infant feeding practices and intestinal disorders were major concerns for physicians, government bureaucrats, and parents, since many infant deaths resulted from diarrhea and dehydration. The breast-versus-bottle debate that had heated up popular and professional medical discourse in the late nineteenth century continued through 1945, but with a critical difference—bottle feeding became the more acceptable and, for many, a more desirable choice. The decline of breast-feeding among the middle class and the wealthy was in part a result of the increasing popular acceptance of medicine and nutrition as "scientific" in the late nineteenth and early twentieth centuries. For working-class women the shift to bottle feeding was linked to this culture-wide faith in science, the increased availability of cheaper bottles and other feeding paraphernalia, and the necessity for many of these women to work outside the home. Some physicians buttressed their arguments in favor of bottle feeding by erroneously warning that working-class women's breast milk was probably less healthy than scientifically developed "formula." They maintained that the diet of the adult working class was likely to be deficient in "vital" substances, especially the new miracle "vital amines," or vitamins, that were first isolated in the early twentieth century.

Formula, or "percentage," feeding was based on laboratory analysis of breast milk for fat, sugar, casein, and protein content. Properly supervised commercial production of products with exactly the same ratios as the average healthy woman's breast milk was considered a giant step toward lowering the rate of infant mortality. The revelation that raw cow's milk (an alternative some women had tried) was loaded with bacteria and was in any case difficult for infants to digest without alteration helped establish formula as a desirable alternative to breast feeding. In addition, the widespread availability of pasteurized cow's milk in most cities and towns by 1915 aided efforts to decrease infant mortality. With a fuller understanding of the ways in which diseases were spread and the methods by which bottles and nipples could be sterilized, infant mortality for Americans as a whole (but not African-Americans and American Indians) dropped radically.

Some physicians attacked the new science of artificial feeding as unnatural and indicative of an overcivilized and "soft" America. They were particularly scornful of middle-class and wealthy women, since they did not work outside the home and still chose to bottle feed. But the critics were no match for white coats and gleaming labs. Formula feeding was so closely linked to the power of science and the Progressives' drive for better health, sanitation, and overall social and economic efficiency that breast-feeding was easily linked to the "old-fashioned," poverty-stricken, immigrant, and other "inferior" types. Ironically, immigrants who often could least afford formula bought and used it even if the mother did not work outside the home. They associated formula with science and perhaps with the United States and a better life. The emotional bonding argument in support of breast-feeding was unveiled in the late 1920s, but it gained relatively few adherents.

The shift to bottle-feeding, after a brief initial period of breast-feeding, and the sanitation crusade meant altered procedures in middle-class and wealthy homes from almost the day infants were born or came home. Professional advice and traditional wisdom sometimes competed for attention in the determination of exactly the right time to transfer the infant from breast to bottle, but whatever the decision about timing, bottle feeding meant different work and routines. Junior still got fed every four hours and sometimes on demand, depending on the mother's predilections. Ideally the kitchen was then transformed into a miniature laboratory and the bedroom or nursery into a domestic hospital room, though working-class families often could not manage to give up the space or the time to meet the new standards. The concern for cleanliness necessitated the organization of a home sterilization system. Usually this meant a large pot of boiling water on the stove, and tongs to remove the glass bottle and nipples once boiled. Commercially produced formula or warmed pasteurized cow's milk diluted with water and sometimes fortified with sugar was then to be ladled or poured into the sterile bottle, and the nipple attached by means of a screw cap over the rubber part. It was much like canning fruits and vegetables in a hot-water bath (with less hot water), and since some women still canned or once had, the task was familiar. Once cooled to a temperature the infant could tolerate, feeding began.

Sterilized bottle-feeding was a constant chore, at least until the baby progressed to strained and solid foods. By the end of the 1920s commercially produced mashed, strained, and otherwise pulverized fruits, vegetables, and meats were widely available, and pediatricians recommended that infants begin eating these concoctions at about six months. These goods and this advice further damaged the case of the advocates of breast-feeding, since it undercut the idea of milk as the sole and best source of nourishment for the very young.[2]

The everyday experience of child-rearing, at least for the middle class and the wealthy, was also altered somewhat by the increasing popular awareness of the work of child psychologists. As they had a century earlier, Americans of the era perceived a "wave" of crime threatening to overwhelm them, and sought answers for the seeming increase in lawlessness in the childhood experiences of the outlaws. Countless sociological studies of adult prison inmates helped generate a multitude of articles in popular and professional journals, nearly all of which linked antisocial behavior to economic, social, and emotional deprivation in childhood. Sensationalist newspaper stories, the actions of the underworld, and movies also turned attention to the child as the source of future antisocial behavior. Movies such as *Angels with Dirty Faces* (1938) and *Dead End* (1937) portrayed children as basically good, but corrupted by their environment. The burden of blame rested upon the parents. Feed the little tykes the wrong stuff, avoid playing with them, take little interest in their studies, and a potential Al Capone, Bonnie Parker, or Clyde Barrow was liable to emerge. Advice was easy to find: Columns in newspapers and in periodicals such as *Ladies' Home Journal* abounded. *Parents* magazine began publication in 1926.

EDUCATION

Improving primary and secondary education was for many policymakers and parents a critically important element not only in crime prevention but also in the achievement of the

more positive goal of increasing the general welfare of the
nation. When the United States began to mobilize for battle in
1917, standardized intelligence testing of recruits revealed a
shockingly high percentage of men who appeared to be of sub-
standard intelligence. These tests and statistics confused intelli-
gence with education, and took no account of the quality or
availability of education for the recruits, but the results led to
a call for wide-ranging educational reform.

After 1915 teacher training standards were raised, research
in learning skills and styles increased, states and localities
lengthened the school year, and the minimum legal dropout
age was raised. Only about 7 percent of all Americans between
fourteen and seventeen years old attended high school in 1900;
by 1915 that figure had doubled. The curve of high school
attendance continued on roughly that path until 90 percent
were in school in 1960. Children who thought about skipping
school faced more numerous and more efficient truant officers.
In urban areas of most states kindergarten for five-year-olds was
introduced, and more training in the trades and vocational skills
was included in the curriculum. By 1930, 90 percent of all
grade-school-age children were attending school, up from approximately 75 percent in 1920.

Immigrant parents often made great financial sacrifices
to send their offspring to private, usually church-sponsored
schools. In Chicago in 1930, twenty Irish Catholic and thirty-
three German Lutheran and Catholic schools were operating.
Polish and Czechoslovakian church-run schools also were organized and popular with Czechs and Poles. These schools were
a way of keeping elements of home-country culture alive, and
parents took comfort in the fact that the school and its related
activities constituted a pool of potential marriage partners
within the ethnic and religious group.

In rural areas educational reform proceeded more slowly. In
many of these areas, and especially in the South, education for
African-Americans meant segregation and, for both races,
sometimes a school year that was often only three months long.
The school was usually a one-room building, and most students
had to walk each way—often several miles.

I went to an old country-style schoolhouse. . . . One building that had eight rows in it, one for each grade. Seven rows were quiet while the eighth one recited. . . . The woman teacher got the munificent sum of $30 a month . . . she taught every subject, and all eight grades. This was 1929, '30, '31. . . . At the back corner was a great pot-bellied stove that kept the place warm. It had about an acre of ground, a playground with no equipment. Out there were the toilets, three-holers.[3]

Landlords often pressured families to take children out of school to work on the farm, and the pull of an extra hand to possibly increase crop yields or fend off insects and other marauders often convinced parents to curtail education beyond the sixth grade. Those black families that could manage to let children off from fieldwork to go to high school often found that there were none to attend. Only two were open to black Marylanders in the 1920s: one in Washington, D.C., and the other in Baltimore. Eventually the automobile and the school bus put nearly all of the one- or two-room schoolhouses and their one- or two-teacher staffs out of business. Stricter attendance requirements and more and better teacher education also improved the educational standards and benefits of the rural child.

More affluent white farmers' children took advantage of education in agriculture and home economics through the efforts of the Grange and 4-H clubs. By 1929, 750,000 boys and girls were 4-H members. They went to weekly or monthly meetings and learned about scientific agriculture and how to best show their stock at the county and state fairs that took place late in the summer. Their parents learned from agricultural extension agents, who, equipped with literature from the home office, regularly visited, bringing news of the markets, recipes, preserving tips, new machines, and scientific advances.

In the larger northern cities de facto and de jure segregation limited access to high-quality education for almost all black children. Not until 1954 would the idea of "separate but equal" be overturned by the Supreme Court. For white middle-class and wealthy children in cities, towns, and suburbs the educational experience was vastly different. Parents pressured their

form of announcing one's intentions—almost always by the
male—was not practical or desirable for young people living in
crowded urban centers. Moreover, calling meant visiting a
woman in her home; dating meant going out and escaping the
watchful control of the parents and chaperons with whom Victorian American youth had struggled. Dance halls, cars, speakeasies, restaurants, and especially the darkened moviehouses
were haven and heaven for couples, but all required an additional element to make the experience possible—money.

With limited financial resources, most urban working-class
men had few dates, and had to content themselves with "making time" at work or with visiting women at home or in social
surroundings such as the union hall and church. The latter were
multigenerational and courting was therefore more difficult.
Movies were inexpensive and popular with the working-class
young, not only for their entertainment value but also because
they were the cheapest path to privacy. For young people in
rural areas the opportunities to meet (and be alone with) eligible members of the opposite sex were more limited: visits to
town, church, yearly fairs, the Grange, and the occasional picnic. Scattered throughout the countryside with often great distances between them, young people in the country faced dim
prospects for meeting the right man or woman. Organizations
such as the Grange or the American Country Life Association
recognized the problem and its seemingly inevitable consequence—young rural Americans leaving the farm for the city.
"If the flight to the city . . . shall go on as rapidly as it has in the
last few years," wrote the president of the American Country
Life Association in the proceedings of its 1929 annual meeting,
"the next generation will witness a farm population largely
composed of the physically and mentally unfit." The solution to
the impending crisis, the association agreed, was "organization":

> Organization means the difference between the mob and a highly
> organized, progressive society. The psychologists tell us that in the
> unorganized mass of men the primal instincts have full sway. There-
> fore, he who appeals most strongly to the passions of the unorgan-

ized mass influences them most. Reason, justice, mercy, all the finer qualities which civilization has evolved are swept away by the rising tide of primitive passions of men.[6]

Using references to the basic elements of Freudian psychology, this passage demonstrates the pervasive fear of demagogues and the masses that gripped many elite urban and rural Americans between 1915 and 1945 as well as an almost desperate call for the realization of a nostalgic agrarian world that was disappearing or had already vanished.

RULES OF THE GAME

Because it was public and a part of consumer culture, dating became a form of competition for both men and women. Getting a date—or even better for women, many requests for the same night—was seen as a personal triumph, a quantifiable measure of self-worth. Advice columns on dating etiquette proliferated in the pages of the newspapers and magazines directed at women. The message seemed to be that the actual experience—the film, the dance, or the dinner—was secondary to getting a date, having a lot of money spent on oneself, and being seen. Women were warned not to be too cheap a date: "I know I don't give many second dates to boys unless they can take me to keen places," wrote one woman. Men were advised to aim for beautiful women if they were going to part with much cash. ("Any chicken has to be a Lana Turner or a Hedy La Marr [sic] to rate more than a buck seventy-five or two bucks for a usual date.") Given parental (and many young people's) concern about premarital sex and pregnancy, the public elements of dating could have been a clever hedge against too much privacy and too little control. But the cash calculus that some men and women saw in dating might also have established a scale of sexual permissiveness based on the expense of the date. "If [a woman] had two drinks with [a man]," recalled Chicagoan Kid Pharaoh, "and she didn't lay her frame down, she was in a serious manner. She could have one, and explain she made a mistake by marrying some sucker. . . . But in the Thirties, if you had a second drink and she didn't make a commitment where she's going to lay her frame down for you the entire matter was resolved quickly to the point and could end in mayhem."[7] Class distinction and consciousness also figured into the sexual element of a relationship. Men who considered themselves of a higher class than their companion often thought they deserved more sexual activity from their partners than they might have from women of their own or a wealthier class.[8]

Dating many men—rather than pairing off—was pitched by advisors and parents as not only a smart way to enjoy oneself and prepare to meet the right man, but also as a way to limit the probability of sexual intercourse. "General popularity," rather than one suitor, was the goal recommended, and was considered a measure of self-worth. Warnings against "cheapness" abounded, and the confusion of economics and self-worth embodied in the term further revealed the era's equation of sex, morality, and money. "Too many late hours lower your value. Reprice your line," wrote Elizabeth Woodward in the May 8, 1942, issue of *Ladies' Home Journal.*[9]

SEX

This cacophony of advice was akin to closing the barn door after the horses have bolted. The new sexual norms for which the young of the 1920s are remembered were a result of the popularization of elements of Freudian psychology, in particular the idea that sex could be pleasurable for women, and that the act of coition could be physically separated from the responsibility of reproduction by the use of newly mass-produced contraceptive devices. Necking (physical contact above the neck) and petting (activities below the neck) were such common practices after 1915 that magazine articles openly discussed them. Floyd Dell's "Why They Pet," an article in the October 1931 issue of *Parents,* might have shocked a few readers, but for most it offered information about a younger generation that parents did not comprehend. And *Parents* was hardly a radical magazine.[10]

Contraceptive devices transformed sexual behavior by the 1920s. They were available in most gas station rest rooms and even in the Sears, Roebuck mail-order catalog, and contraceptive information was available, if sometimes difficult to find.[11] Throughout the era the middle class used condoms, diaphragms, coitus interruptus, abstinence, and spermicides. Lehn and Fink, manufacturers of Lysol, gradually transformed their advertisements to euphemistically suggest what the public already had decided about the stuff—that it not only worked as a disinfecting and deodorizing douche, but also that its germ-killing action could help alleviate "calendar fear," or the terror of late menstrual flow and unwanted pregnancy. The Lynds found that more than one-half of Muncie's working-class women favored contraception and nearly all of the city's business-class women did so. They discovered that seventy percent of Muncie's young middle class had sexual relations before marriage. Declining birth rates among all classes in city and country throughout the 1920s can hardly be attributed to mass abstinence or more accurate knowledge of the conception cycle.

The limits of necking, petting, and coitus were allegedly set by women, and the boundaries of behavior were based on the assumption that men would not force themselves on women after an inexact but generally acknowledged number of protestations. Physical and economic power were male attributes and advantages, but the responsibility for chastity ("keeping one's worth") rested with the women. "A man is only as bad as the woman he is with," wrote the author of *How to Win and Hold a Husband* in 1945. More blunt was the famous arbiter of good behavior and taste, Emily Post: "Petting and cuddling have the same cheapening effect as that produced on merchandise which has through constant handling become faded and rumpled, smudged or frayed and thrown out on the bargain counter in a marked-down lot."[12] What a fate. The price reductions on the "sales tag" of virtue were visible, it seemed. The continuity of this warning against sexual activity by the young is an indirect but credible indicator of the persistence of premarital sexual intercourse.

As Paula Fass has demonstrated in *The Damned and the Beautiful,* critics who worried about lost virginity among the collegiate were right about students' sexual activities about 50 percent of the time. And students were not the only people who were hopping into bed with someone who was not their spouse. A Southern Methodist University study of 1935 discovered that 75 percent of Dallas area motel business was accountable to men and women who stayed only a short time—less than a day, and seldom a night. J. Edgar Hoover, the director of the Federal Bureau of Investigation, thought most motels were "dens of vice" catering to the "hot pillow trade." A 1928 study found that approximately 25 percent of all married American men and women admitted to at least one adulterous love affair.[13]

CLOTHING

Critics and the young of the 1920s exaggerated distinctions between generations in matters of sex, but there were generational differences in clothing preferences. In the 1920s young women rejected shoe-length skirts, choosing above-the-knee hemlines and rolled stockings. Loose chemises replaced the corseted clothing that emphasized a matronly bust and hips. Bobbed hair—which some critics derided as an invitation for men to "take liberties"—was in vogue, in lieu of long, upswept, and pinned hairstyles. Amply endowed women flattened their breasts with elastic girdlelike apparatuses or simply bound them to give a more boyish flat-chested appearance.

By the 1930s most of the presumed wildness and boyish enthusiasm of the young had vanished. Fashions accentuated rather than flattened breasts; double-cup, underwired brassieres were fashionable, and the motherly figure again returned as the ideal. Fitted waistlines on women's dresses returned, skirt and dress hemlines fell to about one inch above the floor, and padded shoulders were common by 1940. The "sweater girl," a 1940s euphemism for a busty woman in a tight sweater, was further proof of the return of the bosom as a marker of womanhood, although some critics thought such garb was a "distraction" for men, especially in the workplace. The fashion changes suggest a more serious approach to the role of women and especially motherhood than in the 1920s. Middle-class men in and out of work wore conservative dark suits if they could. Skimmers and boaters were not much in evidence after the crash, except among some of the very wealthy who not only missed getting hurt by the Depression, but in some cases actually profited from it.

"MODERN MARRIAGE"

In the 1920s the young heading toward marriage encountered a new set of arbiters of convention. Academics—sociologists and some health professionals—studied courtship and issued manifestos that identified the secrets of a happy marriage and effective child-rearing. Colleges and universities began to offer courses in "modern marriage." The first such offering was probably at the University of North Carolina in 1927. Ernest Groves, a prominent sociologist who had written a textbook on marriage in 1926, was hired to teach the course, which had been offered at the request of senior men. A product of the new sexuality, the course also owed some intellectual debt to the continuing power of eugenics and high school hygiene courses that touched lightly and cautiously on matters of anatomy and sex. Ten years later more than 200 colleges and universities offered similar courses. The University of California at Berkeley registered 12,000 students for the course between 1939 and 1945. As impressive as these statistics are, however, the students represent but 2 percent of all Americans between the ages of eighteen and twenty-four in any given year between 1939 and 1945. Groves did reach a broader audience with his "lecture" in *Good Housekeeping*'s "College Courses on Marriage Relations," which began in September 1937.[14]

"Companionate marriage" was the fashionable term for the ideal marriage relationship of the 1920s. A "good sport" and shared interests, rather than the nineteenth-century concept of "separate spheres," were the keys to happiness. Promoters of the new kind of relationship encouraged couples to socialize together with other couples, instead of the traditional middle-class and wealthy social practices that separated the sexes. Reformers criticized men who were constantly slipping off to clubs, bars, or golf courses that excluded women, and they attacked women who for their social lives relied primarily on entertaining other women at home, or on meeting them in restaurants or department store salons, or at their own clubs. The companionate marriage concept explains the surge in middle-class women's interest in sports they could play with their husbands or boyfriends, such as golf and tennis.

The working-class marriage received far less attention from these reformers, and couples probably experienced this ideal less than did those who were more affluent. Traditional gender roles remained strongly entrenched among urban immigrant workers and African-Americans, as well as the white urban industrial working class that had been born in the United States. In part this was a result of the exigencies of trying to eke out a living. Leisure was a scarce commodity, and the free time that the middle class and the wealthy enjoyed simply did not exist for workers.

Companionate marriage was a way that the well-off sought to distinguish themselves from the poorer sort, who did not experience as much of the flush times of the 1920s. In the 1920s, at least, the idea was also carefully linked with eugenics and racial and ethnic nationalism, pitting the middle class and the wealthy against the urban and rural poor and those who held to traditional gender roles. For all that, companionate marriage bestowed considerable benefits for those women who gained a greater measure of equality in their marriages and freedom in their daily lives.

Religion, Aging, Dying

FAITH IN AND OUT OF THE HOME

Almost all the advocates of companionate marriage identified religious devotion as an important family activity. Organized religion played a distinguishable and significant part in the everyday lives of most Americans, even if they only went to their place of worship occasionally. In addition to their functions as places for prayer, marriages, christenings (or brises), communions (or bar mitzvahs), and funerals, churches and synagogues were social gathering places. Most offered their members the chance to participate in organized sporting events, clubs, picnics, and potluck suppers, and in times of trouble many churches and synagogues provided free food and shelter. One Polish immigrant boy remembered that "church was almost a second home to us. I mean we never miss[ed] a novena or any service at all." But others fell away from the fold. Another immigrant's husband "stopped going because you just get so much of it. . . . My oldest son also enlightened me when he was sixteen and gradually we stopped going altogether."[15]

Many rural white and black Americans were periodically gathered to the religious fold in the revivals that occurred every summer, particularly among the Baptists and Methodists. Urban revival meetings also netted converts and backsliders throughout the period, especially in the Depression, when many down-and-out people looked to the church for comfort and some sustenance. African-Americans could boast that Harlem's Abyssinian Baptist Church, with 14,000 members in the 1930s, was the largest Protestant congregation in the United States. The services and music of many of the northern Methodist and Baptist churches that served black parishioners tended to be less demonstrative than their southern counterparts, and after the great migration began during World War I, many newly arrived blacks established churches with more outwardly emotional services and music. In the South black worshipers usually prayed in small and modestly appointed one-room churches that were also centers of African-American culture and tradition. Many churches organized the "homecomings" that nearly every year brought families together for music, food, dancing, socializing, and church services.

Americans of all classes included some physical reminders of religious affiliation in their homes. Even in the poorest abodes walls were often decorated with items such as framed prints and calendars depicting biblical events, needlework or printed mottoes such as "God Bless Our Home," and crucifixes. Religious statuary or menorahs often graced parlors and dining rooms. Americans considered these images and other objects powerful reminders and statements of their faith and important instruments of civilization.

Jews came to the United States in two great bursts of immigration. In the middle of the nineteenth century thousands of German Jews settled all over the country, especially in the cities. Always a minority and usually singled out—sometimes brutally—by the Christian majority, they held on to their culture and built synagogues from the eighteenth century onward. Some succeeded in agriculture, and some in finance and industry, and many of the latter were particularly significant in the financial sector of the southern cotton economy before the Civil War.

The second large immigration occurred between 1890 and 1920, when thousands of eastern and southern European Jews fled pogroms and poverty. Most entered the United States through New York City and settled in northeastern and upper midwestern cities, and others landed and settled in south Texas, Washington, D.C., and the Far West. Many were rural peasants or urban artisans in the service trades, such as tailoring or shoemaking. Like African-Americans, and to a lesser extent Roman Catholics, Jews were harassed by bigots such as the Ku Klux Klan and other exclusionists, who branded the Jews as "Christ-killers" and "alien reds." Synagogues and neighborhoods were places of refuge as well as areas of conviviality and devotion.

HOLIDAYS

For Christians, the most important home and church intersection occurred at Christmas. For centuries an important holiday for Roman Catholic, Russian Orthodox, and Greek Orthodox families, Christmas was not celebrated by American Protestants in the northern states with much fanfare, if any, until the middle of the nineteenth century. Southerners who were descendants of an Episcopal tradition had more boisterous and revelrous celebrations, often consuming huge amounts of liquor, especially the appropriately named "punch."

By the early twentieth century, however, feasting, drink, presents, and gifts to the poor were entrenched throughout the country. The Germans had introduced the Christmas tree by the 1850s, and printers such as Louis Prang had met the demand for Christmas cards in the late nineteenth century. By that time, the jolly rotund Santa Claus or Saint Nicholas—a derivation of a painting and engravings by *Harper's Weekly* cartoonist Thomas Nast—had replaced an earlier figure associated with the holiday, Ruprecht. The older figure was more of an angel of punishment than a "jolly old elf," as Clement Moore referred to him in his mid-nineteenth-century poem "The Night Before Christmas."

Gift-giving formed a central part of the celebration, and for the middle class and the wealthy there was a special significance attached to the homemade gift. (The working class had neither the time nor the inclination for this practice, since homemade was what they got more often than they would have liked anyway.) Middle-class complaints in the early twentieth century about cheap store-bought gifts that were simply "gimcracks" were swept aside by the 1920s enthusiasm for domestic appliances as gifts for women. During the 1920s and 1930s, magazines such as the *Women's Home Companion* and *Good Housekeeping* were loaded not only with advertisements for appliances as Christmas gifts, but also with articles that listed desirable gifts for women. Presumably wives were to show their spouses the articles to discreetly help them find the right electric toaster, clothes iron, curling iron, vacuum cleaner, and, if they were lucky, clothes washer. Advertisements and store clerks pushed perfumes, toiletries, and tablewares on men for the women in their lives, and women were urged to buy or make clothes for their spouses and fathers. Books were popular gifts for both sexes and especially for children, who were also showered with toys if the family could afford it.

GROWING OLD

The holidays Christians and Jews celebrated reaffirmed the family's ties and marked out the cycles of the year, much as the seasons did. But growing old was not cyclical and renewing; it was linear and, for many, threatening. In the United States between 1915 and 1945 aging was eased if one had money or a family that was willing and able to provide care when it was needed. But most older Americans had little money and thought that dependence on their children would be an imposition and a hardship. Moreover, moving in with the children was not an option many older Americans wanted—in their children's homes parents had to respect the wishes and rules of their children. For many it was humiliating to accept an inferior role. Advertising presented the elderly—when depicted at all— as objects of nostalgia or anachronisms—background subjects present for effect.

There were few if any "safety nets" for the older American until Social Security became law in the mid-1930s, and even that was little help to those already old, infirm, and poor. The working class, especially in the extractive industries, often suffered from job-related injuries or chronic disabling conditions that aged them prematurely. Miners hacked from black lung or silicosis. Farmers often lost digits or limbs in machines, or contracted lung diseases from the dust raised while working dry ground or harvesting grain and hay, or became deaf as a result of driving tractors that normally had no muffler. Few workers had company pensions, and those who did found them to be meager.

But aging was not simply a tale of woe and unmitigated disaster, even for the working class and the poor. When the last of the children left home it was the beginning of a time of freedom as well as the end of an era. And not all children disappeared from their parents' lives. Many settled near their siblings and their parents, especially since working-class children starting out on the job often did so in the same place where their parents or relatives already worked. Even in the Depression, when the aged suffered terribly and thousands of young people bummed it and rode the rails, and husbands sometimes took off from the rest of family, the majority of American families stuck together and in some way took care of each other.

There were some organizations that provided social comforts, if not physical protection, for the older American. Synagogues, churches, and fraternal groups such as the Knights of Columbus, the Elks, the Moose, the Odd Fellows, the Grange, and the Masons provided camaraderie and understanding for their members. Older women had fewer structured opportunities for socializing, but had more continuity in their social relationships, since many had for years centered their social lives in their homes and neighborhoods among friends their own age. Excluded from many clubs and lodges because of their gender, they built networks of women friends and neighbors as they grew old.

DYING

When death visited a family, it brought them together in a community of grief, and also into contact with a funeral director. Then the nation's more than 15,000 funeral directors prepared the body for interment, sold caskets, and laid out the dead in the home or, in a small but steadily increasing number of cases, in funeral "homes." Until about 1850 embalming was regarded as an exotic, ancient, and curious procedure, but it became the norm by 1920 in all regions except the South, where the old method of wrapping and rapidly burying the corpse persisted. Embalming had become an acceptable choice for the bereaved because most Americans wanted to view an opened casket at the funeral and nearly all wished to see the dead as "asleep." In addition, the old way of preserving the body until burial did not always prevent some discoloration and putrification, conditions that were extremely upsetting to the mourners and, in the case of decay, a potential health risk. Cremation appealed to only a tiny fraction of Americans, in spite of advocates' arguments that the process was more sanitary and less expensive than embalming. Cremation was too radical a step for those people who on some level were certain that resurrection included a physical aspect or for those who viewed cremation as barbaric or in opposition to their religious traditions.

By 1915 the rectangular metal-lined and upholstered casket had replaced the six-sided wooden coffin at nearly all funerals. The concern for preservation and sanitation that had made embalming the choice of mourners also sold funeral directors' customers on the casket. In addition, the attention paid to the design and the decoration of caskets—elaborate hardware of precious metals, fine woods, and expensive fabrics—directed attention from death itself and to the trappings of the event.

Nearly all religions, ethnic groups, and classes in some way gathered to honor the dead at graveside services. Ministers, priests, and rabbis had by 1925 begun to alter their presentations so that the idea of death as retribution for human sins was replaced by a more consoling and positive interpretation of dying. The funeral services also became more private, isolating the family and intimate friends from the more public ceremonies of earlier times. Grief was considered a painful and personal affair, an emotion to be overcome as quickly as possible. By the 1920s the practice among women of wearing black and lilac for as long as two years after the death of their husband was discarded except for a very few traditionalists.

Wakes, sitting shivas (for Jewish families), or "at home" gatherings remembered the dead and helped the bereaved go on. The world wars made the process particularly difficult because remains were not always available, and the death that had been feared when the soldiers left occurred far away under unknown circumstances. Moreover, death in war always meant that sons and fathers had died before their time, leaving siblings, wives, and children to mourn at a time in their lives when they never expected to have to do so. The world wars were but twenty-four years apart for the United States, close enough to draw nearly all American families into their shadow. Only a relatively few men were too young to serve in World War I and too old to serve in World War II. Beginning in 1917, two consecutive generations faced up to the complex tangle of emotions, opportunities, and threats of going off to fight.

Wars

WORLD WAR I

When the German government announced in January 1917 that its attack vessels would no longer discriminate between neutral nations and belligerents, direct American involvement in the European war was simply a matter of time. When Woodrow Wilson arrived on Capitol Hill in April of that year to address the special session of Congress he had called, both the legislators and the general public (except for the pacifist and isolationist minorities) had been fired up for battle against the Germans. Riots and petitions against nonintervention had been occurring with frequency in large cities and small towns; there had already been boycotts against German-American businesses and several incidents of destruction of property owned by suspected German sympathizers.

Wilson's war message summoned up the ideals and language of a political generation that remembered the long carnage of the Civil War and the brief, if deadly, adventure in the Caribbean and the Pacific in 1898. Ironic in that it was delivered by a southerner and ardent segregationist, the war message invoked the cadences of the oratory of the Union Army and its defenders. "America is privileged to spend her blood and might," the president intoned, to "fight . . . for democracy, for the right of those who submit to authority to have a voice in their own Governments, for the rights and liberties of small nations, for a universal dominion of right. . . ." They were stirring words, but for the soldiers and for many Americans the war had little to do with those ideals, and the American Congress's rejection of Wilson's League of Nations after the signing of the peace treaty was a more accurate symbol of what the war meant for the United States. Lurking in the shadows of the hallways at the Paris peace conference after the war had ended was the realization that it had all been a huge waste. European national economies had been laid waste, and a generation of European men had been slaughtered. In the Congress lawmakers were convinced that Europe was an unregenerate decayed culture that threatened to suck the United States into a vortex of murderous chaos.

But in 1917 it was not difficult to sell Americans on entering the war. Wilson tried to ensure that the effort would be a popular success by creating the Committee on Public Information, headed by journalist George W. Creel. The CPI enlisted Hollywood and the music industry in its campaigns. Filmmakers produced scores of works with such titles as *The Claws of the Hun,* and the biggest industry stars—Mary Pickford and Douglas Fairbanks—toured the country to sell war bonds to their adoring fans. Ragtime and romantic ballads with patriotic messages abounded, and the sheet music industry turned out hundreds of songs with posterlike covers depicting soldiers and women (with little children in their arms) draped in the flag. The CPI paid approximately 75,000 speakers to deliver short pep talks in moviehouses and vaudeville theaters. Political cartoonists all over the country pictured the Germans as baby-killers and barbarians. In May 1917, Congress passed the Selective Service Act. Twenty-three million men registered; 2.8 million were inducted into the armed forces, and a total of 5 million served. The First Army Division marched through Paris on July 4, 1917. By September 1918 "Black Jack" Pershing, the American commander-in-chief, commanded an army of 1.2 million men and American forces held 85 miles (about one-fourth) of the Western Front.

For most Americans the war was a great crusade to be supported in as many ways as possible. The men going off to Europe to do battle were the most obvious American contribution, but the home front paid its price as well, if not in lives and wounds. The economy was unprepared for war, and would not be in full wartime swing for almost a year after the American entry. Wilson's conservatism led him to a policy of voluntary restraint to control consumption and the promise of high profits as the incentive to raise production. The War Industries Board, composed of a hundred businessmen led by Bernard Baruch, set prices and tried to increase efficiency in production and distribution of goods for the war effort. Other boards Wilson created effectively nationalized the railway system, allowing high profits and high wages while authorizing $500 million for repairs and new equipment. To conserve coal and other fuels, Americans were encouraged to turn out all lights at night and to use no gas on Sundays.

Not everyone agreed with the decision to intervene. The pacifist contingent was never very large, but it was vocal. Prominent socialist Eugene Debs saw the war as another chapter in the international capitalist struggle for world domination, to be conducted at the expense of the laboring poor. Militants such as "Big Bill" Haywood of the International Workers of the World and anarchist Emma Goldman shared Debs's analysis, and advocated resistance by all means, including violence if necessary. Some moderate and conservative reformers were not uniformly in favor of the war. Jane Addams, of Chicago's Hull House fame, opposed the war because of her pacifist convictions. Intellectual Randolph Bourne warned of the results of entanglement in the war at the expense of the nation's internal divisions and needs. In the Midwest, with its strong German and Scandinavian Lutheran presence, the Non-Partisan League, a farmer and laborer political party, advocated a pro-German foreign policy rather than the pro-English policies they perceived to be behind Wilson's neutrality.

Women could not serve on the front lines or in the medical corps, but thousands volunteered for work as Red Cross nurses at home and in Europe. "Gray ladies" gathered together and prepared bandages for the boys wounded "over there." Other women took newly available jobs in defense and other industries, as they would in World War II. The war effort in part aided women in their quest for the vote. Some suffragettes refused to support the war until women were guaranteed the right to vote, but most backed the effort with the understanding that they were to be heard from when the crisis was over. Many western states had already passed laws enabling women to vote, and Rhode Island and New York had done so in 1917. In 1918 even the conservative Wilson came out in favor of votes for women. In 1919 Congress passed the nineteenth amendment. In the summer of 1920 the ratification process was complete.

When the fighting stopped on November 11, 1918, it seemed to Americans that their boys had made the difference, and those at home were only too happy to claim the victory. After all, had not the hostilities ceased within eighteen months of American entry and four months after the major American-Allied offensive of the summer of 1918? Had not the French army mutinied in 1917 and the Russians left the war in 1918? And had not the Central Powers been fingered with the blame for the war and made to pay in both territory and tribute? But it was a naive vision. The European world had changed in more ways than the defeat of the Central Powers and the drawing of new boundary lines. Gone were the monarchies that had ruled most of Europe and parts of Asia for centuries: the Hapsburgs, the Hohenzollerns, the Romanovs, and the Ottoman Turks. But most menacing for Americans, or so they thought, were those who replaced the czars.

Nations girding for war and the necessity of sending an army off to the killing fields cast the conflict in terms of absolute good versus utter evil. On the home front this almost always results in the persecution of nonbelievers and pacifists—and, in the case of the United States, of immigrants and natives of the "villain" states' extraction. German-Americans were harassed; the German language was banned in some schools, German-American musicians were not allowed to perform, Bach and Beethoven disappeared from symphony halls, sauerkraut became "liberty cabbage," dachshunds were called "liberty hounds," pretzels disappeared from "free" lunches in saloons, and enthusiasts of German artists and literary figures were accused of nonsupport or even treason, as were those who refused to buy war bonds. Strikers and pacifists were beaten. The critique of all that was German shocked some German-Americans and affirmed the fears of others once war had broken out between the United States and the Central Powers.

WORLD WAR II

As horrible as World War I had been, with its rat-infested and slimy trenches, barbed-wire no-man's-land, and endless slaughter for minimal territory, it was a mere preface for the next generation's more sophisticated carnage. The world—or much of it—gradually went to war long before the United States entered the conflict in December 1941. Japan invaded Manchuria in 1931, and soon after the Japanese army had moved southward, seizing much of the Chinese coast. Hitler had come to power in 1933, renounced the Treaty of Versailles that had been signed after the armistice, and began to rearm Germany in 1935. In 1936 the German army took the Rhineland; Italy, under the leadership of Mussolini, attacked Ethiopia; and the Spanish fascists, with aid from Germany, began their war against the republicans. Japan pressed farther into China in 1937, and in 1938 Hitler seized the Sudetenland area of Czechoslovakia and took over Austria. The 1939 attack on Poland brought the English and French into the war and generated American internal controversy over "collective security" or "America first." In 1940 France fell and Japan occupied Indochina.

Molding public opinion for another war in Europe—and in the Far East—had begun long before Pearl Harbor. In the 1940 presidential election, both Roosevelt and challenger Wendell Willkie promised to avoid military intervention in either Europe or Asia. But some elements of American popular culture did not shy away from advocating American entry into the war. In September 1939 *Time* published and distributed 4.5 million copies of *Background for War,* a five-cent pamphlet that reprinted a series of articles on the European political situation from World War I to 1939. Advocating the immediate intervention of the United States against the Axis, it was to that time the largest printing and distribution of any single-issue pamphlet in American history.

Some Americans worried about the American intervention in still another chapter of the European penchant for self-destruction; and in a Depression-era distortion of Darwinian evolutionary biology, critics of involvement maintained that American forces would be allowing unfit and unregenerate Europeans to survive at the expense of American lives. Moreover, there did not appear to be a consensus among the populace about the identity of the most dangerous enemy. Surveys of public opinion on the Spanish question revealed that a majority of Roman Catholics supported the Franco forces, while a majority of Protestants supported the Republicans. Opinions on the dangers of Hitler and Mussolini divided the country, and many German- and Italian-Americans found themselves in the uncomfortable position of having to reject the homeland in which many still had relatives.

The Japanese attack on Pearl Harbor on the morning of December 7, 1941, eliminated nearly all controversy about entry into the war. The December 11 declaration of war on the United States by Germany began America's four-year struggle with Japan, Germany, and Italy. As in World War I, the government marshaled a multitude of tools to bring public opinion together behind the war effort. The Special Service Division of the War Department hired famous Hollywood director Frank Capra, best known for his comedies, to complete a seven-part series of one-hour films entitled *Why We Fight*. The series rearranged some of the facts of the conflict, and portrayed the Germans as evil marauders bent on enslaving defenseless peoples such as the Danes and the Norwegians. With the Germans sneaking into Scandinavian harbors with warships disguised as merchant vessels, and aided by treacherous fifth columnists such as the infamous Quisling, free and democratic Europe was presented as no match for the deceitful, organized, and technologically superior Nazis. The quick fall of France to Panzer divisions that swept around the "impregnable" Maginot Line and broke through at the town of Sedan was attributed to the weakness of a "cynical and disillusioned nation" that had been corrupted by amoral leaders and that had lost its younger generation in World War I. The fate of France, the films warned, could be waiting for the United States if it too was unprepared and pacifist.

As in World War I, the nation girded its loins with armor, and its psyche with the vision of a crusade against the absolutely evil enemy. And the Nazis made it easy to portray them as such. The German bombing of Rotterdam after the surrender of the Netherlands, in which 30,000 were killed in ninety minutes, was described in the "Divide and Conquer" segment of *Why We Fight* as "one of the most ruthless exhibitions of savagery the world has ever seen." Bombing cities and towns to drive refugees onto roads and thereby snarl the movement of war materiel was termed "a new low in inhumanity." Peace between the Nazis and the Vichy government was labeled the "final price of French disunity." The warning was clear. The media campaigns in service of the war effort—especially in the omnipresent warbond posters—sold the war against the Axis as a fight to defend mothers and daughters from the salacious drooling Germans and the buck-toothed, milk-bottle-bottom-eyeglassed white slavers of the Orient.

Why We Fight was the War Department's version of Hollywood director Michael Curtiz's *Casablanca*. Rick, played by Humphrey Bogart, begins *Casablanca* as an isolationist. "I stick my neck out for nobody," he deadpans, as Ugatti (Peter Lorre), the thief of letters of transit out of Casablanca to the free port of Lisbon, is hauled away screaming, "Rick, help me!" Rick's background is mysterious, but the film reveals that he ran guns for the Republicans when the fascists would have paid more for them, and that he had run when the Germans occupied Paris. Once he resolves his injured past with Ilsa (Ingrid Bergman), he and the French prefect of police (Claude Rains) embark upon "a beautiful friendship" against the Nazis. (Rains had, until the climax of the film, congratulated Rick on his neutrality, calling it a "wise foreign policy.")

With nearly 17 million men gone to Europe and the Pacific, nearly all American women were left to wonder. Virginia Purul, born in 1920 in Philadelphia, had her three brothers and her husband go off to war. She quit her job to take care of her parents. "I'm telling you it wasn't easy. I went through hell worrying about my husband and my brothers in the service. Whenever a man came down the street with a telegram you would bless yourself and hope to God he wasn't coming here and you had the strength to face it." More than a quarter of a million of those telegrams—announcing the death of a service-man—were delivered.[16]

Marriage and birth rates skyrocketed during and after the war. "Good-bye babies" were a sort of insurance policy in case the father died while in the Armed Forces. Other couples with the husband at home got married and had children as soon as the economy picked up in the 1940s, since many young people had deferred both marriage and starting a family during hard times. Military allotments were higher for married men and increased proportionately as the number of children in the family increased, and this also furthered family expansion among military families. The scarcity of men once the Armed Forces had been mobilized also promoted fears of "theft" of a husband by other women. "Huntresses," "highjackers," "man-stealers," "vamps," and "pals" were everywhere, or so the popular media wanted married or otherwise attached women to think.

THE HOME FRONT, 1941–1945

The demand for materials and technology for the war effort created a shortage of consumer goods. Prices rose dramatically—18 percent between late 1941 and the beginning of 1943. Moreover, the military demand for vast quantities of food, fuel, and weapons pushed the government to encourage saving all sorts of materials for reuse and to limit consumption of items necessary for the war effort. Scrap metals were obviously important, but so too were common goods such as meat fats. Chicago newspaper columnist Mike Royko remembered that "we were all supposed to save fat—bacon grease and chicken fat. We believed it would be used to make nitroglycerin. . . . In our back yard, we had big coffee cans of fat and grease. The rats in the neighborhood must have had a hell of a good time."[17] In Portsmouth, New Hampshire, a major navy yard, corner grocery store owner Bertha Abbott kept her grease can in the kitchen, next to the candy display.

The seriousness of the materiels crisis and the unpredictability of voluntary regulation impelled the government to ration certain goods to consumers. Cards necessary for obtaining sugar, butter, cheese, meat, bacon, canned foods, shoes, gasoline, and alcohol were issued in 1942. A pain in the neck for retailers and a new racket for petty crooks, the ration coupons were a sign of the domestic contribution to the men at war. War bonds were pitched to the working class as well as the wealthy, and by 1942 Congress made it even easier to not spend too much money by rewriting the tax law so that from 1943 onward anyone making more than $642 annually had a flat tax of 5 percent withheld from his or her paycheck. Price and wage controls brought inflation under control, but pleased almost no one. Workers put in longer hours—the average work week jumped from thirty-eight to forty-seven hours—and the nation reached full employment as a result of the 17 million new jobs created by the war and the nearly 17 million men and women who joined the military. Soon after the hostilities began, Americans were required to "black out" their lights to save energy and to hide from the enemy that many feared would bomb the United States.

Even after the horrors of the Nazi death camps were revealed in 1944 and 1945, George Gallup found that 80 percent of Americans surveyed thought the Japanese were crueler than the Germans. The hatred of the Japanese exhumed old racist antagonisms that had haunted them wherever they had settled. Frank Keegan, from San Francisco, recalled that "we were dreadfully frightened of the Japanese. For years we were told of the yellow hordes. We had the Oriental Exclusion Act. Even before Pearl Harbor we were scared of them." Once the war began, all Japanese-Americans became suspects in ways German-Americans and Italian-Americans did not. Japanese-American fruit farmers, store owners, lawyers, businessmen, physicians, and their families were harassed, beaten, and arrested.[18]

The proof of the racist nature of the American response to immigrants from the Axis powers was that, with few exceptions, only Japanese-Americans were interned. Yuriko Hohri, who was twelve years old and lived with her family in Long Beach, California, when the war broke out, saw FBI agents come to her home, ransack it, and ultimately take her and her family away.

> A black car came right into the driveway. One man went into the kitchen. As I watched, he looked under the sink and he looked into the oven. Then he went into the parlor and opened the glass cases where most of our treasured things were. There were several stacks of *shakuhachi* sheet music. The man took the music. . . . My father was at work. He took care of the vegetable and fruit sections for two grocery stores. He was brought home by the agents. He was taken to a camp in Tujunga Canyon. . . . There was a tall barbed-wire fence, so we were unable to touch each other. . . . We went to Santa Anita. We lived in a horse stable . . . there was no privacy. . . . We left Santa Anita in October 1942. . . . We wound up in Jerome, Arkansas. It was in the swamps. The toilet facilities had not been finished.[19]

As they had when the United States entered World War I, African-Americans hoped that battle experience would bring opportunities that racism in civilian life had denied them. Again they were mistaken. Even with a tremendous surge in employment that occurred after the war began, black Americans were the last hired and the first fired. Confronted with this racism as American policymakers denounced Nazi racism, some black leaders decided to take a stand. A. Philip Randolph, president of the Brotherhood of Sleeping Car Porters, threatened the government with a march of 150,000 black Americans unless discrimination was ended in the war industries. Washington bureaucrat Joseph Rauh recalled the frenzy Randolph's threat caused. "I got a call from my boss. 'Get your ass over here, we got a problem. Some guy named Randolph is going to march on Washington unless we put out a fair employment practices order. . . . We got defense plants goin' all over the country, but no blacks are bein' hired. Go down to the Budget Bureau and work something out.' "[20] Roosevelt issued an executive order that banned discrimination in the defense industries and that created the Fair Employment Practices Commission.

On the home front, African-Americans faced the same sort of antagonism they had encountered during World War I and the intervening years. Attempts at integration, a housing shortage, and new antidiscrimination orders antagonized racist whites. Race riots broke out throughout the country. Thirty-five blacks and nine whites were killed in a Detroit riot over housing. Harlem, Los Angeles, Beaumont, Texas, Mobile, and other cities also exploded. Similar riots pitting white sailors against Mexican-Americans erupted in Los Angeles in 1943.

A NEW AGE?

The war in Europe ended on May 8, 1945. Roosevelt had died in office, and was succeeded by Harry Truman. On August 14, 1945, the new president went on national radio and announced that the Japanese had surrendered. Two million people came together in New York City's Times Square for a celebration. All over people honked horns, thanked God, and listened to church bells tolling. Factory worker Peggy Terry recalled, "Oh, the beautiful celebrations when the war ended. They were selling cigarettes in Paducah. Up until that hour, you couldn'ta bought a pack of cigarettes for love or money."[21]

Six million men were discharged from the military in 1945, 4 million more in 1946. Nearly all the interned Japanese-Americans were freed in 1945; a few were unaccountably kept in prison for a few weeks or months after the surrender. Life did not return to "normal," if prewar America could be called that. Upon their return to the United States, many single servicemen reentered the search for a mate, and resented the idea that they were expected to resume the "competitive" money-oriented dating of the prewar years. Nearly 100,000 soldiers did not have to contend with that question: They brought wives back home with them, half of them Englishwomen, the rest European and Australian. Many European women had treated American G.I.s as conquering heroes rather than as the failed breadwinners of the Depression. For many of the Yanks, the foreign women were exotic and unconcerned with material finery. Unlike some American women, they made no complaints about the nylon stocking "crisis" when the material was essential for making parachutes. European women had witnessed the war's devastation and death, and were thus easier to communicate with, or so it seemed to many soldiers. And many veterans thought European women were more adventurous about sex than their American counterparts. (A 1946 survey of servicemen's attitudes found, however, that some soldiers were disgusted by European women's allegedly less inhibited sexual practices, since these men wanted hugging and sympathy from them, rather than intercourse.)[22]

For many Americans the war was a rite of passage into a different sort of adulthood than they had imagined. The Depression was a memory, but it was a deep wound in the psyche of the people, made with the dull blades of poverty and fear. In 1945 *House Beautiful* magazine urged women to adapt their home to their man's wants. Although 70 percent of women employed outside the home during the war wanted to remain on the job after the war ended, they would not get their wish. As in World War I and its aftermath, they would be pressured back into the parlor and kitchen. The birthrate soared—a postwar baby boom. In 1945, 22,000 servicemen went to college on the G.I. Bill of Rights, which had been enacted in 1944. One million would do so by 1946. The bill also guaranteed home loans, and a building boom began. There was prosperity. The United States had the only atomic bombs on the planet. It seemed that God was in his kingdom, and the earthly abode of the Divine was right where those Puritans thought it might be in 1630—in the New World, and more precisely, in the United States of America. Or so it seemed.

5

THE HEALTHY TABLE AND
THE HEALTHY HOME

T HE TYPICAL American diet underwent a revolution of sorts between 1915 and 1945. The spearheads of the great change were the advocates of the "new nutrition." The goal of their crusade was to convince Americans to jettison the greasy meat-and-potatoes diet that had been popular for decades in favor of a "balanced" program of fruits, vegetables, carbohydrates, and proteins. The critics were most successful among the middle and wealthy classes, but the "new nutrition" also affected the diet of the poor to a limited extent.

Changes in Americans' eating habits were intertwined with efforts to analyze and improve Americans' overall fitness and the delivery of health care to the population. Technological changes in the production and preservation of foods and the attempts of producers to consolidate their operations and rationalize the marketplace led to an alliance of science, medicine, and business that produced both hucksterism and innovation. Vitamins and minerals, fiber and temperance, malnutrition scares and created "diseases" were part of a drive to build a healthier America, fit for the struggle to survive in war, economic downturn, and the socioeconomic marketplace. Healthy food was considered a fundamental building block in the edifice of health and medicine that was altering Americans' lives in this era, from birth through death. With more hospitals and more sophisticated diagnostic tools, physicians were treating more patients with greater success than before. But there was a dark side to this optimistic situation: The poor were largely still de-

155

prived of medical care, since there were few if any ways to deliver treatment that did not require them to pay. Because many lived perilously close to the edge of existence, most of the poor had to do without the shining successes of modern medicine.

Clothing fashions and recreation alternatives and attitudes were additional important elements in development of a new interpretation of health and its importance, and may have been the catalysts that transformed a half century of professional and quasi-professional complaints about Americans' physical condition into altered behavior. By 1920, the successful man was depicted in advertising and other forms of popular culture as slender, clean-shaven, and slickly groomed, a stark contrast to the turn-of-the-century identification of corpulence with success. For women, the ideal body form of the Gilded Age— rounded, corseted, and bustled—evolved first to that of the cinched but active "Gibson girl" and, by the 1920s, to the boyish-bodied "flapper" or streamlined body of the movie queen and the athlete.

Cooking

THE ANGLO HERITAGE AND REGIONAL FOODWAYS

In 1915 most of the white Anglo-Saxon middle class and wealthy equated good cookery with English foodways. Roasted joints and fowl with heavy gravies, raw oysters, piquant relishes, scalloped side dishes, loads of butter and sugar, fruited sauces, and lots of sweets were the order of the day. The regional cultural pride and nostalgia for Olde England and colonial America that had been evident in literature, architecture, and furniture styles for at least a quarter of a century reinforced this equation, and stalled the work of health and dietary reform. In 1923, when breakfast cereals were already in their heyday (critics called it—and the products—a hayday), the magazine *The Nation* commissioned proponents of regional cuisine to come up with a list of "home dinners" typical of the regions of the United States. In Baltimore, Chesapeake Bay oysters, terrapin

Maryland style, and roasted wild duck were noted; in New England, the favorite regional dinner included broiled scrod, doughnuts and coffee, boiled dinner, fish chowder, baked beans, spareribs, potatoes, biscuits, pumpkin and apple pies, and Indian pudding. Tennesseeans picked fried chicken, boiled ham, sweet potatoes, butter beans, okra, hot biscuits with cream gravy, and tomatoes; New Orleans residents included in their typical cuisine oysters, crawfish bisque, pâté de foie gras, filet mignon bordelaise, roast mallard, stuffed eggplant, roast veal, and candied yams, or, for the less well off, gumbo, red beans and rice (with ham hocks), corn fritters, and cow peas. Rural Alabamians opted for sow belly, greens and pot liquor, string beans, snap beans, boiled onions, corn pone, coffee, and fried chicken. Roast pork and sauerkraut were the favored foods of Pennsylvania Germans, and tortillas, frijoles, chilis, and the chocolate-based mole sauces were characteristic of the Spanish-influenced Southwest.[1] Clearly there was work yet to be done for the grease crusaders.

Americans' penchant for cakes, pies, and fried foods clogged their arteries, rounded their bodies, and drove nutritionists, physicians, and fitness advocates crazy. Lard was the favorite shortening of the American public, and continued to be long after World War I, when Procter and Gamble spent $3 million to promote its new vegetable-based fat, Crisco. Eventually, and not nearly as quickly as the company thought, Crisco replaced lard in many kitchens, although lard is still found on grocery store cooler shelves in most regions of the United States.

BEGINNINGS OF CHANGE

The broad-based American enthusiasm for fat-laden and greasy, fried foods had been undermined, albeit in a limited way, before 1915. The cereal kings—J. H. Kellogg and C. W. Post were the most famous of the many—had succeeded in convincing many middle-class and wealthy householders that grain products were a healthier breakfast option than meat and eggs, in part because they argued that fiber-rich breakfasts were a counterbalance to the heavier foods that most preferred for lunch and supper. By 1915 an abundance of different kinds of cereals was available. In addition to such standbys as Cream of Wheat, Grape-Nuts, Post Toasties, Corn Flakes, and shredded wheat, the shelves of grocery stores groaned with boxes of Malta-Vita, Cerro-Fruto, Mapl-Flakes, Norka, Malted Oats, Golden Manna, and Vim Wheat Flakes.

An additional factor in the alteration of the diet of many Americans was the European food crisis of World War I, and the work of the Iowan named to run the U.S. Food Administration. Created to contend with the worldwide food shortage of 1916–1917, the USFA and its chief, Herbert Hoover, were charged by president Woodrow Wilson with developing policies to prevent hoarding, food shortages, and, Wilson feared, riots. The Department of Agriculture's Home Economics Division sent out hundreds of canvassers to survey Americans' eating habits in minute detail and to convince Americans to consume less. The Food Administration tried to convince people to sign pledges to reduce their consumption of meats, butter, sugar, and wheat flour and to eat more perishable fruits and vegetables so that the United States could ship staples and preserved goods to Europe, where farming had been disrupted by the war. Taking Hoover's pledges bound Americans to a program of porkless Thursdays and Saturdays, wheatless Mondays and Wednesdays, and meatless Tuesdays. American food exports to the Allies tripled in 1917, domestic consumption declined, and overall food production increased by nearly 25 percent. Prices were allowed to rise, and farmers were guaranteed minimum prices for some foodstuffs. To their great pleasure restaurant owners were encouraged to scale down the size of portions they served (for the same price as before) in the name of patriotism.

World War I army mess also helped change the American diet. The 1916 manual for army cooks stressed the new nutrition idea of balanced meals that included proteins, fruits, vegetables, and carbohydrates. The wartime food experience had its greatest effect on immigrant and southern soldiers. The latter were fed beef, pork roasts, milk, white bread, and potatoes, rather than cured pork and corn meal, the "hog and hominy" that, along with greens cooked with "side meat" (pork fatback), had been the staple of southern cooking. The Army introduced immigrants from eastern and southern Europe to a new meal-time experience; in the military mess hall they found no potato-and-cabbage dishes or pasta and sauce.

Even if southern and immigrant working-class soldiers believed in the new nutrition, it was still army food, not home cooking. In spite of the efforts of Hoover's hustling crusaders, the working class in the cities and the rural folk who did not go off to war not only clung to older foodways but increased their consumption of the very foods the administration was trying to get them to forgo. Ham, fatback, and bacon were still king in the South; beef and pork consumption in 1917 was 11 percent higher than it had been in 1916, even after all those pledge cards had been signed. The higher wages commanded by workers in many trades and the short-lived agricultural boom of the war years meant more and better food for many immigrant and native workers and farmers. In those good economic times, the working class turned the reformers' recommendations upside down. They increased their intake of higher-grade proteins, substituting meat for grains and vegetables whenever they could. They had had years of involuntary simplicity. Meat meant success and health.

Some changes in diet of the middle class came from abroad, or from ethnic enclaves in American cities. Italy's status as an ally helped broaden the popularity of pasta dishes with tomato sauce, especially spaghetti. So popular had the latter become that by the 1930s the tablewares and housewares designer Russel Wright successfully marketed a spun-aluminum "spaghetti set." Red sauce, as Italians had long known, could also be a meat stretcher, and the Food Administration and economy-minded Americans promoted the dish as healthy and patriotic. Women's magazines were full of recipes for spaghetti and its nearly infinite variations.

When middle-class soldiers returned from the war they came home to an environment more receptive to the balanced meal idea than was the working-class household. By the 1920s, the businessman's lunch included more fresh fruits and vegetables than it had in the past. In 1928 all Americans ate 5 percent fewer calories than had their counterparts in 1890; they ate more fruits, especially citrus, more vegetables and greens, more milk and cheese, and less corn meal, wheat flour, potatoes, and sweet potatoes. By 1930 they had cut their annual per capita beef consumption from 72.4 pounds in 1899 to 55.3 pounds.[2]

THE FOOD PROCESSING REVOLUTION

The middle-class household also was transformed, at least in its eating habits, by the increasingly sophisticated processed food industry. In the nineteenth century, canned foods in particular were a mixed blessing, and one not necessarily adopted by the middle class or the wealthy. The processors' claims of labor-saving were accurate, but commercially canned foods had limited appeal because many thought they tasted "tinny" and implied slothfulness. Moreover, many women did not want to give up control over food processing even if they wanted the free time that processed food promised. Working-class women bought canned foods in the nineteenth century because they had neither the time nor the space to prepare and store foods, since many took in laundry and other jobs or worked outside the home.

By the 1920s major changes in the production and distribution of processed foods helped remove the stigma attached to them, if not necessarily the quality problems of earlier years. Food became very big business.[3] Between 1914 and 1929, capital investment in the food industry more than tripled, making it the largest American manufacturing industry. Growers and manufacturers formed institutes and associations to promote their goods and their particular foods, and became the second-largest purchasers of newspaper advertising in the 1920s. "New" foods were introduced, or at least marketed as such to a national and largely middle-class audience. Citrus growers pushed their wares as never before, jumping on the "vitamin" bandwagon. Asparagus was virtually unknown until California growers launched a promotional campaign in the early 1920s. Pineapple became a craze in 1923 when Del Monte began to market the fruit aggressively.

The food processing industry also became more mechanized, as assembly lines and machines replaced hand operations in slaughterhouses and commercial canneries, and prices of many goods dropped. Mass-produced bread also became a staple in American homes by World War I. Baking at home usually took four to six hours, depending on the quality of the yeast, the amount of sugar, the coarseness of the flour, and the number of times a recipe called for rising. By 1915 commercial bakeries in most American cities used huge coal- and gas-fired ovens, high-pressure steam, and automatic slicers and packagers to produce the white frothy bread that became the American standard.

Many immigrants were accustomed to buying a commercially baked loaf every day or two, and the soft American packaged version was an unpleasant surprise to them. As a result many continued to support small-scale local bakers, who made coarser and heftier loaves of rye and other breads.[4] The home bakers and partisans of these breads were a dwindling minority, however: By 1939 the value of mass-produced bread was estimated by the U.S. government to be $514 million, while the value of privately baked bread was estimated at $20 million. Four times as much white pan bread was produced (7.2 billion pounds) as rye or whole wheat or hearth breads (1.7 billion pounds) in the same year.[5]

Americans did not begin to use frozen foods in significant quantities until 1928, three years after Clarence Birdseye had developed a method to quick-freeze foods on a large scale. The slower freezing methods used before Birdseye's innovation had burst the cells of most foods, causing them to turn to mush upon thawing. By 1934 Americans bought 39 million pounds of frozen foods; ten years later they purchased 600 million pounds. In 1936 farmers in the Tennessee Valley, as part of the government's Tennessee Valley Authority cooperative venture, formed organizations to finance the construction of freezing factories. By 1945 upscale New York City apartment houses regularly installed large frozen food lockers in the basement, and provided tenants with one or more drawers or small lockers within a large unit.

Dietary reform was a powerful—but not omnipotent—force for the assimilation of immigrant groups into mainstream middle-class culture. In part the newcomers' acceptance of com-

mercially processed foods was a solution to the twin responsibilities of wage-earning and meal preparation that many immigrant and working-class women faced. For them products such
as gelatin, white bread, canned soups (Campbell's soups cost
twelve cents a can in 1929), bottled condiments such as
ketchup, mustard, and pickles, and quicker meals such as sandwiches and broiled rather than roasted meats may not have
been as satisfying as old-country cuisine, but they shortened the
day's work.

More instruction in and more information about mainstream
middle-class cooking was reaching immigrant households as
states and the federal government began to impose more limits
on children's labor and mandated longer attendance in schools.
Unable to leave school to earn wages or do housework until
their mid-teens, immigrant and working-class women learned
about Anglo-American cooking and processed foods in home
economics classes. In addition, mass circulation magazines,
which by the 1920s were more common in working-class homes
than they had been before the war, were also vehicles for the
transmission of ideas between classes and ethnic groups. Information about Anglo-American cooking thus penetrated workers' homes from two new fronts after 1915, pitching the benefits
of new methods and new nutrition, making these changes both
a cause and an effect of more time away from the cookstove.

WORKERS' FARE

For some immigrants, food in the United States was a bounteous
experience. "We ate like kings compared to what we had over
there," wrote one Czechoslovakian immigrant who landed in
1914. "Oh it was really heaven."[6] But if the American working-
class diet was more lavish than that of its European counterpart,
it was still wanting, as government and private foundation surveys conducted throughout the era revealed. In part these con-
clusions were due to cultural distinctions unappreciated by eth-
nocentric investigators; in part they resulted from changes in
nutritional values and standards that were publicized in the era;
and in part they reflected the hunger and suffering that regularly visited working-class households.

Studies such as those of typical Chicago stockyards-district households and New York City workers in 1914 found that only a small percentage of income (2 to 4 percent) was spent on fruits and vegetables. By 1928 New Yorkers were found to be spending more on milk, cheese, fruits, and vegetables, and less on grain, flour, and cereals. It would have been easy to conclude that the overall dietary condition of working-class Americans had improved, but a Brookings Institution study of 1929 found otherwise. Seventy-four percent of nonfarm families, according to the study, could not afford "an adequate diet at moderate cost." This confirmed and reinforced earlier studies of specific groups, such as a 1920 investigation of Italian-American households that found them "suffering from cold and lack of food, buying one or two ounces of Roman [sic] cheese and a small quantity of olive oil. . . . [In] many homes . . . housewives bought no milk at all because they thought it too expensive and at the same time were buying a small piece of cheese at $1.25 a pound."[7]

But nearly all these studies failed to see the economies of stews, borschts, minestrones, goulashes, and pasta dishes, and did not recognize the values of herbs and spices, especially garlic. All were thought too "stimulating." Spiced sausages and peppered meats that were favorites of the poor and the immigrants had little appeal for middle-class and wealthy reformers who visited the working-class homes. Reformers tried to accomplish, as Pearl Ellis called it in her 1929 book's title, *Americanization Through Homemaking.* Mexican-American girls were taught to cook with Anglo white sauces (flour, butter, and milk) and hard sauces (butter and sugar), rather than traditional red and green sauces that were higher in vitamins and in some cases proteins and calcium than the "white" counterparts. Chilis and hot sauces, reformers thought in a literal equation of food and politics, stimulated behavior consistent with the fire of the condiment: revolution and banditry. Such instruction happily ignored the tendency of butter to spoil in hot climates.

The Anglo reformers often encountered resistance among the cooks they wished to convert. The constraints of time and the power of the educational mass media did not completely overwhelm traditional and old-country cooking. Family members expected it on weekends, holidays, and other special occasions, such as weddings and bar mitzvahs. "Whatever you do, make it taste Polish," was one Polish woman's advice in a 1918 settlement house cooking demonstration. "Put cabbage in." Italians valued certain seafoods—such as squid and octopus—that made reformers uneasy, and their penchant for garlic and olive oil constantly provoked those who would teach them the joys of English and American fare. Italian immigrants held closely to their network of greengrocers and bakers, as well as their suppliers of pasta and other specialties. Jews ate more beef in the United States than they had in Europe, and the best kosher butcher shops and delicatessens were measured first by their corned beef and second by their pastrami, the pepper-coated meat brought to the United States by Rumanian Jews. Smoked salmon, whitefish, and chubs from the Great Lakes or the ocean were also favorites, although the salmon was expensive.

When times got hard, the poor fell back on what was inexpensive, what they could grow, and what they knew. Potatoes; day-old bread spread with lard, olive oil, bacon grease, or rendered chicken fat; damaged and scavenged fruits and vegetables; and marginal poultry or meat parts, such as chicken feet, ham hocks, and head cheese (a conglomeration of gelatin and pork snouts, ears, and whatever else could be ground up), dominated the diet of the poor.[8]

FARMERS AND THE RURAL POOR

Southern tenant farmers of both races sometimes had the opportunity to raise some of their own foods. Typical crops for those with their own gardens included corn, cabbage, parsnips, turnips, carrots, onions, beans, black-eyed and green peas, tomatoes, and peppers. From the orchards of the larger farms that they worked, damaged fruits were sometimes available if they were not pressed for juice. Most poor farmers tried to grow at least one hog annually, which they usually slaughtered in late autumn. The hams, bacon, and most of the other parts were salted down, stored for two months, and then smoked over sassafras, apple, or hickory fires. Hung on hooks sunk into rafters of the house or in separate sheds on the property, these meats were an important source of the family's proteins for the year. Fowl—chickens, turkeys, and ducks—ranged free during the day and were penned at night so that foxes, weasels, and other predators were hindered if not entirely thwarted. A cow—for dairy products and meat—was less common, because they ate so much feed and grass that the poorest tenants and sharecroppers could not afford the animals. In theory most of these poor farmers might have been able to build a balanced diet, but in reality most subsisted on corn meal and pork products—"hog and hominy"—for much of the year. Inadequate storage facilities for perishable produce, virtually no cash to buy most goods, and the necessity of devoting the bulk of their labor to grow crops that would pay off their debts consigned poor southern white and black farmers to a diet of deprivation. State and federal government studies in the 1920s and 1930s found a high incidence of pellagra (a condition caused by B-vitamin deficiency) and other diseases among poor southern farmers.

Many American Indians of the plains, whose diets before white intrusion had been heavily dependent on the low-cholesterol meats of the buffalo, the deer, and the elk, were by 1920 in a nutritional crisis. In a 1927 article in the *Journal of the American Dietetic Association*, Jesse Stone and Lydia Roberts found that the staple food of a Sioux reservation in South Dakota was "grease bread," or white flour bread or biscuit dough fried in fat. Potatoes and beans were the only vegetables most of the tribe consumed, and squash and tomatoes were eaten by only a few of the tribe. The inhabitants consumed virtually no green vegetables, fruits, milk, eggs, butter, or cheese. Meat came from the monthly government ration of twenty-five to forty pounds of beef per family on the ration roll. Theoretically the allotment might have been sufficient, but those not on the ration roll usually moved in or ate with the recipients of the meat until it was gone, usually in about two weeks. For the remainder of the month daily fare consisted of grease bread. Tribes near water fared somewhat better if they fished, and some had rights to continue to take fish even when the government-regulated season was not open. In the Klamath River in the Pacific Northwest and the lakes of Minnesota and Wisconsin, for example, salmon, pike, and other food fish were harvested by Indians throughout the year, or for as long as the weather permitted. Although year-round fishing was guaranteed in treaties with the federal government, it annoyed the increasing number of white sport fishermen, who viewed the Indians' behavior as injurious to their interests.[9]

Mexican-Americans, living primarily in the Southwest but as far north as the mining towns of Montana and Colorado, continued to eat corn tortillas (made from masa flour, which is ground from corn soaked in lime), beans, chilis, tomatoes, and very little meat, eggs, milk, or other dairy products. Their diets lacked the amino acids not found in beans, and the vitamins and minerals found in the bananas and plantains they had trouble finding as they ventured farther and farther north of the Mexican border.

Rural Americans who were more well off than sharecroppers, tenants, and migrant workers ate a more varied diet. A typical Mississippi truck farmer's breakfast in 1927 consisted of fried eggs, flour muffins with butter and molasses, coffee, and milk. Lunch was robust: roast pork, sweet potatoes, cabbage, corn bread, and custard or other pie. For supper, commonly a less important meal than that of midday, spaghetti with tomato sauce, fried sweet potatoes, biscuits and butter, fruit preserves, and milk constituted typical nutrition. Substitutions for pork included fried chicken and, less often, beef cuts.[10]

Numerous studies of white farm families' diet found that milk and dairy product consumption was widespread among all but the poorest farm families. In 1930, only 10 percent of the rural population of South Carolina had no cows or purchased no milk at all. Ninety-four percent of the farmers who owned land in two cotton-growing areas of Mississippi owned at least one cow. Farther north, earlier studies had discovered that only 29 of 1,331 farm households (2.2 percent) surveyed in Kansas, Missouri, and Ohio in 1922–1924 had no cows or bought no milk. In 1935, another survey found that 73 percent of 895 New Hampshire farm households owned cows and/or drank at least one quart of milk daily. While this was encouraging to reformers, especially since milk came to be identified as an essential and perhaps "perfect" food, there were other signs of trouble, especially among the outlanders. Southern Illinois "river bottom" white people rejected foods such as catfish, possum, and muskrat as "nigger food," choosing instead less healthy and more expensive canned salmon, hamburgers, and canned chili con carne. A 1940 study found that class and race prejudice got in the way of nutrition among whites in the Southeast. Poor farmers in the Carolinas, Georgia, and Florida preferred processed urban foods over less expensive homegrown goods and traditional foods that they tended to denigrate as "old-timey," "country," and "nigger." Canned rather than country hams were chosen by these people, as were beef and canned salmon rather than fresh-caught fish and fresh pork.[11]

RESTAURANTS AND SALOONS

Restaurants helped standardize the definition of "good food," and the successful eatery combined familiar home cooking with new and difficult-to-prepare foods. Going out for a meal—especially supper—became more popular as the range of restaurant options increased, as middle-class living standards improved, and as women pushed for relief from cooking. Restaurants in the 1920s promoted themselves as less work and a social experience. Gus Mann's Chicago seafood restaurant was a big success after its opening in 1923, in part because of the fishnet and nautical decor. Others followed suit, and Roman villas, haciendas, Chinese temples, log cabins, and other such architectural renderings appeared in cities and towns all over the country. W. C. Lape introduced "Barkies," a chain of sandwich shops distinguished by a storefront with a huge pup with the identifying sign in its teeth. Patrons entered by walking between the canine's front legs. In 1921, the first drive-in restaurant, Royce Hailey's "Pig Stand," opened in Dallas, and for not much money barbecue or a chicken-fried steak with cream gravy could be had. Most theme restaurants, with the exception of Chinese and Italian eateries, served food that bore little relation to the ethnic or regional decor. If they tried for genuine cooking, the food was usually a pale imitation of the real thing. Often the special meals on the menu coexisted with traditonal American cuisine. The regular dinner at Ching Wah and Company's restaurant in Pittsfield, Massachusetts, in 1920 featured "New American and Chinese" fare for forty cents.[12]

White Tower, probably the first fast-food franchised restaurant, appeared in the late 1920s. Built to be movable and all white to signify cleanliness, the castle-shaped joints were a cheap alternative to eating at home, and were affordable to all but the poorest people. A sliced sausage type of "hamburger" was the Tower's specialty, but the restaurant fare that was closest to homogenized America was probably found in the now venerable diner. Often shaped like the streamlined railroad diner cars or house trailers of the 1930s, diners served a modicum of regional foods but for the most part served up Anglo-American grub at its best and worst. Coffee and doughnuts or pastries or eggs and some form of meat and toast constituted breakfast; sandwiches and one or two hot specials defined lunch; and meat loaf, turkey, or some form of spaghetti were the dinner choices. For dessert, pies were inevitable, along with rice pudding, Indian pudding, bread pudding, or custard. Those wanting a lighter finish could order gelatin, cubed and served in small heavy white dishes.

Prohibition had an immediate effect on the restaurant trade. Many hotels, which had made money off drink but lost it on elaborate restaurants, closed down their bars and transformed both rooms into cafeterias and lunchrooms to serve middle-class office workers and women about the town. Shorter lunch periods (a result of the increased influence of efficiency experts) and an increased number of office workers meant that those venturing out of the office for the midday meal had to get service quickly. In midtown Manhattan, restaurants commonly served previously prepared hot table d'hôte meals at a fixed price. The necessity for a speedy lunch helped launch the chain restaurant with standardized menu and food preparation techniques. By 1923 the Waldorf chain had 112 branches nationwide and was doing an annual business in excess of $14 million.

The desire for speed also meant the acceptance of mechanization and a decline in the number of service personnel in some establishments. Horn and Hardart launched the "Automat" in 1903, in which a nickel inserted in a slot got one the sandwich or dessert displayed in the little chrome and glass cubicle. Initially the Automat served cold lunches only and was a limited success. Trade quickened after steam tables to serve hot foods were installed to cater to the traditional hot lunch trade, but they were used with less frequency when cold lunches became more acceptable in the 1920s. Even drugstores got into the act. Counters with syrup taps and light lunch fare became common. By 1929 an estimated 60 percent of drugstore sales took place at the lunch counter, and 67 percent of those sales were of food. Of all restaurants that opened in the twenties—and the number of restaurants in 1929 was three times that of 1919—48 percent were lunchrooms, 26 percent were coffee and sandwich shops, 8 percent were cafeterias, and 11 percent were full-service establishments.[13]

Saloons that had offered "free" lunches (which usually cost five cents to keep out the freeloaders and down-on-their-luck types) and four- to five-course "businessman's lunches" had been the stiffest competition for middle-class restaurants, but prohibition killed them. For those that tried to stay in business, fruit syrups and soda-dispensing machines replaced the beer taps; soda "jerks" replaced barkeeps, and the "luncheonette" was born. Gone too, until 1933 and repeal, were cigar smoke, spittoons, and the ornate mirrors and paintings of female nudes that had hung over the bars of these male-dominated areas. Few of the beer joints and gin mills became "tea rooms," but some of the hotels did, catering to the middle-class and wealthy women who were their primary clientele.

SCHOOL LUNCHES

The school lunchroom offered no competition for the luncheonette, the diner, the tea room, or the restaurant, but it was perhaps as important an indicator of the increasing homogenization of American everyday eating habits. Children's school lunches for little or no money were first served in Boston in 1894. By 1912 more than forty cities across the country had similar programs. For about ten years the number of schools serving cheap lunches grew slowly, if at all, but in 1922–1923 the effort gained new life from a new definition of malnutrition. The new program was first established in those schools populated predominantly by poorer children, but eventually it was a fixture in nearly all American schools, save for the remaining one- and two-room schools in rural areas.

Anglo-American foods were served more often than not: chicken croquettes, scalloped everything, and such treats as salmon loaf and various other ground-up and formed combinations of mysterious raw materials greeted schoolchildren at midday from Monday through Friday. White bread was the standard additional carbohydrate, which pleased both the kids who wanted to eat it and those who recognized that it made far better spitballs than did the crusty and heavier fare of home-made bread.

Sometimes school lunch managers ran into trouble with the scientists of good eating. The "new nutrition" stressed the benefits of lower caloric and protein intake, hardly the characteristics of many school lunches. Reformers had for years tried all sorts of techniques to convince the working class that they should not emulate the rich foods of the wealthy. In 1916 Metropolitan Life Insurance Company distributed 300,000 copies of *Food Facts,* a pamphlet that summarized the tenets of the new nutrition and contained several recipes based on the plan. The same concern for overeating and health can be found in the cookbooks aimed at the middle class.[14]

Reform

THE "NEW NUTRITION"

The school lunch programs of the era and the "new nutrition" were products both of a general attempt at reforming the eating habits of the working and middle classes and of the "malnutrition scare" of the early twentieth century. In 1907 chemist Frank Underhill was commissioned to estimate the amount of money necessary for a person to maintain a healthy diet. Using

Dr. Wilbur Atwater's elevated nineteenth-century estimates of necessary daily nutrients, Underhill concluded that a minimum of twenty-two cents per day was needed. Since one-third or one-fourth of the population (depending on which calculations one believed) did not make enough money to support this minimum, reformers and others became convinced that the American working population was significantly undernourished. Quality of food, rather than quantity, was important in this crusade. "Undernourished" and "malnourished" replaced "underfed" as the characteristic problem, reflecting the new definition. In New York City in the early teens, 225,000 schoolchildren were diagnosed as malnourished. The scare cooled somewhat with the development of a new standard promulgated in 1915. The Dumferline scale measured height, weight, eyesight, muscularity, "mental alertness," and rosiness of complexion against models of healthy white Anglo-Saxon or northern European middle- and upper-middle-class children. The last component of the standard clearly showed the bias toward children with light skins: Italian and Jewish children, for example, were often too darkly complexioned to measure up. And African-American youth befuddled examiners. Stacia Treski recalled that she was always labeled "malnourished" by school doctors in Pennsylvania. Each year her parents were told she needed milk. "Well, my mother would go out and buy one quart of milk and that's the last quart of milk you'd see for months."[15] At first the new scale was a comfort. In 1915 only 4 to 5 percent of New York children were in jeopardy. But in 1916 the examinations showed a sharp increase in malnourishment, doubling in New York, Boston, and Philadelphia. After much debate and the disappointing results of army physicals for service in World War I, the school lunch program was identified as an important solution.

For the middle class the problem was not undernourishment or perhaps even malnourishment, but nourishment that was not good enough to ensure success in the uncertain world of business. "Good health is magnetism," claimed an ad for the California Fruit Growers' Association's Sunkist oranges in the November 29, 1924, issue of the *Saturday Evening Post*. "It wins people to you, makes it easier for you to influence others, whether you are a salesman, department head, manager, or chief executive." Women's magazines such as *Women's Home Companion* and *Ladies' Home Journal* carried articles warning parents of the dangers of ill-feeding and stunted growth. By 1920 food manufacturers and processors began to hawk their goods armed with a new weapon against the evils of "bad" food—vitamins. Invisible and seemingly immeasurable, these compounds—originally termed "vital amines"—were the advertiser's dream. Like the panaceas offered by patent medicines of the previous century, extravagant claims that were unprovable yet irrefutable were made—and believed. Elmer McCollum, the "father" of the American vitamin movement, used laboratory testing of rats to show that the absence of certain substances, rather than only the addition of bacteria, could cause disease. In 1916 McCollum showed the connection between the absence of vitamin B (which he isolated in 1912) and beriberi; in 1922 he showed the link between the absence of vitamin D and rickets. The exact amount of these compounds needed on a daily basis was unknown, but the sources of the wonder materials had been identified. Milk, grains, and citrus were key foodstuffs. Although very few Americans ever saw anyone with beriberi, rickets, or scurvy (or would have recognized the maladies if they saw them), the threat was sufficient to alarm all sorts of Americans.

MILK AND "VITAL AMINES"

McCollum's rats with full diets were robust and healthy, those with incomplete diets thin and sickly. Milk became one of the basic foods in the campaign against malnutrition, since it contained so many crucial vitamins and had been the object of a highly publicized national purity effort. In the early twentieth century, discoveries of all sorts of microscopic contamination in milk had shocked Americans. The culprits in this scandal were the retail sources of milk for most Americans—itinerant milk peddlers and store owners who dispensed milk with dippers from bulk storage cans. But by 1920 improvements in commercial pasteurization and packaging and the "Pure Milk" crusade of the previous two decades allayed many consumers' fears of contaminated milk.

The consolidation of the dairy industry into a few giant producers also aided the promotional and purity efforts. National Dairy Products (Sealtest) and Borden became huge holding companies that bought up smaller producers, with whom they could not necessarily compete on a local level but who could not afford to retool to meet government sanitation standards established after the passage of the Pure Food and Drug Act in 1906. In 1928 Borden brought fifty-two small companies in one week. The conglomerates used McCollum's rat photos to show that milk was a miracle food. State agricultural departments, scientists, agriculture departments of universities, dairymen's leagues, and big business joined together in the promotional effort, establishing the "quart a day" standard, especially for growing children. And if the little ingrates did not like the stuff, there were additives to con them into drinking it: Cocomalt, Ovaltine, and manufacturers of all sorts of chocolate syrups and powders pitched their wares at the guilt feelings of mothers worried about their kids' inability to make the big money later because they failed their offspring when they were tots. By 1925 Americans consumed 800 pounds of milk per capita.

The health reformers' first concern in 1915 was for the poor, but by the early 1920s good health as a product of the right foods was a middle-class fetish. Restaurant menus in the more fashionable areas of the country included calorie counts with the description of the dish, as well as a vitamin rating. (A capital V signified lots of the essential compounds, a lowercase v fewer vitamins.) Food producers and processors seized upon middle-class and wealthy Americans' fears of failure and pushed their goods with shameless abandon. Morton salt promoters salivated over the connection between iodized salt and the avoidance of goiter in their advertisements for "health salt." Sunkist lemons' marketing wizards cooked up a new disease—"acidosis"—a debilitating condition brought on by not eating enough acidic fruits. Welch's grape juice ads crowed about the vitamins and minerals in the purple liquid, as well as the "laxative properties you cannot do without."

"AUTOINTOXICATION" AND OTHER SCARES

The manufacturers and promoters of Fleischmann's yeast were perhaps the most notorious of the hucksters that used the health movements for all they were worth. Prohibition—which was the law in many counties and municipalities scattered throughout the United States long before it became the law of the land—and the decline in baking at home had seriously harmed the company's profit margins. By 1919 the firm had a strategy in place that it hoped would open new markets. A free promotional pamphlet, *The Healing Power of Compressed Yeast*, claimed that three cakes of the stuff eaten daily would cure "Pimples, Blackheads . . . Boils, Carbuncles, Constipation . . . Gastro-Intestinal Catarrh," and would "tone the general health, build up impoverished vitality, probably due to its richness in the cell-body substance, Nuclein, and in vitamin properties."[16] In 1920 the company pushed even harder, hiring the famous advertising firm the J. Walter Thompson Company to run their campaign.

Fears of what Fleischmann's termed "intestinal intoxication" and the popular press called "autointoxication" were pervasive in the United States. The idea that one could be poisoning oneself by not evacuating properly and often enough stung a middle class that was always looking for an edge on the competition and constantly mindful of being pushed out of their seemingly precarious socioeconomic position.[17] Like other food and health product producers, Fleischmann's hit upon the autointoxication issue as well as the vitamin enthusiasm of the day to increase its sales by 130 percent between 1923 and 1926. The firm used physicians' testimonials in its pamphlet in 1919 and in magazine ads by 1927, with superimposed diagrams of human intestines in the latter to dramatically "show" the point. A full-page ad in the September 4, 1933, issue of *Time* ran a banner headline atop the page: "That coated tongue may indicate *serious trouble*—" The photograph on the top half of the page shows Dr. Edouard Agasse-Lafont, "a chevalier of the Legion of Honor and Ancien Chef de Clinique of the Faculty of Medicine of Paris," examining a woman's mouth. The text affirms the great fear—"auto-intoxication." "My advice," the doctor writes, "is to eat fresh yeast. It gently stimulates the intestines. . . ." American physicians often refused substantial payments to provide such endorsements, so companies and advertising firms increasingly began to recruit English and European physicians, who may have believed in the manufacturers' claims for the product.[18]

Undaunted by the criticism of physicians, Fleischmann's further embellished its claims as a health food by promising that its allegedly additional vitamin A helped cure colds. Pet milk boasted that it was irradiated with vitamin D. Listerine, the flagship product of Lambert pharmaceuticals, pushed its profits from a paltry $100,000 in 1920 to $4 million in 1927, almost entirely as a result of Listerine. Originally marketed as a mouthwash and oral antiseptic, Listerine was also successfully promoted as a cure for dandruff, colds, and body odor (another new "ailment"), as well as an effective after-shave and astringent.

That Americans of the middle class needed some sort of cleansing restorative was not a new idea in the late teens and twenties. From the late nineteenth century onward the problems of "softness" and "nervousness" had been a plague that had bedeviled these men and women. Sport and the "strenuous life" ideology promulgated by Theodore Roosevelt and others, dietary reform, and various medical and quasi-medical treatments were applied with vigor and hope. The Boy Scouts were formed in 1911 after the English model; Girl Scouts and other such groups soon followed. In addition to the cures for the real or imagined diseases conjured by ad men and manufacturers, exercise and fitness activities became cures for weary desk-job Americans and their wives and children. Suntanning became a fad in the 1920s, and the bronzed complexion replaced white skin as a mark of beauty and health. "Nature's restorative" contained vitamin D in its ultraviolet rays, and it was not long before the panacea manufacturers came out with an assortment of ultraviolet and violet ray machines in (usually) black-clad boxes filled with glass tubes in various shapes to massage the allegedly healthful rays all over the body. Civilization may have consigned one to a desk and may have processed the vitamins out of canned foods, but science and technology (or their bowd-lerized offshoots) could and did bring back the healthful aspects of nature when one could not partake of the outdoors or of sport. Cereals, vitamin supplements, laxatives, irradiated milk and dairy products, and the hidden benefits of common foods were answers.

DRESS REFORM AND THE NEW BEAUTY

One happy prospect for the worriers about American fitness was the alteration in the nature of fashionable clothing that had taken place by 1915. The stiff corset, the bustle, and the volumi-nous skirts of the nineteenth century gradually faded from pop-ularity until by 1915 they were uncommon. The expansion gir-dle still firmed up and occasionally packed in both women and men with more around the middle than they cared to reveal in their dress, and women office workers still wore long black skirts and white blouses with stiff collars and black ties (men's uniforms were similar—black or dark suits with white shirts and ties), but heavily boned clothing was disappearing from most women's wardrobes. The new sexuality among the young—even if only in talk—and the acceptance of the desirability of pleasurable sexuality in marriage meant that men and women more than ever fretted about their body shape and size, hoping to conform to the models of ideal form defined by the adoles-cent youth culture that was so powerful in the 1920s.

Cosmetics sales dramatized the increased concern for a new youthful and healthy beauty. The cosmetics industry did $180 million worth of business in 1930. There were 40,000 beauty parlors in operation in that year, eight times as many as in 1920.[19] For men the pressure to be active and youthful was also intense. Their new heroes were not captains of industry with ample girths, bearded faces, and fat cigars, but actors such as Douglas Fairbanks and, to a lesser extent, Rudolph Valentino—slender clean-shaven "suaves" who got the girl. Three-hundred-and-fifty-pound William Howard Taft was the last cor-pulent president to serve; he was replaced in 1912 by the lean Woodrow Wilson. By the mid-1920s the desirability for slender bodies among the middle class and wealthy became an obsession, and this weight consciousness helped transform the American diet for all but the poor. For the middle class and wealthy, breakfast commonly consisted of dry cereal with milk and fruit, citrus fruit or juice, or eggs and toast, juice, and coffee. The popular lunch was now a cold one and was often encased in bread; dinner ("supper" to the working class, who continued to call the midday meal "dinner") was commonly a roast or boiled meat with potatoes and vegetables, or in some cases spaghetti and a tomato meat sauce accompanied by a light dessert such as gelatin.

Weight consciousness also altered restaurant menus in some quarters, as did the related pure-food scare of the 1920s. French food was rejected by many as too fattening and too stimulating. Meat consumption in restaurants declined by nearly 50 percent between 1920 and 1930. White bread ceased to be served at the table in many eateries, replaced by rolls and darker breads. By the end of the decade, more than one-quarter of all restaurant patrons ordered milk, an increase of enormous proportions since virtually no one save children had drunk it before 1920. In addition, health-conscious Americans began to insist upon or at least favor restaurants that had decor that suggested cleanliness. White enamel, white tile, and stainless steel became fashionable and waiters and waitresses increasingly dressed in white uniforms. Black service personnel were banished to the dishwashing rooms and kitchens if they had been out front, as if their skin suggested dirt. Condiments on tables appeared in original packaging, signifying that trusted corporations that met Food and Drug Administration guidelines had prepared the goods. Gone were the generic serving dishes filled with ketchup or mustard. It mattered not that in reality the small home-size bottles and jars were filled from the big restaurant-sized vessels and that unscrupulous (or smart) restaurateurs could substitute cheaper bulk brands for the Heinz or French's. The surface and the image were what mattered.

PUBLIC HEALTH AND OLD WAYS

By wars' end the idea of rotundity equaling healthy and slimness equaling weak had been almost thoroughly reversed, except for infants, who were allowed their "baby fat." The slender body was the healthful body, as long as it was not bony and emaciated. But for some Americans, yearning for slimness might have seemed laughable if they knew anyone who did so. A 1928 study of the Sioux found a prevalence of bowed legs, decayed teeth, blindness, and constant eye pain. Twenty-two percent of the women, 25 percent of the men, and 27 percent of the children studied were termed "extremely thin," while, perhaps ironically, 40 percent of the women, 27 percent of the men, and 11 percent of the children were described as "fat." Thirty-three percent of the children on the South Dakota Sioux reservation studied were dead before they were two years old; 50 percent passed away before their seventh birthday.[20]

The plight of the Indians received little attention in the popular press or in the U.S. Congress. Public health issues for the bulk of the white population were largely concerned with three important phenomena: the increasing number of hospitals, the growing professionalization of physicians, and the great influenza epidemic of 1918–1919. Between 1900 and 1920 the number of hospital beds in the United States doubled, as cities and universities built new facilities and expanded older structures to accommodate both the burgeoning urban populations and the more sophisticated medical training of would-be physicians. In addition, the Progressive ethos of top-down reform and its commitment to good health as a necessity for the preservation of American (that is, Anglo-American) culture stimulated the expenditure of public monies for both more efficient city governments and more efficient delivery of health care and, Progressives hoped, less disease.

Medical education had become more structured and rigorous as early as the 1870s, when Daniel Coit Gilman at Johns Hopkins and Charles Eliot at Harvard undertook the reorganization of American medical training, hoping to rescue it from the unlicensed and inconsistent efforts of the past. Formal training that included laboratory work and extended training beyond the classroom characterized the profession, and by 1900 nearly all of the nation's medical schools followed the Harvard-Hopkins example. More effective diagnostic tools, from microscopes of heightened powers to x-rays, as well as laboratory testing on animals, had turned ordinary Americans' attitudes toward physicians from mistrust to near veneration, especially after the isolation of vitamins and the stunning effects of such innovations as sulfa drugs for the treatment of infection.

Cures for dreaded diseases further strengthened the medical community's position in the United States. By the late 1920s typhoid fever, smallpox, and cholera had virtually disappeared from urban and rural America. Tuberculosis, the second most common cause of death in the United States in 1900, was tenth on the list in 1930. The death rate for TB dropped from 150 per 100,000 Americans in 1918 to 98 per 100,000 in 1922. Syphilis was brought under control by the use of Salvarsan, and fortified flour and margarine helped control and nearly eliminate rickets. Infant mortality declined from 100 per 1,000 live births in 1915 to 71.7 per 1,000 in 1925 to 55.7 per 1,000 in 1935. For physicians the growth of hospital care and better diagnostic tools meant long hours, and less of them out of the office on house calls. In 1929 a typical Philadelphia physician's work week was more than fifty hours long, but only six of those hours were spent on visits. The rest were spent in the office, hospitals, and clinics.[21]

The enhanced reputation physicians enjoyed did not completely eliminate the old ways or other methods of treatment. Ray La Marca's father, a barber in the Pittsburgh area, had learned the centuries-old techniques of bleeding in Rome as a young man, and continued to practice the ancient arts for some of his patrons. "If you had pneumonia, they would lay you down on your stomach. They used to get a quarter and dip it in oil and light the quarter. Then they would put a glass on top of the quarter to get all the bad blood in one place. You had to do this two or three times on the back of your spine. And then my dad used to make slices in the skin and the suction of the glass would draw out the blood. The blood was black as anything, you know. Even in the United States my dad couldn't sleep at night for all the people that wanted him to do that for them."[22]

Many women continued to use midwives to deliver their babies, and until 1938 the majority of births occurred outside of the large and sometimes impersonal hospitals. For many, hospitals were fearful places, full of dying and hopelessly diseased people. For immigrant women the reassurance of a midwife who spoke the language of the old country was a comfort, although sometimes the results were disastrous. Rose Popovich's mother had a midwife help her and Rose with the delivery of her third child. But the child was stillborn, and Rose's mother never forgave the midwife, who was allegedly drunk at the time of delivery. By the end of World War II, at least in large cities, hospitals had shed much of their previous reputation, and were viewed as centers of scientific cleanliness and professional care that was superior to home treatment.[23]

SANITATION

After World War I public health issues in the United States included not only the pure milk and food crusades, but also the organization of municipal and town sanitation activities such as regular and expanded garbage collection, the building of water treatment facilities, the expansion of sewage removal lines into poorer areas of cities, and the certification of meat for purity. Beginning in about 1915 street cleaning machines, drawn either by horses or a truck, were replacing hand sweeping. A 1914 survey of ten American cities revealed that 90 percent had taken on street cleaning as a public responsibility and that 50 percent were collecting garbage on a regular basis, especially in the wealthier districts. All streets were flushed daily in New Orleans and major streets three times weekly in Los Angeles. Denver sanitation engineers swept or flushed the streets daily in the summer, and swept them whenever the weather permitted in the winter. Most cities had anti-litter laws on their books, but did little to enforce them. In poorer neighborhoods, where garbage was less often collected and there was much less room to store refuse, the streets and alleys were full of trash, rats, mice, cockroaches, marauding dogs and cats, and occasionally opossums and raccoons.[24]

This environment was interpreted by the less enlightened as simply another example of the equation of the poor, the black, and the immigrant with lower forms of life. But for others it was a clarion call for action to clean up cities and their corrupt and inefficient practices of government. Even if reformers believed themselves in some way inherently or biologically superior to the poor, and reform only a way to prevent the spread of contagion from the poor to their own neighborhood and class, the result was a broad-based attack on dirt, trash, and disease in the cities. By the late 1930s nearly all American cities with populations greater than 100,000 had municipal trash collection on a regular basis throughout their city limits.

Medical care was expensive, and there were few "safety nets" for the poor. Most African-Americans, Mexican-Americans, American Indians, and Asian-Americans relied on their own physicians and cures to treat ailments, and neighbors and family to nurse them, because they trusted their people and because it was often less expensive to do so. The health care of parents too infirm to work or who were out of work because of their age fell to their children if they were nearby. Nearly all Americans—young or old—living in small towns and villages and far-flung farms seldom went into a hospital and only rarely saw a physician. Farm families' health was also sometimes endangered by their living and working environments. Hog and other animal pens near water supplies resulted in the contamination of the water with fecal coliform. Those with a milking cow found it difficult, if not impossible, to avoid contact between soiled udders and the milk. Contaminated water and milk carried bacteria that caused dysentery, chronic diarrhea, hepatitis, and typhoid fever.[25]

Influenza and the Cleanliness Crusade

THE PANDEMIC OF 1918–1920

The isolation of the farm did have one public health advantage, however. The influenza epidemic of 1918–1919 was especially severe in cities. Crowded residential areas and limited knowledge of the disease's method of contagion provided near perfect conditions for mass infection. Hundreds of thousands were struck down by the disease. The January 6, 1919, edition of the Fitchburg, Massachusetts, *Sentinel* reported that in 1918, 111,688 people had died of the disease in the nation's forty-six largest cities. Four days earlier, the paper reported that fifty "new cases" had been reported in two days. "There are now over one hundred houses placarded with the new black and white card which designate them as containing one or more cases of the disease." Newspaper columns and magazine "articles" with the appearance of news pitched patent medicines as cures for the frightful disease. Careful readers found the tiny word "advertisement" or "adv." at the bottom of the ad, however.[26]

Like cholera, which had plagued urban areas in the nineteenth century, the disease came on with fearful suddenness and multiple symptoms: digestive upset and nausea, fever, aches, and dizziness. The medical community could not keep up with the spread of the contagion. People were terrified and tried anything to defeat it or stave it off. Maria Kresic remembered that "If you drank whiskey and tea you weren't supposed to get the flu. . . . So many died from the flu they just rang the church bells; they didn't dare take [corpses] into the church."[27]

Urban sanitation movements and the shock of the influenza experience helped fuel a cleanliness craze in American homes in the 1920s. The quest for hygiene in the home reached its zenith between 1920 and 1940, when youngsters born between 1900 and 1920 began their own families. That generation—especially those who were middle class and wealthy—was the product of an ideology that intertwined health and fitness with eugenics and racial nationalist theories of the late nineteenth century.

PHYSICAL FITNESS AND "RACE CONSCIOUSNESS"

In the United States, news about male fitness for service in the Spanish-American War and World War I and continued concern for female weakness and nervous diseases fueled the argument for "the strenuous life" in the outdoors.[28] Muscle-building gurus such as Charles Atlas, Lionel Strongfort, Earle Liedermann, and the irrepressible and often ridiculous Bernarr Mac-Fadden filled men's magazines such as the *Police Gazette, Pop-*

ular Mechanics, Physical Culture, and even comic books (by the late 1930s) with ads for their bodybuilding formulae. Swimming champion Annette Kellermann posed in form-fitting swimsuits pitching her book *The Body Beautiful,* and ads for gear that claimed to enlarge a woman's bust, straighten either gender's nose, or lengthen a man's penis could also be found, if one looked for them.[29]

Admen and hucksters received support for their claims of doom for the "race" from academics and other seemingly respectable authors. (In the late nineteenth and early twentieth centuries *race* was roughly equivalent to "nationality" or "cultural group," as well as skin color.) Yale physiologist Irving Fisher worried about "race suicide," and became active in the eugenics movement, which sought to limit births among the less "desirable" groups in society. The people to be regulated were usually labeled by their skin color (nonwhite), ethnicity (all but Anglo-Saxons and Nordics), or economic circumstance (poor). Fisher was concerned that white "Nordic" people would "quietly lie down and let some other race run over us." Historian John Fiske, in his 1916 work *The Critical Period of American History,* insisted that the American revolutionary tradition was a white middle-class one, with no proletarian aspect at all. He detested immigrants, particularly Irish Catholics, who had settled and, by 1915, controlled much of the political life of his beloved Massachusetts.[30]

Influential ideas about ethnic and race relations and the health of the predominantly WASP middle class also came from popular writers. Madison Grant's *The Passing of the Great Race,* first published in 1916, synthesized many of the concerns and fears of the middle class and the wealthy into a theory of national rise and decline. Grant tried to show that the most influential and accomplished civilizations in human history were "pure," and that ethnic mixture led inevitably to decay. Moreover, he identified as the best and most accomplished only those civilizations of the "Nordic," or Anglo-Saxon and northern European, peoples, as if the Italian Renaissance had never happened or the Moors had never existed. He declared that the descendants of the seventeenth- and eighteenth-century white settlers of the United States were the last "remnants" of the "great race," and that their numbers would soon be overwhelmed by the new immigrants, who seemed to be producing babies far faster than did the old stock. Self-imposed WASP restraints such as smaller families and contraception, and cultural changes such as women's rights and increased apartment living in cities, were leading, he thought, to "race suicide."

Grant's popular tract was influential and long-lived. In 1921, Albert Wiggam, in an article in *Physical Culture* entitled "Can We Make Motherhood Fashionable?" summarized Grant's theories with references to the latter as if he were known to all. He then asserted that "the only answer [to the race "problem"] is to make parenthood fashionable among people of brains . . . and to encourage birth control among the foolish. . . . In our time the lower, more incompetent *one-half* produce children *three times as fast* as the other half, which is socially more adequate, the net result is that the lower one-half is producing three-fourths of the next generation."[31]

The middle-class home hygienic movement blended racial nationalism, Progressive regulatory legislation, urban sanitation movements, birth control advocacy, and fears of decline and submersion by masses of foreigners and nonwhites together with dramatic material results for the home. If dirt was a sign of moral and parental lassitude and irresponsibility, and in a larger sense evidence of a betrayal of one's assumed superior nationality, then cleanliness was a sign of health, responsible parental behavior, and national identity. An Old Dutch cleanser advertisement in the July 28, 1939, issue of the *Ladies' Home Journal* summed it up: *"The most important thing you can put into your refrigerator is Healthful Cleanliness"* (emphasis in original).

THE SANITARY HOUSEHOLD

For most Americans cleanliness equaled whiteness. White tile floors and walls, white enameled metal appliances and kitchen tables, stainless steel—all the accoutrements of the sanitary restaurant and hospital—were the sure signs of care and cleanliness. When pastel color-coordinated kitchens and bathrooms became popular among the affluent in the mid-1920s, sanitation was not compromised because the new shades were light enough to show dirt. The pastels constituted a middle ground between the hospital and the home.

This increased both the burden of guilt on mothers and young women and the pressure to perform more work in the home. Gleaming white or pastel fixtures and floors were meant to show dirt. Cleaning the bathrooms—never a pleasant job for most—came to mean both visible dirtlessness and invisible sanitizing. Products such as Lysol succeeded because they promised disinfectant powers. Bathing assumed even greater significance, not only as a way to remove harmful bodily dirt that could "clog pores," but also as a way to distinguish oneself from the poor, who allegedly washed less often.

This concern for cleanliness and social acceptance sometimes went to extremes. Lysol was also promoted as a disinfectant necessary for feminine hygiene. The firm offered a booklet (by mail order, in a "plain envelope") that gave "the facts—frankly, explicitly, and reliably." Kotex, probably the first successful mass-market sanitary napkin in the United States, similarly confronted the "embarrassing" problem of trying to control or at least conceal menstrual flow. Mothers were often depicted in these ads as uninformed or incompetent, and the corporation was portrayed as a scientific (and therefore knowledgeable) and anonymous (and therefore less embarrassing) advisor.[32]

Business and government efforts to bring sanitation and better overall health to the household were loaded with political meaning as well as genuine concern for extending life. Efforts to change the foods Americans ate, the shape of their bodies, and the condition of their homes became an obsession after 1915, and ultimately reached all classes of Americans, in the mass media if not in fact. In reality most of the poor received limited if any benefits from these activities, except for recipients of New Deal relief efforts, especially the Civilian Conservation Corps and Public Works Administration jobs that were militarylike in their feeding and housing of the workers. When World War II began, eventually the 17 million men and women who served in the Armed Forces (and those of their immediate

families who were able to relocate to a military base) were
provided with facilities, food, and medical treatment that often
exceeded their previous experience. In World War II the "doctor's draft" brought many physicians into the Armed Forces,
and the military once again introduced many recruits to more
advanced—if mass-produced—medical care and nutrition.

6

✼

IN THE three decades preceding the end of World War II the amount of time expended at ease and the variety of leisure activities had expanded for millions. Innovations in the industries of play were both enduring, such as radio and the talking cinema, and faddish and ephemeral, such as mah-jongg. Americans of nearly all classes experienced in one way or another what has been rightly termed the "golden age" of sport and dancing. Prohibition may have cramped the style of some for a while, but speakeasies and other "clubs" eased that difficulty. A drink could be had with considerable speed in most cities if the thirsty knew where to look and were stout of heart, since the quality of the hooch was often frightening. Ultimately there were enough forms of entertainment that were cheap enough that many of them became true mass media and mass diversions, in spite of the Depression.

The Radio Age

A CULTURAL REVOLUTION

The most important leisure-time innovation of the era was the radio. For Secretary of Commerce Herbert Hoover in 1921, it was "an instrument of beauty and learning." But for others, such as Bruce Bliven, editor of *The New Republic,* radio programming was "outrageous rubbish, both verbal and musical."[1] Undaunted by Bliven's condemnation and perhaps encouraged by Hoover's hyperbole, the popularity of radio grew rapidly. By 1924, 5 million homes nationwide had at least one set, and Americans had spent $350 million on radios and radio parts, or one-third of all the money spent on furniture. Within the first eight years of the industry's life it had become a $500 million industry with more than 500 local stations. For every 1,000 Americans in 1928, 50 radios were owned. A January 1, 1929, survey conducted for the National Broadcasting Company by Massachusetts Institute of Technology professor Daniel Starch found that one-third of all American homes owned a radio, and that 80 percent of all radio owners listened daily. In addition, he found that rural and urban listener programming preferences were virtually identical, which suggested to some optimists that radio programmers had discovered—or created—some of the unifying elements in American culture.

The severity of the Depression did not slow radio's phenomenal growth. By 1934, 60 percent of all American homes had radios, and radio listening had become Americans' favorite pastime, according to a survey conducted by the National Recreation Association, published as *The Leisure of 5,000 People*. Americans owned 43.2 percent of all the radios in the world. By 1939 the number of radios in American homes totaled 44 million, 86 percent of all households owned at least one set, and the average listener tuned in for four and one-half hours daily. There were, in addition, 6.5 million radios in automobiles. In 1940, the entire population spent 1 billion hours weekly listening to the radio, about seven times as much time as they passed at the movies.[2]

Working-class Americans often saved money by building their own sets. After buying a germanium crystal for about $2 at a hardware or department store, the do-it-yourself radio builder only had to connect it to a wire wound in a coil, and attach the whole thing to a board. Then, after wiring a headset into the apparatus and twisting the coil until sound began to crackle, all that remained were adjustments until a comprehensible sound came through. Putting the headset in a hollow vessel created a loudspeaker of sorts.

EARLY PROGRAMMING

Radio in the 1920s was for the most part a local affair, and it reflected the interests and talents of either urban neighborhoods or farming areas. Much of the early urban programming was nonprofit, operated by ethnic, religious, and labor groups. In 1925, 28 percent of the nation's 571 stations were owned by educational or religious groups. Many predominantly English-language stations broadcast "nationality hours" in the languages of the most powerful or most numerous ethnic groups of the cities they served.[3] In the countryside commercial stations were at first more common, for the most part because businesses were about the only source of capital available to those who wanted to begin operating a station.

Commercial radio soon infiltrated all areas of the country, because broadcasting in areas in which people were highly concentrated could be very profitable. The commercial alleged to have been the first of the genre was aired on August 28, 1922. It was for real estate, and was broadcast over station WEAF in New York City. By the mid-1920s radio station managers discovered that manufacturers would pay for air time providing they could have some fraction of a fifteen-minute time slot to pitch their wares. Some advertisers at first declined to use the medium, fearing that the radio ad was too much of an intrusion into the intimacy of the parlor or bedroom. But by 1927, when the National Broadcasting Company established the first national network, the advertising business had shed its reservations. The radio was an immediate personal experience—as the cinema was not—and was for many advertisers a dream come true. One slick trick was to buy enough time to name the show after a product. The *Eveready Hour* debuted in 1926 on fourteen stations, and in the 1927–1928 season thirty-nine companies sponsored shows on NBC, while four did so on the newer Columbia Broadcasting System. The next year sixty-five sponsors bought time from the networks for a total of more than $25 million.

By the 1930s, tuning in the radio (which was at times a testing task requiring an attentive listener) brought Americans advertisements that were louder, more frequent, and more boisterous in their claims for products than the subdued descriptive ads of the late 1920s had been. Radio ads took up an increasing percentage of corporations' advertising budgets, and led to a corresponding drop in monies spent on advertising in other media. Between 1928 and 1934, radio ads grew 316 percent nationally, newspaper ads declined by 30 percent, and magazine ads dropped 45 percent; 246 daily newspapers ceased publication, in part a result of the Depression and in part because of their losses in advertising revenue.

Early commercially made radio sets were often crude, industrial-looking objects, conglomerations of dials, diodes, wires, resistors, capacitors, and speakers. At first, and until about 1927, the technology of the thing was miraculous, and the look of it was properly scientific and laboratorylike. But by the late twenties diodes were not enough of a statement: The miracle of sound was taken for granted, and a newer sign of the future and of technology was marketed. The workings, like those of the appliances of the era, were encased in new materials, such as Bakelite, or in basic box furniture forms designed to indicate "future" or "modern." Veneering the cases with different colored woods using the linear and streamlined decorative designs of the era's graphic arts gave a sense of movement to radios, and many floor consoles were designed to look like a piece of parlor furniture that was more tech-moderne than a sofa. The latter merely provided a comfortable place to sit or recline; the radio cabinet contained the wizardry of science and technology. Machine-age designs did not appeal to every radio owner, however. "Colonial" and other "historical" forms were also broadly popular, in spite of the incongruity of encasing a thoroughly modern communication system in furniture that represented the preindustrial world. Perhaps these forms of eras long gone were an unconscious comfort to those who wanted the benefits of the new technology and the illusion of "simpler" times before machines and industry had taken over American culture.

Music was the most common form of programming broadcast in the early 1920s. Sporting events and plays were distant second and third most common broadcast genres, and news reports occurred every hour on the hour. In cities classical music dominated early radio programming, consistent with the conviction that the medium had its greatest potential as an agent of uplift and that classical European music was the best form of "higher" culture. The first live symphony concert was broadcast in 1926, as Serge Koussevitzky led the Boston Symphony Orchestra in a concert heard by an estimated 1 million listeners. Music appreciation shows and weekly concerts were aired through the 1930s, and the Metropolitan Opera began broadcasts in 1931. In 1938 an estimated 12 million people heard the Met broadcasts regularly during the opera season. WQXR, New York, began a classical-only program in 1937, and the New York Yankees baseball team sponsored a program of classical music interspersed with major league scores.

Popular music gradually surpassed, but did not completely supplant, classical music on urban radio stations. In 1938 the Federal Communications Commission conducted a survey of the content of 62,000 radio hours, and found that one-third of the air time was devoted to commercials. Of the remaining 40,000 hours, one-half were devoted to music, and popular music dominated that segment; 9 percent of the time was for drama, 9 percent for variety programming, 8.5 percent for news and sports, 5.2 percent for religion, 2.2 percent for special events, and 13.7 percent for "miscellaneous," mostly talking, shows.[4] Country music stations operated in nearly all the nation's rural areas, sometimes bringing the music of Nashville's Grand Old Opry (which began broadcasting the show under that name in 1927, after a few years as station WSM's "Barn Dance"), but usually carrying the performances of itinerant singers and bands that played at the station for a week or two and then moved on. West Virginia miner Aaron Barkham remembered when "the first radio come to Mingo County . . . in 1934. That was a boon. It was a little job, got more squeals and squeaks than anything else. Everybody came from miles around to look at it. We didn't have any electricity. So we hooked up two car batteries. We got 'Grand Old Opry' on it."[5]

The radio brought a new style of singing, termed "crooning," to Americans, in addition to comic songs, ditties, and country music. The most famous of the crooners—Bing Crosby and

Rudy Vallee were two of the best known—developed a slow and smooth delivery that featured sliding into notes as opposed to the clipped style of more formal singers. In 1935 another unique American form of music and song joined the airwaves when the "singing cowboy," Gene Autry, began his evening show and enormously lucrative career as movie star, singer, and entrepreneur. Radio play of recorded music did not actually cut into record or sheet music sales, but record sales became the measure of how often and for how long tunes were aired.

AMOS 'N' ANDY; THE "SOAPS"

Perhaps as significant because of their national popularity, if not their percentage of the air time, were two other types of programs—comedy and daytime drama. The great age of radio comedy began (on a national scale) in the summer of 1929. Just a couple of months before the crash, two Chicago radio actors went national with a show that had been a local success for a few years. Freeman Gosden and Charles J. Correll "blacked up" their voices as Sam 'n' Henry, two "indigent colored boys" known as "the Gumps" in Chicago.

After changing stations in Chicago, and their names to Amos 'n' Andy, they linked up with NBC and shuffled into American homes with the help of Pepsodent toothpaste. The most popular radio show of the 1930s, it eventually dominated the listening lives of middle-class and working Americans, including some African-Americans, in spite of the show's demeaning racial stereotypes. First aired at eleven P.M. eastern time, the network switched to seven because parents complained that their children refused to go to sleep until the show was over. When people in the mountain and Pacific time zones complained that they were still at work when the show aired, the network broadcast it again at eleven-thirty P.M. eastern time. Restaurants broadcast the show, and movie houses scheduled showings around the fifteen-minute adventures of the two urban hustlers, sometimes actually stopping a film to bring in the broadcast. Telephone calls dropped off precipitously at seven and eleven-thirty, and only the president had air rights over them.[6]

Amos 'n' Andy succeeded brilliantly among the white middle-class audience that loved them because they epitomized coping with the Depression in a manner that posed no threat to the established order. The black protagonists—one a middle-class aspirant who never quite got it right in spite of his schemes (Amos), and the other a lazy, clownish, but ultimately shrewd manipulator (Andy)—were obsessed with money and money-getting. The show's hokey moralism reinforced the idea that hard work and industriousness (and implicitly not labor organization or strikes) were the keys to success. Their struggles were those of the population as a whole, but they were depicted as if the scuffling of everyday life were appropriate for them, and not for the white folks. Three-quarters of a million blacks didn't think so: They signed a petition protesting the depiction of African-Americans on the show. Nothing much happened. *Amos 'n' Andy* became a television show after World War II, still steeped in stereotypes, but at least with black actors.

Other comedy shows brought vaudeville performers such as Eddie Cantor and George Burns and his allegedly dingbat wife, Gracie Allen, to the radio, and made-for-radio shows such as *Fibber McGee and Molly* made fun of everything about American married life, often with barely disguised slights of ethnic groups.

Daytime drama programs, originally sponsored by soap companies, seized a significant market share during the afternoons. Figuring that the bulk of the listeners at home during the day were women, and that they were the major purchasers of soap products, the companies put their money behind an array of extremely successful serial dramas that soon after their introduction were termed "soap operas." Three such shows were on the air in 1931. There were ten in 1934, nineteen in 1935, thirty-one in 1936 and 1937, and sixty-one in 1939.

Most offered plots revolving around personal struggle—with finance, with lovers and husbands, or between classes. Most had strong women as central characters, reflecting the gender, the problems, and the desires of their listeners. The shows' formulaic plots oversimplified the problems of personal interaction, and in keeping with the experience and identity of their working- and middle-class audiences, the characters were plain simple folk. Like "Old Ma Perkins," they embodied the mythic American culture that had been overwhelmed by the greedy and unprincipled economic onslaught that had caused the Depression.

Ma Perkins was a widow who had "spent all her life taking care of her home, washing and cooking and raising her family." When her husband died she took over the lumberyard that he had run.[7] She was a fountain of down-home wisdom in Rushville Center, reaffirming the "basic" social values of accommodation, cooperation, and comfort with one's social and economic position. In these dramas men were largely irrelevant, or absent, with the exception of older, nonthreatening figures. What order there was in the turmoil of Rushville Center or in the class-conscious lives of Stella Dallas, Helen Trent, or Our Gal Sunday (other famous "soap" heroines) was the result of wise, struggling, and strong women. Maybe the promise of the machine and the modern was a hollow one after all, a slick urban sophisticated hoax on the basically sound values of town, farm, and village. The villains were the easily identifiable (and overdrawn) stereotypes of city life: rich men, hollow socialites, painted women, shysters, crooks, hoods, and hustlers. Amos 'n' Andy were urban but safe: They were clownish, almost rural chicken-stealers in the city, nonthreatening because they were black, unsuccessful, and segregated. In the "soaps" the greedy high-rollers were white, successful, and everywhere.

Evening radio serial dramas often starred motion-picture cowboy heroes such as Gene Autry or radio creations such as the Lone Ranger. The masked man was a typical Depression-era hero: a renegade Texas Ranger who rode with an outcast and sage Indian who had rescued him and nursed him back to health. The Lone Ranger, like Dashiell Hammett's Sam Spade and other detectives in the popular mystery novels of the era, was an outlaw, and a symbol of a society with little faith in its established institutions. The regular lawmen in this and other western series were usually good men at best buffaloed by crime, and at worst simply inept and occasionally crooked. The Ranger was a vigilante, and potentially a dangerous example of the man who took the law into his own hands, a Machiavellian do-gooder who rejected the limitations of law and law enforcement, even though his goals were justice. By the middle of 1939 the Ranger had ridden more than 1,000 times, on hundreds of stations, as often as three times in a week. For the Lone Ranger, Gene Autry, and other western heroes, as well as for Ma Perkins and the rest of the "soap" heroes, the key was to return, if not to "those thrilling days of yesteryear," as the Ranger and Tonto did, then to the values of those years, as Ma, Stella, and Helen did.

NEWS AND SPORTS

News and sports shows were often spectacularly popular, gathering as much as one-half the audience if the event was truly monumental. These were often one-shot affairs, such as the second Joe Louis–Max Schmeling heavyweight fight, which got a "Crosley" rating of 57.6 percent of the radios turned on and measured by the Crosley company. Politics entered the radio era in 1928, when an estimated 40 million listeners heard Al Smith and Herbert Hoover speak on election eve. The largest single line item (20 percent of the total) in the Republican party's campaign budget in 1928 was for radio ads. The Republicans bought 30 more hours of radio time in 1932 than they had in 1928, when they purchased 42.5 hours, to the Democrats' 51.5 hours (the same amount as in 1928). It backfired on Hoover, who came across as stodgy and distant in the face of a great human crisis. Roosevelt used radio to convey a personal and caring presence. Later, his "Fireside Chats" were also big scorers, garnering 30 to 40 percent of the listening audience. The World Series, the Kentucky Derby, and the Rose Bowl were similar big winners. Workers in the plant and on the farm regularly listened to baseball games all through the spring and summer if they could bring them in on the radio.

Listeners perhaps were comforted by the repetition of the hourly news that punctuated the day. News stories did not break with regularity or very often, but the news bulletin and its dramatic urgency (especially as World War II began to take shape in 1938 and 1939) kept many radios on, even if the listeners were only half attentive. In 1934 there were 4,670 interruptions of normal programming for news bulletins, nearly one-half of them relating to the "crime of the century," the kidnapping and death of the Lindbergh baby.

The war in Europe provided radio news with its greatest opportunity to establish the medium as the most reliable medium for the delivery of information. The crisis of the late 1930s also provided CBS with the opportunity to make up ground on NBC, the first and largest network. Pictures did not lie, but they were not instantaneous and they were not personal. Live reporting brought the crisis home and did it with immediacy and drama. A legendary group of reporters—among them H. V. Kaltenborn, Edward R. Murrow, and Robert Trout—brought interviews with political leaders, battlefield reports from Spain in 1936, and later from eastern Europe as Hitler began to overrun the region. Daily broadcasts from Berlin, Prague, Rome, London, and Munich began in 1938, and bulletins from two minutes to two hours in length during the Czechoslovakian crisis of September 1938 established news as more popular than entertainment and CBS as the top news network. Murrow's famous "This is London" opening brought the reality of the Blitz to Americans in a way that complemented and perhaps outdid the power of the photograph. In early 1938, the Columbia University Office of Radio Research reported that its surveys found that less than one-half of the public preferred radio to print journalism; after the Munich crisis, two-thirds preferred radio news to newspapers and magazines.[8]

THE RADIO AND THE PHONOGRAPH

Until radio burst upon the leisure and educational scene, music in Americans' lives came from live performances, or from phonographs. Pianos and organs were still popular among those who could afford them, but the parlor organ had been declining in popularity since 1900. More common in middle-class homes was the pianola, or player piano. Introduced in 1898 by the Aeolian Company, within twenty-five years "automatic" pianos accounted for 50 percent of all pianos produced in the United States.

The phonograph was introduced on a mass scale at the turn

of the century, and it was both a revolution and a revelation. It was a revolutionary instrument because it reproduced and preserved sound. Americans bought the new machine, wax cylinders, and, later, records with verve. They typically spent more on popular music—ballads, songs, ragtime, and marching-band tunes—than on musical instruments, books, periodicals, or sporting goods. But cheap radio sets and free programming ended the record-playing boom: Expenditures for records and record-playing gear in 1930 were one-twentieth of what they had been in 1920.

American popular music on record and radio was heterogeneous. Regional variations and ethnic and racial specialty music sold briskly. "Race records" were those cut by African-American performers for a primarily black audience. In Harlem alone Mamie Smith's rendition of "Crazy Blues" sold 75,000 copies in one week.[9] African-Americans bought more than 5 million records in 1925, according to Howard Odum and Guy Johnson's study of three record companies. "Jazz" records, first marketed under that name in 1917, were produced by both black and white bands. Black Swan Records was the only major black-owned record company; the white-owned companies— Paramount, Columbia, Victor, and Okeh—turned out records for both black and white audiences, including songs with overtly racist lyrics that appealed to whites and to many ethnic groups that competed with African-Americans for jobs and social position.

The technology of early recording was not particularly complex or expensive to set up, and a multitude of small recording companies were also established to meet the demand for traditional country and gospel music. The fiddle and banjo music that was to evolve into bluegrass was popular among country people and among some of the city residents who for fifty years had been leaving the farm for the city, but who still longed for the music of their home. Gospel recordings appealed to some whites but primarily to black audiences, especially those who had moved north during the migration that began during World War I.

Reading

NEWSPAPERS

The radio helped kill off more than 200 daily newspapers, but the daily and the weekly survived as a form, and still occupied a significant place in Americans' daily lives. William Allen White's Emporia, Kansas, *Gazette* has become the most famous of the small papers, both for the quality of the reporting and for White's articulate thoughts about the importance of local news and local issues for such papers. In out-of-the-way towns and villages, weeklies thrived and often competed with one another for the same limited market. Foreign-language newspapers continued to serve the immigrant populations long after the newcomers had become settled in the United States. They provided not only the news for those who had not yet learned English, but also offered information about the location of hard-to-find ethnic goods and services.

The newspapers that survived and thrived after World War I offered a form of reading material—in addition to news, advertisements, and features—that was to become a part of the everyday life of most reading Americans, even if they could barely make out the English language. Comic strips—which may have saved some papers from extinction—had been introduced in 1895 when Richard Outcault's *Down Hogan's Alley* was first published. The strip's main character, the "Yellow Kid," inspired toys, games, and other goods in much the same fashion that an earlier comic creation in book form, the Brownies, had. *The Katzenjammer Kids* (1897), *Happy Hooligan* (1899), *Alphonse and Gaston* (1899), *Little Nemo* (1905), *Krazy Kat* (1910), *Bringing Up Father* (1912), and others appeared, and each snagged a loyal following. As their titles suggest, many poked fun at immigrant groups, and these probably had minimal attraction for the subject group. There was enough diversity in most papers' strips to provide white readers with the chance to snicker at others, especially African-Americans, who were usually lampooned if they appeared at all.

After World War I many papers published a "comic page"

that included older humorous strips and new dramatic strips such as *Gasoline Alley* (1919), *Little Orphan Annie* (1924), *Tarzan* (1929), *Dick Tracy* (1931), *Mandrake the Magician* (1934), *Prince Valiant* (1937), and *Rex Morgan, M.D.* (1945). *Little Orphan Annie* was the most popular drama strip of the 1930s, and the kid and her mutt also appeared in two movies and had their own radio show. Politically conservative in its message, the strip characterized the unemployed as lazy and content with relief. Aggressively anti-union, *Little Orphan Annie*'s creators consistently mixed stories of their heroine's trials with barely concealed assertions that workers should stop striking, go back to work, earn their keep, and shut up.[10]

MAGAZINES

Newspapers were the most common reading matter in most Americans' lives, but magazines increasingly began to occupy reading time. Magazine circulation reached 80 million in 1930, according to an independent survey conducted by the Audit Bureau of Circulations in 1934. There was a slight drop in the mid-1930s, but by 1942 circulation had risen to over 100 million. The new and successful magazines of the era—*Time, Reader's Digest, Esquire, The New Yorker, Fortune,* and *Life*—joined established periodicals such as *The Saturday Evening Post, Harper's, The Ladies' Home Journal, Good Housekeeping,* and pulp fiction and self-help magazines such as *True Story* and *Physical Culture.* The slicker urbane qualities of most of the newer magazines (*Reader's Digest* was the exception) appealed to the white middle class and to middle-class aspirants. The Curtis Publishing Company's flagship magazine, *The Saturday Evening Post,* suffered after the crash. The magazine's folksy rural nostalgia perhaps seemed inappropriate as farmers went bust in a cloud of dust.[11]

Time was first published in March 1923. Its irreverence and slick—or smug—tone and its departmental organization (like that of a university) were designed to appeal to the affluent and the urbane. The magazine's popularity grew steadily through the 1930s; its predominantly Republican and upscale philosophy appealed to a large chunk of the middle class. By the end of 1924 *Time* had 70,000 subscribers; by 1930, 300,000; and by 1937, 650,000.[12]

Founded in 1922 by DeWitt Wallace, *Reader's Digest* hoped to provide readers with articles that would be uplifting. Essentially conservative in political stance and, as the title indicated, digested, the little magazine was composed of articles culled and expurgated from other periodicals. Less nostalgic and not as folksy as the beleaguered *Saturday Evening Post,* the *Digest* sold well and consistently increased its circulation and profits.

Home workshop and do-it-yourself magazines were popular in the 1920s and 1930s. They brought suggestions and instructions for household jobs to eager readers who had time on their hands, not enough money to pay professionals to do the work, and desires for a new way to make a few bucks. Throughout the pages of these magazines were countless come-ons for the would-be small independent businessman, who was promised a pile of income from fixing locks, radios, small engines, and nearly everything else imaginable. The December 1935 issue of *Modern Mechanix* magazine, for example, contained ninety ads for job opportunities or education that could bring a new and steady (a key word) source of income, and seventy-six ads for all other sorts of consumer products. In addition there were nineteen "self-help" ads promising solutions to everything from blemished skin to physical weakness. Perhaps the most far-fetched was the full-page ad for the "new uncrowded industry" of raising giant frogs. Sponsored by the American Frog Canning Company of New Orleans, the ad promised that a "backyard pond starts you" on the way to "make big profits!"[13]

In addition to "smart" magazines, *Reader's Digest,* and do-it-yourself magazines, sensational and marginally risqué periodicals also had booming sales throughout the era. These sexually suggestive and sometimes implicitly violent mass-market magazines owed much to the success of the *Police Gazette,* a decades-old rag whose quickly tattered issues piled up in barbershops, saloons, pool halls, and other male-oriented places. The number and circulation of these magazines expanded after the professional strong man and health-obsessed Bernarr MacFadden launched *True Story* in the 1920s. The genius of *True Story* was in its cross-gender appeal, and especially in its appeal to women, who had only limited public access to salacious literature until MacFadden's efforts.

True Story and magazines like it were formulaic in their articles and in their visual appeal. Like *Physical Culture,* the covers often depicted beautiful young women showing enough skin to be suggestive without getting the magazine pulled from the shelves. The stories—alleged to be true, and "stranger than fiction"—were generally moral tales of naive good women confused and hurt by a complex modern (i.e., urban) world, much like the dynamic of soap operas. A fall from original grace often occurred, and punishment was certain: shame, ostracism, and, in more extreme cases, loss of a spouse or even death. So effective was the *True Story* formula that by the late 1920s advertisements in all sorts of magazines—including proper periodicals such as *Ladies' Home Journal*—used the confessional style. Tales of woe and rescue by using the right cereal, laundry soap, or toothpaste were everywhere.

Women's magazines published articles on amateur dressmaking, more efficient housecleaning, and cheaper cooking in greater numbers than they had before the crash, but they carried little information about going into business for oneself. Instead the ads and the articles centered on child-rearing and the potential embarrassment of dirty clothing, dirty children, or a dirty house. Reinforcing traditional gender roles, these middle-class magazines offered a higher-end counterpart to the moral tales of the more working-class-oriented confession magazines.

Confessional, mechanics, and smart-set periodicals replaced many of the upright literary journals and compendiums that had been vital since the nineteenth century but which had been steadily losing readers since 1900. By 1940 such venerable titles as *Literary Digest, Review of Reviews, The Outlook, Judge, Delineator, Century, World's Work, Scribner's, Forum,* and *Women's World* were gone, many after as much as a half century of publication. Their tone of uplift and literary appreciation was rendered superfluous in a culture that traded on condensed books and articles and the "quick hit" of the newsmagazines. Many of the expired magazines were victims of their moral tone of restraint, an unfashionable position in the postwar era of automobiles, increasing sexual openness, and resistance to prohibition.

BOOKS AND COMIC BOOKS

The literary magazines also lost ground to the libraries that expanded their services in the 1920s. Not only were library buildings built and enlarged, some public libraries filled trucks with books and sent them on the road to small towns and hamlets. Mail-order book clubs were established in the 1920s to bring less expensive editions of great and popular books to the country and city, thereby increasing sales and, as some book club magnates hoped, a more thorough and widespread knowledge of the classics in the United States.

The classics probably fared better than they might have without these efforts at mass marketing and greater reader accessibility, but popular books of the era were usually of a type other than that of a college literature course. In 1925 and 1926, the best-selling nonfiction book in the United States was Bruce Barton's *The Man Nobody Knows.* Barton, who in 1928 became a founding partner in the eminent advertising firm Barton, Batten, Durstine, and Osborn, described Christ as a businessman trying to make his way through the world. Tales of the Old West and mystery novels were consistently popular fiction genres. Zane Grey's stories of lone lawmen continued to sell long after his death in 1936. Dashiell Hammett's *The Maltese Falcon* (1930) sold well (as did most of Hammett's other works), and in 1933 Erle Stanley Gardner had published the first of his Perry Mason mysteries *(The Case of the Velvet Claws).*

Hervey Allen's *Anthony Adverse* was a fiction best-seller in 1933 and 1934, but the sales of Margaret Mitchell's one-thousand-page saga of the Civil War South, *Gone With the Wind* (1936), surpassed the sales of any novel that preceded it within a year of its release. *Gone With the Wind* was both a love story and a nostalgic tale of preindustrial, agrarian America that evaded the problems of racial inequality in the Old South. Mitchell's work also probably offered some solace and encouragement to white Americans struggling with the effects of the Depression, since it showed the brave face of southerners torn apart by the Civil War but forcefully promising to rebuild.

Some of the artistically and financially successful fiction of the era did confront the problems of class differences, the shallowness of consumer culture, and the poverty, suffering, and struggle to survive of ordinary people. F. Scott Fitzgerald probed the first two issues in *This Side of Paradise* (1920), *The Beautiful and the Damned* (1922), and *The Great Gatsby* (1925). Sinclair Lewis found American business and small-town culture wanting in *Main Street* (1920) and *Babbitt* (1922). By the 1930s, and the deepening of the Depression, many novelists fixed their attention on the real and mythical farmer, unthreatening foreign peasant cultures, and the poor. Much of this popular literature reveals intellectuals' search for answers to the Depression in the culture and values of the common people, or the "folk." Pearl Buck made millions (most of which she donated to care for the destitute) and won the 1932 Pulitzer Prize for *The Good Earth,* her tale of peasant life in China, and Erskine Caldwell's novel about the plight of southern sharecroppers, *Tobacco Road* (1932), sold well. John Steinbeck's *The Grapes of Wrath* (1939) chronicled the lives of the Joad family, blown-out Okies fighting to survive the lean years as migrant laborers in California. It was an immediate success in the literary marketplace, as well as in its movie version, which was directed by John Ford and released in 1940. Common to nearly all these literary efforts was a sense of individual responsibility and a belief in the need for personal rather than systemic changes to produce a more equitable society. Even the more "radical" or at least politically left works, such as *The Grapes of Wrath,* still ultimately concentrated on the family as the bulwark against hard times.

The sense of individual responsibility and heroism—and a lack of faith in the economic and political system—also informed elements of a new form of literature that hit the stores, streets, and newsstands in 1929. Comic books built upon the success of newspaper comic pages, and were immensely popular among children and many adults who would not admit it. George Delacorte's tabloid, entitled simply *The Funnies,* was probably the first of the genre, although it lasted only thirteen issues. But its successors, including *The Shadow* (1931), *Detective Comics* (1937), *Superman* (1938), *Batman* (1939), and other superheroes that appeared by 1940, were successful for, in some cases, more than fifty years. Many of the most profitable and long-running comic books were not "comic" at all, but were dramatic stories that defined many of the social and economic problems of the Depression and war years in simplistic terms and provided solutions that ignored constitutional rights such as due process of law and habeas corpus.

Nearly all of the comic book heroes were men and nearly all were outsiders. Only Wonder Woman broke the gender line, and her uniform—a strapless, tight bodice, shorts, and high-heeled boots—showed lots of skin, thereby mixing the message of her heroic, crime-fighting athleticism. Superman, the first of the Action Comics heroes (1938), was an alien, and many others of the genre were technological creations and mutations with superhuman powers. Often disguised to fit in with everyday life and usually operating in a large impersonal city, they represented wish-fulfillment fantasies of readers caught in a civilization that seemed neither beneficent nor responsive to the efforts of ordinary humans. Western comic book heroes, like the Lone Ranger or Gene Autry on the radio, were able to whip the bad guys because they lived in a less civilized time and place. As in radio dramas and detective fiction, the ordinary lawmen and the judicial system in superhero comic books were unable to cope with the evils around them.

GAMES AND FADS

For those with a bent for more sociability than reading provided, card games such as euchre, whist, canasta, bridge, casino, rummy, and other traditional games were common pursuits, satisfying many Americans' desire for competition and companionship. Entertainment fads such as mah-jongg (introduced in 1923) and crossword puzzles (1924) enchanted many, although the former was passé by 1930. Stamp collecting was probably the most popular hobby in the United States, and could be expensive (as the king of England or President Roosevelt demonstrated), but it could also be a pastime that cost almost nothing, since used stamps were free and albums were not a necessity. Coin collecting obviously took money out of circulation, but one could always start with pennies, which lightened the financial burden of the parents whose children discovered numismatics.

During the Depression poverty and desperation made entering promotional contests an obsession for some. Radio programs began the rage for contests with promotions in the early 1930s, offering cash and other awards (jewelry, cars, trips) for the best advertising limericks, the best explanation of why a product was superior to another, or the reasons the United States was the best place on earth, usually in twenty-five words or less.

The Movies

SILENT FILMS

Motion picture theaters also used contests and promotional gimmicks to encourage patronage during the Depression. On "bank night" patrons drew numbers for cash prizes. Dinnerware was given away or sold at wholesale—one piece per week per visit; those who came back enough weeks in succession could get the entire service. By 1935, 50 percent of the 13,500 movie theaters in the United States showed double features, and 5,000 still used prizes to attract patrons. Forty percent of all American adults spent their twenty-five cents to gain admission to films at least once weekly.

The cinema, like the phonograph, had been part of the American entertainment scene since the turn of the century. Short films were the rule until 1915, when D. W. Griffith broke with past practice and produced the first full-length feature film, *The Birth of a Nation.* Popular among whites for both its racist rendering of the history of the United States and for its new sense of staging and photography, the film was a huge success. The film industry capitalized on Griffith's technical innovations and developed a star system of readily identifiable players who were larger than any of their roles. Rudolph Valentino became a sex symbol in the films of the 1920s, George Bancroft played heavies, Charlie Chaplin and Buster Keaton were the great comics of the period, Mary Pickford and Lillian Gish were the ingenues, and Theda Bara emerged as the most famous temptress and femme fatale of early films.

The integration of sound with the moving image in 1927 had an effect on consumers similar to that of the introduction of the magic box in the parlor, the radio. Between 1926, just before the "talkies" were introduced, and 1930, weekly movie attendance doubled, from 50 million to 100 million, or the equivalent of one night's attendance per week for 80 percent of the population of the country. By 1930 not a single silent film was produced for mass consumption. Warner Brothers, which had been in financial trouble in early 1928, invested heavily in the new technology, and saw their profits rise 60 percent between 1928 and 1929.

FILMS OF THE DEPRESSION AND WORLD WAR II

The Depression at first caused a downturn in movie attendance. By 1933 attendance had fallen 25 percent, to 75 million weekly, and the theaters and studios were losing money. RKO's $3.3 million surplus in 1930 became a $5.6 million deficit in 1931; Fox's $9.2 million surplus became a $5.5 million deficit; and Warner Brothers saw their whopping $17.2 million surplus turn into a deficit of $7.9 million. When the bank scare subsided by the end of 1933, the studios began their recovery.

Comedy, drama, and after about 1930, music and dance spectaculars were the grist for the moviemakers' mills. Gangster films probed the frightening and alluring world of *Little Caesar* (1930) or the *Public Enemy* (1931) and the *Angels with Dirty Faces* (1938). "Backstage confidential" movies such as *42nd Street* (1933), *Gold Diggers of 1933* (1933), and *Footlight Parade* (1933) took viewers behind the scenes of the entertainment industry, and were for the most part Horatio Alger rags-to-riches stories and backdrops for visually spectacular shows impossible to stage in vaudeville theaters or symphony halls. Both the gangster films and the showy extravaganzas affirmed that justice would be served eventually and that faith in the business world would be rewarded. Edward G. Robinson was killed in *Little Caesar;* Jimmy Cagney's sneering Tommy Powers met his end in *Public Enemy,* and the once-religious Irish Catholic Cagney died screaming for mercy in *Angels with Dirty Faces.* Ruby Keeler was the lucky and talented understudy in *42nd Street,* and the ubiquitous National Recovery Act poster all over the sets in *Footlight Parade* promoted the idea that the New Deal, Roosevelt, and Americans' business acumen would bring the country out of hard times.

As in radio programming and comic books, outsiders were often the heroes who got things done, sometimes by ignoring the law in the interest of the general welfare. In *The Maltese Falcon* (1941), private detective Sam Spade (Humphrey Bogart) is "not as crooked as my reputation." He turns in Brigid O'Shaugnessey as the film concludes, telling her, "I won't play the sap for you." The established order—government, or in this case the police—are late or inept, arriving in time to provide escort service for the crook already caught by the private detective or the dedicated amateur with street smarts, as in the Thin Man film series. The Lone Ranger rides again. Individual effort is still the key to success. Crooks will get theirs in the end. Greedy urban capitalism gone wrong brought on hard times; capitalism and pluck (Alger would have approved) were still the right combination for individual success and economic recovery.

Comedy movies and shorts stressed some of the same virtues but with a dramatic irreverence. Following on the visual virtuosity of Chaplin and Keaton, the great comedic discoveries of the 1930s were the anarchist Marx brothers, the bulbous-nosed reprobate W. C. Fields, and the genius of the sexual double entendre, Mae West. Paramount pictures took a gamble on the Marx brothers in 1929, releasing *The Cocoanuts.* After several years as successful vaudeville comics, Groucho, Harpo, and Chico brought anarchy and chaos to the screen, parlaying word and sight gags into a nearly ten-year run of hits. Their only box-office flop, *Duck Soup* (1933), cast Groucho as Prime Minister Rufus T. Firefly of Freedonia, a conniving goof who attempted to wash the country away in a flood of ridiculous protocol and corruption. Too obvious in its satire of politics and statecraft, it did not tempt moviegoers to respond as they had to *Animal Crackers* (1930), *Monkey Business* (1931), *Horse-feathers* (1932), *A Night at the Opera* (1935), and *A Day at the Races* (1937).

W. C. Fields parlayed obvious gags, dialogue directed to viewers, and pompous and flummoxed posturing to an audience that identified with the social embarrassment he continually suffered in his attempts to figure out an angle. In *The Fatal Glass of Beer* (1933), Fields's unrelenting attack on small-town life rivaled the literary slashing of journalist H. L. Mencken. Fields's barbs resonated with that part of the audience that had rejected farms and villages or never lived in either.

Fields, Mencken, and other critics of rural America were representative of American elite and popular cultural ambivalence about the country and the village. Nostalgia for and celebration of the face-to-face community of the farm, village, and small town was counterbalanced by the critics' conviction that the outlanders were narrow-minded, sexually repressed, ill-educated, and hostile to anything that smacked of pleasure. For many the titanic clash of these two ideologies occurred at the 1925 trial of John T. Scopes in Dayton, Tennessee. The teacher was on trial for teaching about Darwin's theory of evolution, an act outlawed in Tennessee. Clarence Darrow, the urbane lawyer for the defense and political anathema of many rural folk, and the erstwhile populist "Boy Orator of the Platte," William Jennings Bryan, trekked to Dayton to lock in combat. Day after day the army of journalists who covered the trial sent out dispatches to eager editors. Fundamentalism, prohibition, and local control of education were at war with the forces of the city and its godless corruption and licentiousness. Bryan won, although Scopes was released from prison on a technicality. The law was not repealed until 1967.

The countryside and residents of towns like Dayton were not the major market for the cinema, but even the "evil" city audience and the profits-only movie business had its limits. Mae West found them. No one delivered as many sexual double entendres per movie and looked like she could handle the consequences—and enjoy them—as did West. She exuded sex and thumbed her nose at nearly every social, gender, and sexual convention. She was in command, and she demanded to be satisfied. In an era in which men were having a difficult time maintaining their sense of worth because of the shame of unemployment, West represented a curious and perhaps cathartic movie experience. Her virtuoso performance in *She Done Him Wrong* (1933), in which she utters the famous line "Why don't you come up and see me sometime?" to a Secret Service man posing as a minister (Cary Grant), almost single-handedly brought censorship to the movie industry. Songs like "A Man What Takes His Time" marked West as the incarnation of evil for many rural conservatives and urban reformers.

Hollywood rushed to control West and the content of films by establishing a production code in 1934. Gone were double beds. Men wore pajamas. Only the slightest hints of illicit sex were allowed, and those involved—especially the women—were surely and severely punished. West's antics also were instrumental in the formation of the Catholic Legion of Decency, which rated films for their moral content. The legion issued not only recommendations for its flock, but also threats of boycotts if the studios did not clean up their act. West's slightly salacious radio skit about Adam and Eve, which aired in 1937 on the popular Edgar Bergen show, outraged the clergy and many listeners, both for its sly sexual innuendo and for West's apparent blasphemy. The skit brought forth an immediate apology from the J. Walter Thompson Company, which had created the ads for the show's sponsor, Chase and Sanborn Coffee. In an editorial in the *Catholic News* that was excerpted in the *New York Times,* the ad firm confessed, "Last Sunday night, with the introduction of Mae West into the program, the 'Chase and Sanborn Hour' descended into the mire."[14] NBC banned mention of West's name on the fifteen networks it owned. She never apologized.

Far more acceptable to the clergy and to most Americans' taste were films that affirmed middle-class values of hard work, individual responsibility for one's fates, sure punishment for transgressors of the law and morals, and the creed that all classes could live and mingle in peace. *It Happened One Night* (1934) was successful (it swept all the major Academy Awards and set box-office records) because it affirmed these values. A wealthy businessman's daughter (Claudette Colbert) runs from her near marriage to a wealthy and idle polo player, and meets an unemployed journalist (Clark Gable) while on the lam. In the famous hitchhiking scene, she humiliates him after he had bragged about his ability to get a ride. Cars whiz past his thumb, but the first driver who catches sight of her exposed thigh screeches to a halt. The wealthy woman shows some street smarts and shows up the nonworking stiff who thought he knew it all.

Too many differences—especially class—separate them at first. She returns home and is about to marry the rich boy when she runs again—after her father tells her she would be a "sucker" to go through with the wedding. This time she and Gable make it, but only because her father—a working rich man, so he is all right—shows respect for Gable and approves of the union. Viewers saw that class distinctions could be surmounted and may not even exist as long as all share the faith in hard work and success.

These messages were repeated—in different dramatic situations—by the child stars of the 1930s, especially Shirley Temple. Her movies cast the little tyke as a paragon of virtue—a latter-day version of that syrupy nineteenth-century good boy, "Rollo"—who was sympathetic, wholesome, and tolerant of class, racial, and ethnic differences. She seemed to know more about the nation's problems and their solutions than did adults. Her child's logic identified occasionally mean-spirited but more often ignorant adults as the causes of the country's ills, and reduced other problems to the appealingly naive need for personal strength and grit to conquer all.

The western films of the era preached a similar set of doctrines. In *The Virginian* (1929), Gary Cooper played an upright lawman for whom civilization was impossible without the law. Gene Autry and other western heroes played to full houses after 1935, and Paramount released two big hits in 1936, *The Plainsman* and *The Texas Rangers*. In John Ford's *Stagecoach* (1939), the passengers are a variety of apparent social misfits—a prostitute, a drunk, a gambler, and a crook—who ultimately show themselves to be virtuous Americans who will sacrifice and cooperate for the common good when crises arise. The western films emphasized the importance of community standards and cooperation and the dangers of corruption, gang violence, and demagoguery at a time when those activities were surely alive in Europe and the United States.

During World War II the film industry, under the watchful and censoring eye of the federal government's Office of War Information, produced films deliberately intended to stimulate support for the war effort. The OWI constantly tried to get Hollywood producers to develop films that would cast the Japanese as guilty fascists, but there was little success in that effort. *Wake Island* (1942) portrayed the Japanese as duplicitous and vicious fighters, as did *Guadalcanal Diary* (1943) and *Betrayal from the East* (1944). The Germans, on the other hand, got off lightly, in spite of the horrors of the holocaust. *The Moon Is Down* (1943) portrayed the Germans as ruthless occupiers of Norway, but also as human beings in some ways trapped by their leaders. A similar treatment of the Nazis was presented in *This Land Is Mine* (1943), a film that identified workers and intellectuals (and not the middle class) as the conscience of society. The OWI was thrilled with *This Land Is Mine,* as it was with *Watch on the Rhine* (1942), the adaptation of Lillian Hellman's successful play of 1941. *Mrs. Miniver* (1942), the story of a plucky British middle-class woman who keeps her family together through the blitz, swept the Academy Awards for 1942. *Mrs. Miniver* and *Wake Island* were the favorite films of American viewers in that year.

Nightlife

"HOT" MUSIC

After World War I, nightlife in urban America usually meant going out to restaurants and cabarets for food, drink (the illegal variety until 1933), music, and dancing. In a typical night spot, small tables surrounded a central floor reserved for dancing and performers.[15] These were the new, sanitized, middle-class urban versions of the rural honky-tonks and urban brothels that had outraged moral supervisors. Jazz and other popular-music dancing (in addition to formal ballroom dancing) had become more respectable in the 1920s, primarily because American young people had broken many of the taboos of Victorian court-ship and leisure.

Jazz and "hot" music traveled with white and black perform-ers from New Orleans to Chicago and other northern and west-ern cities in the immediate post–World War I years. Louis Arm-strong went to Chicago and Jelly Roll Morton went to Oakland, as did King Ory and Mutt Carey in 1919 and King Oliver's Original Jazz Band in 1921. Baron Long's club was a magnet in the Watts section of Los Angeles, and little clubs throughout the Southwest attracted marimba and jazz bands on the circuit in west Texas, New Mexico, and southern Arizona.[16]

One of the great appeals of the new music was that it was rhythmic and interactional. Black audiences and performers had a heritage of "play and response" in musical performances, and white audiences adapted their own dances to the new music. Vernon and Irene Castle popularized not only European "proper" dances such as the waltz, but also more exotic and potentially more sensual dances such as the tango and the max-ixe. These competed with freer-spirited crazes, such as the Charleston, cakewalk, turkey trot, grizzly bear, chicken scratch, kangaroo dip, monkey glide, and lame duck. In rural honky-tonks and gin mills, the two-step and reels continued to be popular, as they were in the country-oriented cabarets, clubs, and dance halls of the cities. Huge ballrooms opened in big cities in the 1920s in order to capture the middle-class crowd that liked dancing but worried about its associations with liquor and prom-iscuity. The Manhattan Casino could accommodate up to 6,000 dancers. The Savoy, also in New York, opened in 1926 with a 200-foot-long dance floor. From eight-thirty to eleven-thirty on any night of the week the halls were full, or nearly so. On weekends, when the middle class went out more often, dancers had to get there early just to get in. *Social Forces* magazine conducted a survey in 1925 and found that 14 percent of Man-hattan's men and 10 percent of the women living on the island went dancing at least three times weekly.[17] Rather than a potentially debilitating and erotically dangerous activity, aesthetic and athletic dancing was considered by many in the middle class as part of a new strategy for an active and healthy life.

Greenwich Village and Harlem in New York, the South Side of Chicago, Culver City near Los Angeles, San Francisco's Barbary Coast, and other urban entertainment districts were often buffer zones between "proper" white business districts and "red light" sections, shady business areas, and African-American neighborhoods. Cities too small to have a full-fledged "district" still had magnetic and memorable places to play, listen, and dance. Atlantic City, for example, boasted of the Elephant Cafe. Willie "the Lion" Smith remembered that "the front of the cafe was fixed up to look like an elephant's ass and one entered by passing under a big long tail hanging between its legs."[18]

GIN MILLS AND BEER JOINTS

Neighborhood bars and clubs formed an important part of the social life of working-class Americans who could not afford the pricier jazz and dance clubs that catered to the middle- and wealthy-class patrons. John Parraccini, an Italian immigrant from Umbria, recalled that "each gang would have its own place to go. Either because you were friends with the saloon keeper or you just started to go there. And you'd go there after work and play a little game of cards and have a beer. And a lot of times they'd have pool rooms and you'd go play a game of pool, have yourself a drink. . . . You don't go riding, because you don't have no automobile."[19] Charles Oliver, who worked as a clerk in a bank, remembered that "after work each day you go to the pub and 'bum' around until seven o'clock. By the time you get done there you get a couple of more on Second Street. By the time you get home it's time to go to bed."[20] Oliver was single at the time, and his pathway to home was like that of millions of other working-class men in industrial cities and towns all over the United States. Married men sometimes followed the same trail, often to the dismay of their wives.

Certainly this routine troubled reformers who tried to "clean up" the habits of workers, especially since many were convinced that no home life of any stability could come from barhopping. The reformers were correct in some cases: Liquor did fracture families and result in battered and bruised women and children. The "Ten Nights in a Barroom" mentality, based on the famous nineteenth-century melodramatic play's indictment of drunkenness, informed the Prohibitionists' crusade, but missed the social and political functions of the saloon and the inexpensive restaurant. The anti-saloon movement was also an attempt to impose a middle-class small-town and suburban vision of community life from the American historical context upon workers who were situated in urban areas more closely resembling European cities in at least one important sense. By the late nineteenth century and certainly by 1915, the American industrial working class was living in conditions so crowded with family and boarders that, for many, housing presented the barest minimum of space for sleeping and shelter. Social and community activities that the middle class, most farmers, and the wealthy encouraged and enjoyed did not occur in the urban working-class home, but on stoops and in streets, saloons, and clubs. Many in the working class were as troubled by drunkenness as were the Prohibitionists, but they nonetheless opposed the reformers, in part because they resented the interference of another class that they knew was patronizing them, and in part because they recognized prohibition as a social limitation on their already constricted lives.

Prohibitionists won their case by constitutional amendment in January 1920, after trying to abolish alcoholic drinks for nearly a century. The nation went "dry," in what some regarded as a victory for the forces of Christendom and others saw as the triumph of narrow-mindedness. But whatever its ideological supporters or detractors believed, prohibition, which lasted until repeal by constitutional amendment in 1933, changed Americans' leisure activities dramatically. Those who wanted liquor could find it, but in different environments than before the amendment passed.

Hotel dining rooms virtually disappeared, since much of their trade depended on the convenience for lodgers of their bar and

Barbecuing steaks, Turlock, California, May 1942. (Russell Lee. *Courtesy Library of Congress.*)

Saturday morning movie crowd, North Platte, Nebraska, October 1938. (John Vachon. *Courtesy Library of Congress.*)

Playing in the community sprinkler, Frederick Douglass housing project, Anacostia, District of Columbia, July 1942. (Gordon Parks. *Courtesy Library of Congress.*)

Cypress Island picnic, August 31, 1915. (*Courtesy Library of Congress.*)

Main Street, Riverside, California, ca. 1915. (*Courtesy Library of Congress.*)

Traffic jam—shift change at Bethlehem Fairfield Shipyards, Baltimore, Maryland, April 1943. (Marjory Collins. *Courtesy Library of Congress.*)

Gas station, Soland, California, ca. 1942. (Russell Lee. *Courtesy Library of Congress.*)

Farm Security Administration photographer being pulled along a muddy road, Little Fork, Minnesota, 1937. (Roy Stryker. *Courtesy Library of Congress.*)

Tourist cabins, Antico, Wisconsin, ca. 1938. (John Vachon. *Courtesy Library of Congress.*)

Baseball game, Dudley, West Virginia, ca. 1938–1942. (Arthur Rothstein. *Courtesy Library of Congress.*)

Jack Dempsey finishing off Jess Willard, Toledo, Ohio, July 4, 1919. (*Courtesy Library of Congress.*)

Miniature golf course at the Bedford Springs Hotel, Bedford Springs, Pennsylvania, ca. 1930. (*Courtesy Library of Congress.*)

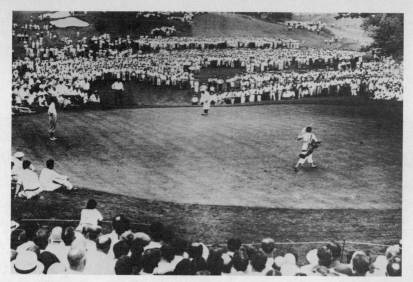

Bobby Jones holing out from forty-five feet for a 287 and his fourth United States Open championship at the Interlachen Golf and Country Club, Minneapolis, Minnesota, 1930. (*Courtesy Library of Congress.*)

Health class, Ocean City, New Jersey, ca. 1925. (*Courtesy Library of Congress.*)

United States Army Air Force, 20,000 feet above Nagasaki, Japan. August 9, 1945. (*Courtesy Library of Congress.*)

dining room. These areas were converted to cafés and soda fountains to compete with the brisk trade enjoyed by owners of cafeterias, department stores, and drugstores. Prohibition also spawned speakeasies, the "secret" clubs ignored by lawmen. Garbage collector Frank Czerwonka's mother ran a speakeasy after her husband died. "Our speak-easy had a candy-store front. That was the come-on. The fuzz wasn't botherin' us. They were just shakin' down the syndicate." "House parties" were another dodge. "They were houses where people lived," recalled jazz pianist "Little Brother" Montgomery. "With a piano in the front room where people danced. And moonshine, twenty-five cents a half pint. . . . The house'd be packed . . . a hundred, eighty people would be in it."[21]

The liquor ban also affected American cooking, not in most homes, but in restaurants that specialized in European cuisine. The ban on drinking also altered the nature of certain ethnic groups' activities. German beer gardens were diluted, and drinking at wakes and weddings was certainly more difficult, if not impossible. It was also more expensive to get the illicit hooch. The nickel beer of the 1920s cost fifty cents in 1930.

Time Off

WORKING CLASS: WEEKENDS AND FESTIVALS

For working-class Americans, Fridays were the big nights on the town. That was generally payday, and was when people felt the most flush. Streets and alleys were alive with play, and stores and night spots stayed open later than usual. In addition to the bars, saloons, and, during prohibition, speakeasies and other "secret" clubs, pool, lodge, and union halls bustled with revelers. Gambling was everywhere. Bingo became a big favorite in the early 1930s, and for about one cent per game, one could get a card at amusement parks, churches, Grange halls, penny arcades, theaters, and carnivals that traveled about from town to town in the warmer months. Slot machines were in bars, tobacco stores, lunch counters, and drugstores, and other gimmicks to get people to part with a little bit of money for a chance at the big score abounded. A 1939 Gallup poll found that one-third of the population occasionally put down a nickel for a chance at a jackpot.[22] In the inner reaches and alleyways of the country's major urban centers, where the middle class seldom if ever ventured, assorted gambling games occupied free time. Craps, numbers, coin pitching, konk, and card games such as blackjack or poker were favorites of the African-American underclass.

For the working class the weekend, which often consisted of Saturday afternoon and Sunday or only Sunday, was a special time of some relaxation, at least for men. Women still had to keep up with the daily regimen of cooking, cleaning, and minding the children, and often had to work extra because of the expectation of a special meal on Saturday night or Sunday. On Saturdays Ray La Marca "used to see that wagon come around full of beer. And they would drop half a keg of beer or a quarter at every other door. And the people used to get together. . . . In the backyard on Sunday they played the guitar and mandolin and cards."[23]

Seasonal festivals, usually associated with the church, provided outdoor street theater and social interaction for urban ethnic enclaves. These were the twentieth-century descendants of the urban fairs and festivals of medieval Europe and the urban counterparts of American county and state agricultural fairs, and usually included music, food, and religious pageantry. The workplace analog of the street fair was the company picnic. Paid for by the firm, these food and drink extravaganzas often turned the activities of the job into contests. Loggers competed in sawing and chopping contests, and miners in drilling events. Pennsylvania coal miner John Parraccini went to many company-sponsored affairs. "There were a lot of picnics. The mines used to hold picnics every year. And then for about a week there was a picnic around. There used to be all kinds of games on those picnics. Many times we used to have big rocks, and fellas would see who [could] drill the hole through first."[24]

Coney Island, near New York, was probably the most famous amusement park in America, but by World War I these combinations of mechanical rides, cheap foods, and games of chance were built in most of the cities of the nation. Often urban trolley companies and amusement park builders formed partnerships, ensuring that a trolley line would be built to serve the park. When there was water around for swimming and bathing, the combination often proved irresistible for both sweltering urbanities and entrepreneurs. Coney Island had seawater; Rochester, New York's Ontario Beach had Lake Ontario. Both were served by public transportation, and both were jammed with people in the summer.

MIDDLE CLASS: MOTORING AND VACATIONS

The middle class, armed with more money (until the Depression) and with automobiles, took to the road for vacations. Before 1915 motoring was too expensive for any but the wealthy to enjoy for recreational purposes.[25] By the end of the war the economic crunch on motoring began to ease. Filling stations and mechanics were more numerous in cities and suburbs, and prices for automobiles and parts were declining, especially for Henry Ford's basic black Model T. For the urban and suburban middle class, the Sunday drive in the country became a ritual in passable weather, as did the one- or two-week vacation, in spite of the challenges of long-distance trips.

There were few paved roads between major cities until the limited number built in the 1920s were finished.[26] The traveler who left the city on a long trip had to be intrepid. Maps of rural America were virtually nonexistent, road signs were scarce, and it was easy to get lost and completely turned around. Mechanics and filling stations were widely scattered and difficult to locate before the advent of roadside advertising signs in the late 1920s. Bridges could be rickety, with no standards of construction or inspection to at least give the impression of safety. Many were built in the distant past, and were meant for the slower and perhaps lighter weight of the horse and carriage. Even in mountainous areas guardrails were the exception rather than the rule. Albert Maltz wrote of a particularly harrowing stretch of West Virginia road in 1935: "From Gauley to Weston is about a hundred miles of as about as difficult mountain driving as I know—a five-mile climb to the top of a hill, then five miles down, then up another. The road twists like a snake on the run and for a good deal of it there is a jagged cliff on one side and a drop of a thousand feet or more on the other."[27]

More than one-half of all American roads that were categorized by local, state, and federal officials were classified as "unimproved." There was no great comfort if one traced an itinerary on a map that stayed on "improved" roads, since that designation was applied to graded dirt and gravel, which could be washed out or a quagmire, depending on the age of the map or recent weather conditions. The federal government had high-minded intentions to connect all cities of greater than 50,000 population with paved roads, or so the Federal Road Acts of 1916 and 1921 intended. World War I hamstrung the first act; lack of funding and the high local funding requirements of the second limited its effects. Only after the New Deal put people to work on the federal payroll did road building take off.

Travelers who made it over the roads and bridges needed overnight accommodations and ample parking space, demands that hotels could not always meet. Hotels were located in city and town centers, convenient to businesses and train terminals. They usually had little space for parking, and could obtain none since central city real estate was expensive and crammed with buildings. Thus the motor hotel, or motel—at first a conglomeration of little cabins placed side by side on major roads outside of cities—was born. Rarely equipped with their own bathrooms or toilets, they were inexpensive and offered more privacy than guest houses, which were usually a family's home that had been turned into a seasonal money-maker. By 1926 (the year the term *motel* was coined), there were an estimated 2,000 motels in the United States, mostly in Florida and the West. In the mid-1920s some cities had opened municipal campgrounds for motoring travelers, equipping the sites with cold-water spigots and outdoor toilets.[28] These became more popular as the car-drawn trailer caught the fancy of many travelers. Seven hundred companies manufactured trailers in the 1930s, and by 1940 more than 100,000 were in use. In 1936 the California Chamber of Commerce estimated that 30,000 families vacationed in the Klamath-Trinity Basin, many in the eighteen private and five government-run resorts and campgrounds.[29] For some of the newly imperiled middle class in the 1930s, the trailer became their only home. During World War II, after prosperity had returned, government rationing of rubber and gasoline further reduced automobile use.

Working-class Americans seldom took a vacation. Often throughout the 1920s and certainly in the 1930s they had too much time off. Even if times were good, many were afraid to take, or suspicious of accepting, a vacation. "A lot of guys," according to Pennsylvania steelworker and union organizer Louis Smolinski, "would never take a vacation because they thought they were doing the company a favor." Distrustful of management, these workers wanted to neither save the company money nor turn their backs by being away. In other cases there was no opportunity. Stanley Brozek knew that "the company never offered you a vacation. My dad started working in 1899 and never got one until 1936. What was the purpose of giving him one? It was to discourage him from joining the union."[30]

Sports

BOXING AND BASEBALL

Vacations may have been inaccessible to many Americans, but sports—either as a participant, a spectator, or a listener to the game on the radio—were part of nearly all male Americans' lives, if they so desired. Historians regard the 1920s and 1930s as a "golden age" of sports, for the most part because of the emergence of identifiable superstars in many different sports. In addition, in two very popular spectator sports—professional baseball and professional boxing—"clean" (or at least not obviously crooked) heroes emerged after a history of scandals. The list of sports greats is impressive: Bobby Jones, Gene Sarazen, and Byron Nelson in golf; Babe Ruth, Lou Gehrig, Bob Feller, Ted Williams, Joe DiMaggio, and the "Gas House Gang" in baseball; "Red" Grange, the "Four Horsemen" of Notre Dame, and Knute Rockne in college football; Helen Wills Moody and

Bill Tilden in tennis; Jack Dempsey, Gene Tunney, and Joe Louis in boxing; Jesse Owens and Babe Zaharias in track and field; and Gallant Fox and Man o' War in horseracing.

Boxing had been on the nether edge of society for as long as anyone could remember—full of shady characters, liquor-laced hoodlums, and dives into the canvas for a few bucks. The sport became more attractive to white audiences when Jack Dempsey, a tough and avuncular white fighter, defeated the black heavyweight champion, Jack Johnson. Johnson was a flashy fighter who provided black fans with a national hero who successfully competed against white men in a segregated society. But he frightened and outraged the racist white American majority with his expensive life-style, his refusal to be submissive to whites, and his penchant for white women lovers. After Johnson was defeated, Dempsey and Gene Tunney—the literate champ who quoted Shakespeare—erased some of the back-alley slugger reputation of the fight game, although attending the battles was still a testing affair for the uninitiated. Joe Louis, the "Brown Bomber," succeeded Dempsey and Tunney as a "clean" heavyweight champ because he was reserved, discreet, and polite—and he did not threaten the values of white society as Johnson had. Before Dempsey's reign, attendance at a prize fight by the middle class and the wealthy was a rare sight. By the mid-1920s, due to some shrewd marketing by promotional wizard Tex Rickard, the "swells"—and their female companions—paid fashionable prices for the finer seats.

There had been high achievers in baseball before the war and just after it, but the professional game had been scarred by the apparent fix of the 1919 World Series, which resulted in the banishment of eight of the Chicago White Sox ball players. Although their cases were thrown out of civil court (evidence unaccountably disappeared), theirs was not the first intimation of gambling and fixed games. Ty Cobb had been implicated—and cleared—and there had been rumors of thrown games for years.

It seemed that the game was tarnished almost beyond redemption. That the national game had become a pawn of big-city gamblers revolted fans. Team owners were in a bind. Be-

ginning in about 1910, many had built new stadia, but attendance sagged during the war years. A few organizational and
some rules changes helped bring attendance back after the war
and the "Black Sox" fix. Promotions such as Ladies' Day and
new club policies that allowed fans to keep foul balls helped.

The game also changed, making it a more enjoyable show for
the fans, if not for the pitchers. The new "lively" balls flew
farther when they were hit—and more balls were used in an
average game. Previously, a ball that remained in the ball yard
was used until it was the consistency of an orange; throwing out
severely abraded or softened balls made it easier for a hitter to
drive pitches great distances and harder for the crafty pitcher to
make his offerings "do tricks"—dipping or curving crazily and
sharply. The rules makers also banned "doctored" pitches—the
spitball, the mudball, the emery ball, and others—although
pitchers did (and still) throw them on the sly.

The result of all this was more runs and more home runs. In
1914 all major league teams combined hit 384 home runs; in
1920, 631; in 1925, 1,167; and in 1930, 1,565. The fans loved it,
and they especially loved—or feared—Babe Ruth, the game's
towering figure between the wars. In 1919 Ruth broke a record
that had stood for thirty-five years when he hit 29 homers. The
following year he hit an astounding 54, and the New York Yankees' attendance doubled. In 1921 he hit 59 into the seats,
drove in 170 runs, scored 177 times, and had a batting average
of .378. No one had ever hit like that before. In 1927 he hit 60
home runs (more than each of twelve teams managed to produce) and accounted for 13 percent of all the home runs hit in
the major league season. He had enormous appetites for food,
strong drink, and women, but moralists couldn't touch him
because he had a genuine soft spot for children. In 1930 he
made the princely salary of $80,000, more than President
Hoover. The situation bothered few Americans because, like
Ruth when questioned about it, they figured that the slugger
"had a better year."

In his virtuoso performance of 1927, Ruth was part of a baseball team and media event that was perhaps an emblem of mass
sporting entertainment in the 1920s. The New York Yankees

were a juggernaut in a decade when baseball eclipsed all other spectator sports. In the huge stadium built in the Bronx to favor the Babe's swing, the Yankees smashed more home runs than any team ever had, and did it with flair. So dramatic and so explosive were they that the term "five o'clock lightning" entered the parlance to describe a late-game Yankees' dismembering of another team that thought it had the game in hand. Their exploits were trumpeted over the airwaves in the year of the first national radio network. Ruth, Gehrig, Tony Lazzeri, Bob Meusel, and the rest were vastly more important popular figures than the dour Calvin Coolidge ever was. The essence of the 1920s bombast and ballyhoo, the Yankees were a consumer product in the great age of consumption. Americans thought they would never come back to earth and never lose, just as they thought the stock market would continue to rise.

The Yankees continued their dominance as the Depression refused to ease and the Midwest blew away. But the order was changing. Ruth, thirty-eight in 1933, still hit mammoth home runs—his two-run shot was instrumental in the American League's victory in the first All-Star game in that year—but Lou Gehrig had become the Bronx team's leader. Jimmie Foxx and Hank Greenberg each hit fifty-eight home runs in 1932 and 1938, respectively, and Bill Terry superseded Rogers Hornsby as the best hitter for average, compiling a .352 batting average in the 1930s. Satchel Paige, Judy Johnson, Cool Papa Bell, Josh Gibson, and Buck Leonard dominated the Negro Leagues. Joe DiMaggio and Bob Feller began their major league careers in 1936, and Ted Williams arrived in Boston in 1939.

Fans in 1941 had two remarkable players to follow. Ted Williams hit well over .400 in May, and chased a .400 batting average all season, finally achieving a .406 figure with six hits in a doubleheader on the last day of the season. No one has hit .400 since. Joe DiMaggio hit safely in fifty-six consecutive games near the beginning of the season, a streak that brought more and more attention to the game and him as he neared and passed the previous record. But when war was declared in December 1941, there was serious discussion of canceling the season until the hostilities ended. Nearly every able player enlisted or was drafted. The game continued, but with players too old for the military, or ineligible for health or other reasons. Attendance declined. When the stars returned for the 1946 season, more than one-half the starting players from the 1945 teams found themselves on the bench, in the minor leagues, or out of a job.

Radio broadcasts brought professional and amateur sports to the majority who did not live in cities with major league franchises. But sports, like politics, were also a local affair. Minor league baseball teams were scattered throughout the country, and rode on the coattails of the "big show." Local teams got as much or more space in the local papers as did the major league teams. Typically a small-town daily would print a column or two with the standings and scores of the majors, and a reference to a team if a local boy had made it. The rest of the page was usually split between reports of local games, box scores, and advertisements.[31]

Semiprofessional and amateur teams abounded in most towns and cities. Some represented industries hoping to parlay support of the club (with equipment, uniforms, and league fees) into support for the company's interests. Others were sponsored by churches, synagogues, ethnic clubs, and groups such as the Knights of Columbus, the American Legion, the Boys' Clubs, the YMCA, and the YMHA. The Ku Klux Klan sponsored a team in the Atlanta municipal league. Their uniforms had the KKK cross emblazoned over the players' left breast. They were good enough to win the 1924 Dixie League title, defeating the Baptist Tabernacle team.[32]

So central to town life was baseball that it was only slightly less important than world-shaking events. On the front page of the May 24, 1919, issue of the Fitchburg, Massachusetts *Daily Sentinel,* immediately under a rare banner headline reading PETROGRAD IN REIGN OF TERROR, was a four-by-six-inch box entitled BATTING ORDER FOR TODAY'S GAME: FITCHBURG V. LEWISTON. The rest of the page was full of articles of international news, such as Germany rejecting the Treaty of Versailles.

BASKETBALL, BOWLING, TENNIS, GOLF

Basketball was the popular winter sport for both men and women soon after its invention in 1891. By the 1920s the quintessentially urban game was played all over the country. High schools and colleges were the centers of organized basketball, and at least at the high school level, boys and girls played. (There were some variations in the rules for the sexes—girls normally played with six players on a side, and few schools sponsored interscholastic competition for girls.) The college game had a substantial following and received media coverage that was modest in comparison to that afforded football, crew, and baseball. Teams of urban universities that either did not play football or that awarded the autumn game only slight attention were the exceptions to this pattern.

Basketball also attracted secular and sacred support sponsors for the many nonschool teams that played. In Worcester, Massachusetts, in 1932, the YMCA and YWCA league teams were organized by denomination: Lutherans, Baptists, Methodists, and Pilgrims (probably Presbyterians or Congregationalists). The YMHA fielded a team that regularly played other YMHAs in neighboring cities; their games were covered only slightly in the general-readership local newspaper, but the teams received more attention in Jewish communities' papers.[33]

As popular as basketball was, bowling was the sport that attracted the greatest media coverage and participation among white urban Americans. The season stretched from early autumn until late spring, and the newspapers were full of charts of scores and averages and details for the duration. Both men and women and some mixed teams played, and the sport offered employment to countless young boys, who dodged the flying pins, gathered them up, and reset them. In 1925 the annual business directory of Worcester listed nine bowling alleys, including those in the YMCAs; there were twelve listed in 1935 and eighteen listed for 1945. In Fitchburg, Massachusetts, the industrial league teams were organized in some cases by craft: The papermakers, finishers, machine shop, and garage were represented, as well as the City Hall bureaucrats and clerks, and united cooperative farmers and united cooperative girl farmers.[34] The sport attracted the wealthy as well as those of more modest means. In the basement of many of the private clubs frequented by elites were one or more bowling alleys.

Introduced in the United States in the latter half of the nineteenth century, tennis gained adherents gradually and steadily throughout the first decades of the twentieth century. Equipment was relatively inexpensive and readily available at local stores or through the mail, and by 1930 many cities had built public courts, some of them lighted for night play. The game's primary audience, however, was the white, primarily Anglo-Saxon elite, and these players dominated amateur and professional tennis. It was primarily a country-club sport, with English roots. The game had a decorum and a white-only dress tradition that operated as a barrier to nonelites. Helen Wills Moody, Fred Perry, and Bill Tilden were the most prominent players of the era, especially when they represented their countries in the Davis or Wightman Cup championships. *Time* put Australian Jack Crawford on the cover of the September 4, 1933, issue of the magazine, and devoted six columns of dense text to the summer's amateur matches and important players.

Like tennis, golf in the United States between 1915 and 1945 is essentially a tale of the achievements and the sporting life of a tiny minority of primarily affluent white men. It was and is a sport that requires a large amount of carefully managed and highly maintained acreage, and therefore a great deal of money. In spite of these elite trappings, its amateur and professional stars stimulated some media coverage and interest among Americans who could not breach the gates of the clubs where most of the rounds were played.

A few cities opened municipal courses for the general public as early as 1900, and caddies—usually working- or middle-class boys—sometimes got a chance to play. Thus when Boston schoolboy champion and caddie Francis Ouimet defeated Britons Harry Vardon and Ted Ray to win the U.S. Open Golf Championship in 1913, it made national news and stimulated a considerable amount of popular interest in the game.

In the 1920s, however, the inspirational player in both the

United States and in the British Isles was the Atlanta attorney Bobby Jones. Jones, an amateur until he retired from competition in 1930, compiled a record of victories and second-place finishes in national championships unequaled by any other golfer in the 1920s. In 1930 he won the "grand slam": the United States and British Amateur Championships and the United States and British Open Championships. No amateur or professional golfer has done it since. Almost single-handedly he stimulated the building of more public and private courses and a surging interest in the game. In 1930 more than three million golfers played the game on over 4,000 courses across the country.

The game lost adherents—or at least players—during the Depression and the war years. Professionals still traveled from city to city "on tour," but interest lagged. Gene Sarazen and, later, Ben Hogan and Sam Snead dominated the game until Byron Nelson, who was unable to join the Armed Forces, overwhelmed all comers during the war. The game slowly won back its players after the defeat of the Axis powers, but did not experience the sort of public boost Ouimet and Jones provided until Arnold Palmer became golf's hero in the late 1950s and early 1960s.

MINIATURE GOLF, THE POOL HALL

In 1929 Americans were seized with enthusiasm for a new game, a hybrid of the amusement park and upper-class sport— miniature golf. The miniature golf fad allowed anyone with a little pocket change to pretend they were competing with the greats. Writing in *Harper's* magazine in 1930, essayist Elmer Davis remarked, "Last winter it was still a toy; by midsummer it was big business, a social problem. In September the Department of Commerce estimated that there were almost thirty thousand courses in operation, representing an investment of one hundred and twenty-five million dollars, and some of them were earning three hundred per cent in a season when most businesses thought they were doing well to keep out of the red."[35]

At fifty cents for each round, it was a bonanza for the thousands of operators who paid as much as $4,500 for the rights to operate a course and for entrepreneurs such as Garnett Carter, who purchased the rights for the entire South and built hundreds of courses that he franchised. With their distinctive fantasyland architecture and the snack bars, lounges, and other "country club" amenities that many operators installed, they were a boon to families wanting a night out, would-be athletes, and young people courting and otherwise getting away from parents and the older generation. Many courses were artificially lighted, and operators found it profitable to remain open all night to accommodate the young and somewhat well off. It was relatively inexpensive and competitive if one wanted it to be so, yet it required no particular athletic conditioning and minimal skill to play respectably.

Billiards and pool were a quite different order of sporting business, although, like bowling, the games were in favor with the wealthy as well as with the poor. The rich owned their own tables or belonged to clubs that did. The poor and the working class shot pool and gambled in urban pool halls, thought by reformers and those concerned with the welfare of young boys to be the schools for a criminal career. The reformers and the Prohibitionists closed the bars and cramped the style of working-class men and boys: The number of pool halls declined precipitously. In the Worcester, Massachusetts, business directory for 1925, thirty-five were listed; twenty-four were open in 1935; nine in 1945.

SCHOOL AND COLLEGE SPORTS

Urban and town high schools tried to provide alternatives to street life, and integrated active extracurricular sports into their educational regimens. These supplemented sports and games that had become mandatory parts of most school physical education classes by about 1910, when they had replaced the calisthenics and gymnastics-only concentration of many programs. High school sports were well covered in newspapers, and in some areas the Thanksgiving Day football championship game became a tradition. Supporters were expected to turn out en masse, even in small towns.

Robert and Helen Lynd found that in Muncie, Indiana, the interscholastic athletic program was a "principal source of civic unity."[36] Like their public counterparts, private schools invested large chunks of the funds they raised in athletic facilities, hoping to trade on the ever-growing cultural concern for fitness and health, and the upper-class Anglophile conviction that the playing fields were the proving grounds of leaders. This attitude about sport permeated intercollegiate athletics, which were avidly followed, not only by the select few with the financial and intellectual resources to attend, but also by former students and people who lived near the college.

Working-class families often could not forgo the extra income of a child who otherwise might go off to college, even if the prospective student was intelligent or athletically skilled enough to land a rare scholarship. Ray Czachowski was recruited for both swimming and football in 1936, but he had to turn the chance away, because "we were in pretty dire need in 1936; we couldn't even raise money for clothes."[37]

Colleges responded to the growing mania for football among alumni and the general public by building huge stadia in the early twentieth century. Harvard built a steel-reinforced arena that seated 40,000 in 1903; other major universities followed soon after. Harvard's trip to the Rose Bowl in 1920 rated front-page headlines throughout most of the Northeast, and Notre Dame's consistently excellent teams made dedicated fans of many Irish immigrants who never attended the university. Recruitment of college football players began in about 1915, as coaches and university financial officers began to realize that they might have a bonanza. By 1930 it was apparent that they were correct. College football, according to historian Allen Guttmann, brought in $21.5 million, or $4.5 million more than did professional baseball in the same year. Coaching staffs were expanded, and scholarships for football and other sports were offered by colleges throughout the country. The activity was not without its critics, however. A 1929 Carnegie Commission termed recruiting practices "disgraceful," and found that many colleges and universities had succumbed so completely to the pressure to win that they were in effect paying unqualified men to play intercollegiate sports.

THE WILD AND THE TAME: SKIING, HUNTING, FISHING, GARDENING

Untainted by such accusations was skiing. While it was an inter-collegiate sport in a few colleges, it was most popular among the Scandinavian immigrants in the upper midwestern states. By the 1930s, however, the sport was gaining devotees in New York and New England. Railroad lines promoted the sport by providing special weekend trains to the Adirondacks, the White Mountains, and the Green Mountains, and the winter Olympics held at Lake Placid in 1932 brought all winter sports to the attention of many otherwise disinterested Americans. The fed-eral government even issued a postage stamp emblazoned with a skier to honor the winter games. By 1940, 2 million Americans were skiing on a regular basis. Still in its infancy, skiing was not yet associated with posh resorts and fabulous chalets. It retained some of its older associations with cross-country skiing, and the equipment was relatively simple: ash or hickory skis and poles and simple leather bindings.

Sport fishing and hunting were popular among people living in the country (many participated not so much for the sport, but for food) and among the urban and suburban wealthy, some of whom were, or were trying to be, part of the Anglo-European sporting and shooting scene. In California, for example, fishing licenses increased 56 percent in the 1930s, while the state's population increased 22 percent. The most desperate for food probably ignored the law and fished and hunted when and where they could.

Like hunting and fishing, gardening—popular among all classes throughout the era—took on new meanings and new immediacy in the 1930s. Working the garden plot could be a money-saving diversion in tough times. Neighbors split the bulbs and tubers of their perennials, and a vegetable garden helped out with the daily challenge of getting food. Working-class people had been growing food in urban yards and on small farms throughout the period. In the 1930s many of the middle class who were newly out of work or underemployed started vegetable gardens. Garden clubs for the still well-to-do also increased their memberships during the Depression. During World War II, when military and overseas demand for food pushed farmers to their limits, the government encouraged Americans to grow as much of their own food as possible. Millions of "victory gardens" were planted, and by 1945 approximately 40 percent of the vegetables grown in the United States for domestic consumption were harvested from them.

The Depression blurred some of the lines between recreation and survival, and for many there was also an occasional blending of work and play. Some aspects of play changed very little in the first half of the twentieth century, yet others were greatly altered, often by new technologies. The radio brought music, drama, news, and sports into the privacy of the home and, with its myriad of commercials, helped stimulate a consumer boom in the 1920s. Like the radio, the cinema brought a special sort of patterned "escape" that reflected and refracted American values.

The three decades after 1915 were also a boom time for spectator and participatory sports, replete with new heroes. The *Recreation Yearbook* of 1939 estimated attendance at public beaches and pools in the United States at 200 million, players on public baseball and softball diamonds at 30 million, players on public tennis courts at 11 million, and rounds of golf on public courses at 8 million.[38] Miniature golf became, for a few years, a fad of enormous proportions, as had mah-jongg. Other fads—contract bridge and crossword puzzles—became traditions. The leisure industries took their beating in the 1930s, as did almost every other sector of the economy, but the die had been cast. By 1945 these industries and activities had assumed their place as major segments of the American economy and of everyday life.

THERE IS NO defining symbol or event that illuminates everyday life in the United States between 1915 and 1945. Historical perspective yields a multitude of possibilities that seem so powerful that they should function as keys to the culture of the era, but attaching central significance to one or the other creates a distorted image of the era. The Depression is surely of signal importance: It lasted for over a decade and left an imprint on almost the entire population, even those who did not suffer hardships. The nation fought in two world wars, and the second in particular altered the nation's place in the world and therefore Americans' lives, not only because it launched the country on an aggressive foreign policy that would enmesh the United States in wars and major "police actions" approximately every ten years, but also because a growing defense budget drew money from other programs, or increased taxes, or increased the national debt.

But as important as the Depression and the wars were, it is impossible to ignore the pervasive and powerful impact of technological innovation and mass production of goods in these three decades. New forms of communication—the radio and the telephone became available to masses of Americans for the first time—and electric power for illumination and for driving machines of all sorts entered the daily lives of the multitudes in this period. So great was the cultural impact of technology and so great was many Americans' faith in technology that the two most important public statements of the country's image of itself—the Chicago Century of Progress Exposition of 1933 and the New York World's Fair of 1939—highlighted and congratulated the nation for its accomplishments and laid out a plan for the future that was wholly committed to the visions and skills of engineers and designers.

The 1939 World's Fair took as its slogan "The World of Tomorrow," and as its symbol the futuristic Trylon and Perisphere. The federal government issued postage stamps honoring both fairs, a small green stamp emblazoned with a frontier blockhouse and a similar-sized blue-gray stamp showing a skyscraper for the Chicago exposition and a larger stamp in blue portraying the Trylon and Perisphere for the New York fair. The pavilions installed by various companies and countries in Chicago were up to date in their designs, and the buildings and exhibits at the 1939 fair were futuristic and more like the worlds of such science fiction characters as Buck Rogers or Flash Gordon than they were like the everyday experiences of Depression-era Americans. The New York fair was perhaps the ultimate expression of the sensibilities of industrial designers Walter Dorwin Teague, Robert Dreyfuss, and Norman Bel Geddes.

Most celebrants at the New York fair and most of its organizers quickly lost sight of the fact that it was to be as much a celebration of the sesquicentennial of the Constitution and of Washington's inauguration as it was of American technology and science. Grover Whelan, the dapper man-about-town and promoter who assumed most of the responsibility for raising money and attendance at the fair, cheerfully hyped the effort to build the future—or models of it—on a reclaimed dump in Queens. He was aided in his effort by the considerably talented and forceful Robert Moses, who masterminded much of the planning and physical construction of the project. Crowds of people went to the fair, and marveled at the miniature cities, the RCA television, and other wonders. But Whelan failed; attendance was less than anticipated, and the fair did poorly economically.

Keys to understanding the successes and failures of the fair lay in the social and economic realities of Depression America and in the population's ambivalent attitude toward all that futuristic machine-age gear and design. On the most basic level, attendance lagged because New Yorkers and other Americans could not afford to come to the fair. Millions were still out of work. On a deeper cultural level, it seemed clear to some Americans that science and technology had not proven to be the boon they had promised to be: The Depression was a decade-long misery by 1939, and hardly a sign of the human race's best efforts at planning and managing. In addition, another war had commenced in Europe and Asia, one that would certainly be more horrible than the Great War of 1914–1918 had been, precisely because the technology of weaponry had improved in its efficiency to kill and destroy.

Science and technology also seemed to offer both hopes and perils in Americans' everyday lives. The radio and the movies brought entertainment and information into the home and onto the screen, yet by the early 1930s the airwaves were full of commercials. The cinema offered cheap escape, but until 1934 was unregulated. It confirmed some parents' worst fears: Some films were openly risqué—which critics thought gave viewers ideas they did not have previously—and the darkened theaters provided the young with a modicum of privacy to act on their new inspiration. The automobile made life easier and richer in all sorts of ways, but it also made it less difficult to move from country to city, which helped depopulate the countryside, much to the dismay of supporters of country life. The car also gave sweet freedom to young adults, who at least claimed or were accused of greater sexual license by their critics. And if automobiles made movement more easy, it also made getaways by crooks that much more efficient.

Household technology in the form of new appliances such as the refrigerator and the washing machine certainly eased elements of middle-class women's work in the home, but their advent was accompanied by an increasing responsibility for the success of a woman's husband and children in a world that seemed to become a more Darwinian struggle each day. The mass media and the slicker advertising moguls discerned the value of insecurity, and used it to sell consumers products that they may not have needed, but that seemed an insurance against failure and loss of status. Even the foods women had traditionally fed their families, and with which they had grown up, were challenged and marked as potentially unhealthy. That the working class continued to eat such meat and fatty foods— even increasing their consumption of them in good times— perhaps reassured the middle class of their alleged superiority if they thought about the workers at all.

At least leisure and sport seemed dependable, and the mass media made heroes out of a multitude of high achievers. Some stars of sport were clearly upper middle class or wealthy, such as Bobby Jones, Helen Wills Moody, and Bill Tilden. But sport crossed class boundaries, at least on the surface, with heroes such as Babe Ruth, Ty Cobb, Dizzy Dean, Joe DiMaggio, Babe Zaharias, Jack Dempsey, Gene Tunney, Joe Louis, and Jesse Owens. The Yankees proved to be a dependable powerhouse throughout the 1920s and 1930s, marching from one superstar-led team to another. But even in sport nothing was certain. The Chicago "Black Sox" threw the 1919 World Series. Lou Gehrig, the brilliant Yankee first baseman who played in over 2,000 consecutive games, died on June 2, 1941, seventeen days before his thirty-eighth birthday, a victim of amyotrophic lateral sclerosis. Even the "Iron Horse's" determination was no match for disease and chance.

After the Japanese attack on Pearl Harbor on December 7, 1941, it did not seem certain that the Americans would turn world events to their favor and prevail, as they had when they entered the Great War in 1917. "Over there" were the jungles and islands of the Pacific, and a juggernaut that continued to march to victory after victory in 1942. There was real fear in Washington in that year that the United States would lose the war, although policymakers were careful about revealing their misgivings.

For working-class men and women World War II brought more work and the end of the Depression, but it also brought separated and broken families. Millions of men went off to battle and millions of women went off to work in jobs not open to them before. How would family structure and relationships change—if at all—when mobilization ended and men returned? Some women with the taste of freedom and responsibility that they achieved in the workplace saw the world differently. One thing did seem certain: Organized labor had won battles during the Depression. Labor–management relations had changed, it seemed, forever. But events of the 1980s and early 1990s indicate that even that assumption might have been too confident.

One of science and technology's most obvious triumphs, and one which opened up a new age for Americans, landed on the cities of Hiroshima and Nagasaki in August 1945. The atomic bomb certainly ended the war with Japan, and seemed to ordain the United States as the premier power on earth, alone in its mastery of the destructive power of the atom. The new president, Harry Truman, went to the final conference of the Allied leaders in Potsdam, Germany, with the attitude of a gunslinger who was convinced he was quicker on the draw. Now began the American century, or so he and many others thought.

We now know that the American arrogance of 1945 was myopic. The Russians had their own bomb within a few years, and Stalin gave little or nothing in negotiation at Potsdam. Mao Tse-Tung threw out Chiang Kai-Shek in 1949, in spite of American support for the latter. By the 1950s a new "red scare" was under way, born of the idea that the new enemies could only succeed if the United States had been compromised from within.

The idea of internal subversion as the explanation for the uncertainty of world events is grounded in Americans' simultaneous acceptance of two conflicting visions of the historical process. Their concept of history as continuous and linear allowed them—a people fortunate enough to never have had their homeland decimated by modern, twentieth-century warfare—to assume that they had arrived at the pinnacle of history as a result of their own virtue and a Darwinian natural selection among nations and peoples.

But a linear historical process also assumes further movement, further change, and an uncertain future. Empires have risen and fallen. How could this pattern be stopped? Unless it were stopped or at least controlled, unless history were made to be discontinuous in some way, would not the United States fall too? Perhaps this need to break out of the apparent linear process explains the nation's continuing fascination with its own mythic past.

Throughout the three decades following 1915 various modes of expression of this historical yearning emerged. The most ironic, perhaps, was the hell-bent collection and organization of artifacts of the past (including entire houses) by the champion of mechanization and mass production, Henry Ford, who began his Greenfield Village project in the 1920s. He of course was not alone in this compulsion: Henry Francis DuPont, of the gunpowder and chemical fortune, assembled Winterthur; the Metropolitan Museum of Art in New York and the Museum of Fine Arts in Boston, among others, began to assemble collections of American arts and antiques; the Wellses collected for Old Sturbridge Village; the Flynts for Historic Deerfield; the Clarkes for the Farmers' Museum and Folk Art Collection in Cooperstown (which had been erroneously but officially designated the home of baseball, America's mythic game); the Webbses collection of Americana became the Shelburne Museum; and the Rockefellers assembled the collections for the Colonial Williamsburg and Sleepy Hollow restorations. All these efforts were those of elites with the money and time to collect the materials, and their museums were popular from almost the day they opened.

Ersatz and accurate colonial-style furniture and architecture—even if only in decorative accents on plain industrially produced forms—was popular throughout the period, and could be had in inexpensive mass-produced versions available in mail-order catalogs and stores. The quest for the "colonial" and the "simpler" and naively rural past was culture-wide from the 1920s on. Aaron Copland composed *Appalachian Spring* in the late 1930s and Martha Graham choreographed it in the early 1940s. The Newark, New Jersey, Museum opened a landmark exhibition of American folk art in 1931. *Drums Along the Mohawk* was a hit, both as a novel and as a movie. While the government celebrated the Chicago and New York fairs with three postage stamps, between 1915 and 1945 the Post Office

Department issued thirty-five commemorative stamps for colonial and Revolutionary anniversaries, as well as twenty-five other historical celebrations, not including the numerous "regular" issues that in 1932 celebrated the bicentennial of Washington's birth.

The history of the nation became a mooring for many Americans, but it was a nostalgic vision of a past that never happened so cleanly and so clearly. American Indians could take little or no comfort in this safe haven, because their recent history was a tale of almost continuous defeat. Their solace was in their golden age before contact with whites. Black Americans had a difficult relationship with the American past because most had been enslaved and nearly all still suffered from discrimination in their daily lives. First-generation immigrants confronted the cultural conflict between keeping elements of their homelands' history alive and blending in with the Anglo-American mainstream that celebrated a past that was not theirs, yet which many newcomers thought was instrumental in providing them a new chance in a new land.

Even in the best of situations history is an uncertain venture, since the evidence is always fragmentary and that which does survive often has done so by accident or the actions of the privileged. By making history a certainty, Americans eviscerated it of accuracy and continuity, but empowered it with great cultural and political force. The history presented by the films, radio programs, and literature of the 1915–1945 period was not necessarily composed for vicious, paternalistic, or controlling reasons. But by affirming a special sanitized vision of their nation as a chosen people in a chosen land, Americans unwittingly set a standard for behavior that the people of the present could not attain, and precluded their ability to comprehend that their culture and the world were changing at the very moment they wished—and assumed—history would stop.

NOTES

INTRODUCTION

1. Kenneth T. Jackson, *The Ku Klux Klan in the City, 1915–1930* (New York, 1967), 4.

2. *Negroes in the United States, 1920–32* (Washington: U.S. Bureau of the Census, 1935), Table 10, p. 55.

3. Jackson, *The Ku Klux Klan in the City*, 175.

4. *Historical Statistics of the United States* (Washington, D.C., 1975).

5. In 1980 but 3 percent of the American work force farmed. The decline in the number of farmers had been steady and pronounced for more than a century, making it perhaps the most profound change in American life.

6. Alice G. Marquis, *Hopes and Ashes: The Birth of Modern Times, 1929–1939* (New York, 1986), 119.

7. Ruth S. Cowan, *More Work for Mother: The Ironies of Household Technology from the Open Hearth to the Microwave* (New York, 1983).

8. *Historical Statistics of the United States*, 213.

9. Sixteenth and Seventeenth Decennial Census of the United States, quoted in Cowan, *More Work for Mother*, 194.

10. In 1940, for example, *Fortune* conducted a survey that revealed that nearly 80 percent of the American population considered itself "middle class." This seems a startlingly high figure, given the modest material conditions found in the census of 1940. Burton Bledstein, *The Culture of Professionalism* (New York, 1976), 3.

11. Loren Baritz, *The Good Life,* (New York, 1988), 77; T. J. Jackson Lears and Stephen Fox, eds., *The Culture of Consumption* (New York, 1983), ix–xvii.

12. Roland Marchand has termed this the "democracy of

goods." Roland Marchand, *Advertising and the American Dream: Making Way for Modernity, 1920–1940* (Berkeley, 1985), 218.

13. Wristwatches were first used by artillerymen in World War I, and became status symbols soon after. The necessity to know the time implied that the wearer was in a responsible position or his or her own boss, rather than a worker whose labor was supervised by another.

14. Marchand, *Advertising and the American Dream*, 12.

15. Christine Frederick, *Scientific Management in the Home: Household Engineering* (Chicago, 1920); Mary Pattison, *Principles of Domestic Engineering: The Business of Home Management* (New York, 1915).

16. Adrian Forty, *Objects of Desire: Design and Society from Wedgwood to IBM* (New York, 1986), 221.

17. For a more detailed discussion of these points see Johan Huizinga, "The Tasks of Cultural History," in *Men and Ideas* (New York, 1970), 17–76.

CHAPTER 1: *Work, Struggle, Intolerance*

1. Irving Bernstein, *The Lean Years: A History of the American Worker, 1920–1933* (Baltimore, 1966), 55.

2. Adrian Forty, *Objects of Desire* (New York, 1986), 120–55.

3. Quoted from the "Minutes of the Monday Evening Meeting" in Marchand, *Advertising and the American Dream*, 13.

4. Marchand, *Advertising and the American Dream*, 354–55.

5. Estimates by Daniel Pope as quoted in *Ibid*, 6.

6. That contention was specious at best, as Vallee admitted in an interview on National Public Radio late in his life.

7. Marchand, *Advertising and the American Dream*, 20.

8. Gallup poll, March 4–9, 1939, cited in Baritz, *The Good Life*, 105.

9. U.S. Department of Commerce, Bureau of Statistics, *Sixteenth and Seventeenth Decennial Census of the United States*, in Cowan, *More Work for Mother*, 194; Marchand, *Advertising and the American Dream*, 64.

10. Bernstein, *The Lean Years*, 59.

11. John Bodnar, *Workers' World* (Baltimore, 1982), 27, 22–23, 17, 87.

12. *Ibid.*, 79, 117, 57.

13. Jennie Lee, "A Diary from a Kentucky Mining Camp," in *The Strenuous Decade: A Social and Intellectual Record of the Nineteen-Thirties*, eds. Daniel Aaron and Robert Bendiner (Garden City, 1970), 43.

14. Studs Terkel, *Hard Times* (New York, 1986), 90; Bodnar, *Workers' World*, 96–97, 19, 55.

15. Quoted in Kenneth T. Jackson, *Crabgrass Frontier: The Suburbanization of the United States* (New York, 1985), 182.

16. Cited in *Ibid.*, 182.

17. The other side of the discrimination black soldiers suffered was that, for the price of humiliation, their families at least knew that their sons, brothers, and fathers had a better chance of surviving than did the soldiers in the trenches.

18. *The Statistical Abstract of the United States: From Colonial Times to the Present* (Stamford, 1966), 462, 470E.

19. Spencer Crew, *Field to Factory* (Washington, D.C., 1987), 6–9ff.

20. Bodnar, *Workers' World*, 136.

21. *Ibid.*, 116; Blue Jenkins, interview conducted by M. Roeder, Racine, Wisconsin, January 3, 1974. Quoted in Crew, *Field to Factory*, 48; Bodnar, *Workers' World*, 35.

22. "Some Hazards of Street Cleaning," *Survey* 38 (April 14, 1917), 42.

23. Arthur F. McEvoy, *The Fisherman's Problem: Ecology and Law in the California Fisheries, 1850–1980* (New York, 1988), 170; Fitchburg, Massachusetts *Daily Sentinel*, 29 January 1919, p. 1; Bodnar, *Workers' World*, 91–92, 93, 46, 69.

24. Quoted in Stanley Coben, *A. Mitchell Palmer* (New York, 1963), 198.

25. For more on the problem of crime in turn-of-the-century America, see, for example, Robert Dugdale, *The Jukes: A Study in Crime, Pauperism, and Disease* (New York, 1910); Cesare Lombroso, *Crime: Its Causes and Remedies* (Reprint edition: Montclair, 1968).

26. Berkshire *Eagle*, 3 January 1920, p. 1. The listing revealed that Springfield, Worcester, and Lynn joined Boston as hotbeds of radicalism in Massachusetts. Nashua was far and away the "red" capital of New Hampshire, and Providence accounted for most of Rhode Island's paltry contribution. The paper's lists also showed that New York, Brooklyn, Detroit, Chicago, Philadelphia, Milwaukee, and Buffalo were the real trouble spots.

27. John Bodnar, *Workers' World*, 74, 73, 148.

28. *Ibid.*, 54, 95.

29. Jackson, *The Ku Klux Klan in the City*, 195.

30. McEvoy, *The Fisherman's Problem*, 124, 173; U.S. Department of Commerce, *Historical Statistics of the United States* (1970), 177–178.

31. Bernstein, *The Lean Years*, 377–81; Kentucky miner to Ar-

thur Garfield Hays, n.d., *Nation* 134 (June 8, 1932), 651, quoted in *Ibid.*, 377.

32. Edward Levinson, "Labor on the March," *Harper's* 174 (May 1937), 642–46.

33. Quoted in Baritz, *The Good Life*, 134.

34. Quoted in Carey McWilliams, *Ill Fares the Land: Migrants and Migrating Labor in the United States* (Boston, 1942), 301.

35. U.S. Department of Agriculture, *Technology and the Farm* (Washington, 1940), 136. Hybrid corn yields were as much as 30 percent higher than regular corn, but there was a catch: The next generation of seeds were not hybrids; thus farmers had to buy from seedsmen each year to enjoy the potentially bountiful harvest.

36. Terkel, *Hard Times*, 240.

37. Interview with Herman Green, West Seneca, New York, January 1979; Bodnar, *Workers' World*, 57, 117–18.

38. Quoted in Kenneth Allsop, *Hard Travellin': The Hobo and His History* (New York, 1967), 71.

39. Terkel, *Hard Times*, 407.

40. Frank J. Taylor, "California's 'Grapes of Wrath'," *The Forum* CII (November 1939), 232–38.

41. Quoted in Allsop, *Hard Travellin'*, 133.

42. Quoted in *Ibid.*, 117.

43. George McDaniel, *Hearth and Home: Preserving a People's Culture* (Philadelphia, 1982), 157.

44. *Historical Statistics of the United States* (Washington, 1976), 14; U.S. Bureau of the Census, *Negro Population in the United States, 1790–1915* (Washington, Reprint: New York, 1968), 486; McDaniel, *Hearth and Home*, 187.

45. McDaniel, *Hearth and Home*, 161.

46. Terkel, *Hard Times*, 46.

47. *Ibid.*, 229.

48. *Ibid.*, 243.

49. Frank J. Taylor, "California's 'Grapes of Wrath,' " quoted in Daniel Aaron and Robert Bendiner, *The Strenuous Decade* (Garden City, 1970), 256.

50. Bodnar, *Workers' World*, 115.

51. *Ibid.*, 77.

52. *Ibid.*, 22, 25, 42; Albert Maltz, "Man on a Road," *Proletarian Literature in the United States*, quoted in Aaron et al., *The Strenuous Decade*, 239.

53. Jennie Lee, "A Diary from a Kentucky Mining Camp," 42–43.

54. McEvoy, *The Fisherman's Problem*, 123.

55. *Ibid.*, 130.

56. *Ibid.*, 137.

57. *Ibid.*, 141.

58. Robert S. and Helen M. Lynd, *Middletown: A Study in Modern American Culture* (New York, 1931), 27; *The Smith and Telfer Photographic Collection of the New York State Historical Association* (Cooperstown, 1978), 40; Bodnar, *Workers' World*, 58, 34, 35.

59. Alice Kessler-Harris, *Out to Work* (New York, 1982), 217–30.

60. Baritz, *The Good Life*, 178.

61. Census and other figures quoted in Marchand, *Advertising and the American Dream*, 202, 203.

62. U.S. Department of Agriculture, *Time Costs of Homemaking . . .* (Washington, 1944), 6–7; see Cowan, *More Work for Mother*, 178.

63. Forty, *Objects of Desire*, 208; Mary Roche, "Designs for Living," *New York Times Magazine*, 10 June 1945, quoted in Siegfried Giedion, *Mechanization Takes Command* (New York, 1948), 621.

64. *Historical Statistics of the United States*, 420. The bureau also estimated that 79 percent of all households owned electric irons; 52 percent owned electrically powered washers; 52 percent owned electrically powered refrigerators; and 47 percent owned electrically powered vacuum cleaners. The total value of electrical appliances produced similarly reveals the revolution that had occurred after 1915; $23 million worth of these tools had been produced in 1915; $83 million worth in 1920; and $180 million worth in 1929.

65. Forty, *Objects of Desire*, 214. Advertisers seem to have ignored one disturbing possibility in their campaign for the mechanical servant. The fearful consequence of technology gone out of control that the "Sorcerer's Apprentice" fable details was of sufficient importance that the Walt Disney Studios made it one of the segments in the animated masterpiece of 1940, *Fantasia*.

66. Bodnar, *Workers' World*, 46.

67. Margaret Byington, *Homestead: The Households of a Mill Town* (Pittsburgh, 1974; Reprint of 1910 Edition), 145.

68. Cowan, *More Work for Mother*, 91.

69. Quoted in Harvey Levenstein, *Revolution at the Table: The Transformation of the American Diet* (New York, 1988), 107.

70. Bodnar, *Workers' World*, 62.

71. Roland S. Vaile, *Research Memorandum on Social Aspects of Consumption in the Depression* (New York, 1972), 19.

72. *The Statistical Abstract of the United States: From Colonial Times to the Present*, 462, 470E. From 1930 through the end of the war

there was one car registered for every five Americans. By contrast there were, in 1930, 42 Britons, 135 Germans, 37 French, 59 Swedes, and 225 Italians for each registered car in their respective countries. B. R. Mitchell, *European Historical Statistics, 1750–1970* (London, 1975), 350–354.

CHAPTER 2: *Crash*

1. Terkel, *Hard Times,* 60.
2. Bodnar, *Workers' World,* 145.
3. McEvoy, *The Fisherman's Problem,* 144.
4. Quoted in Terkel, *Hard Times,* 218, 242.
5. Michael Williams, *Americans and Their Forests: A Historical Geography* (New York, 1989), 271, 273, 309, 461.
6. Jeanette Griffith, "Dug-Outs and Settle-Ins," *Survey,* LXVII (January 1, 1932), 381, quoted in Aaron et. al., *The Strenuous Decade,* 38; Terkel, *Hard Times,* 50.
7. Bodnar, *Workers' World,* 55; Terkel, *Hard Times,* 214.
8. Jackson, *Crabgrass Frontier,* 193.
9. Bodnar, *Workers' World,* 73; McEvoy, *The Fisherman's Problem,* 144.
10. "The Falling Off of the Marriage Market," *Literary Digest* 116 (July 22, 1933), 7; Bodnar, *Workers' World,* 71.
11. Baritz, *The Good Life,* 125; Jackson, *Crabgrass Frontier,* 187.
12. Bodnar, *Workers' World,* 24.
13. *Ibid.,* 59, 61.
14. Terkel, *Hard Times,* 107.
15. *Ibid.,* 122; Kenneth Allsop, *Hard Travellin': The Hobo and His History,* 179–180, 187.
16. Bodnar, *Workers' World,* 145, 61–62.
17. Terkel, *Hard Times,* 46, 16.
18. Bodnar, *Workers' World,* 71.
19. *Ibid.,* 99.
20. *Ibid.,* 146, 51, 22.
21. *Ibid.,* 71, 116.
22. Frank Moorhead, "Broke at Fifty-Five," *The Nation,* CXXXII (May 13, 1931), 528–30, quoted in Aaron et al., *The Strenuous Decade,* 34–35.
23. *Ibid.,* 36.
24. Gerald W. Johnson, "The Average American and the Depression," *Current History* 35 (February 1932), 671–75, quoted in Aaron et al., *The Strenuous Decade,* 6.

25. Robert S. and Helen M. Lynd, *Middletown in Transition* (New York, 1937), 126, 24.

26. Terkel, *Hard Times*, 42; Bodnar, *Workers' World*, 116; Mirra Komarovsky, *The Unemployed Man and His Family* (New York, 1940), 77, 75, 74.

27. *Fortune* (February 1933), second cover, reproduced in Marchand, *Advertising and the American Dream*, 327.

CHAPTER 3: *Houses and Homes*

1. Baritz, *The Good Life*, 120.

2. Bodnar, *Workers' World*, 180; Baritz, *The Good Life*, 72, 73.

3. Jackson, *Crabgrass Frontier*, 205.

4. Wright, *Building the Dream*, 199, 196–97, 198, 213.

5. Mabel Hyde Kittridge, "The Needs of the Immigrant," *Journal of Home Economics* 5 (1913), 308; Jackson, *Crabgrass Frontier*, 201; Margaret Byington, *Homestead: The Houses of a Mill Town* (New York, 1910), 53.

6. Bodnar, *Workers' World*, 66.

7. Bodnar, *Workers' World*, 44, 46, 47; Levenstein, *Revolution at the Table*, 107.

8. Bodnar, *Workers' World*, 105. The record player was an important accoutrement for the immigrant, the African-American, and the rural migrant, since it enabled them to listen to foreign-language records, black performers, and "hillbilly" music.

9. Byington, *Homestead*, 145.

10. Between 1910 and 1920, the number of horses in New York City dropped from 128,000 to 56,000; in Chicago from 68,000 to 30,000; in Baltimore from 15,000 to 7,000; and in Cleveland from 16,000 to 4,000. The elimination of the horse signaled the decline in a major environmental problem—manure—and a new supply of space, as stables and carriage houses were no longer necessary. Jackson, *Crabgrass Frontier*, 184.

11. Rebecca Taylor, interview by Myrna Wasserman in Plainfield, NJ, March 10, 1980; quoted in Crew, *Field to Factory*, 41; quoted in Cohen, "Encountering Mass Culture at the Grass Roots," 16; Bodnar, *Workers' World*, 36; quoted in Jackson, *Crabgrass Frontier*, 208.

12. Gladys Sellew, *A Deviant Social Situation: A Court* (Washington, 1938), 58–70, quoted in Borchert, *Alley Life in Washington*, 69; Marion Ratigan, *A Sociological Survey of Disease in Four Alleys in the National Capital* (Washington, 1946), 86–94, in *Ibid.*, 93, 95. Ratigan determined the mean number of furnishings per household as follows: 1.6 stoves, 2.2 bedsteads, .97 iceboxes, 1.6 tables, 1.3 dressers,

5.1 chairs, 2.9 pictures, 0.14 radios, 0.1 victrolas, 0.01 pianos, 0.01 telephones, and 0.2 sets of overstuffed furniture. The chairs were portable and were moved out to a stoop for socializing in good weather. The low number of electrical goods reveals that power may not have been available to these residents, as well as the expense of the goods.

13. Wright, *Building the Dream*, 178–86.

14. Rosanne Currarino, "Matters of the Heart: Everyday Life and Culture of a Working-Class Community: The French Canadians of Lowell, Massachusetts, 1890–1928," unpublished M.A. thesis, Northeastern University, 1991.

15. R. O. Eastman, Inc., *Zanesville, Ohio and Thirty-Six Other American Communities* (New York, 1927), 69–71.

16. U.S. Department of Agriculture, *Farm Housing Survey* (Washington, 1934), passim, cited in Cowan, *More Work for Mother*, 185.

17. Martha Hagood, *Mothers of the South: Portraiture of White Tenant Farm Women* (Chapel Hill, 1939), 99; McDaniel, *Hearth and Home*, 17, 5.

18. Terkel, *Hard Times*, 155.

19. McDaniel, *Hearth and Home*, 150–93, passim.

20. Jackson, *Crabgrass Frontier*, 185, 175.

21. *Ibid.*, 166.

22. See Susan Williams, *Savory Suppers and Fashionable Feasts: Dining in Victorian America* (New York, 1985) and Katherine C. Grier, *Culture and Comfort: People, Parlors, and Upholstery, 1850–1930* (Rochester, 1988) for analyses of the importance of these two rooms in Victorian America.

23. R. O. Eastman, Inc., *Zanesville, Ohio and Thirty-Six Other American Communities*, 69–71. See also Alfred Hopkins, *Planning for Sunshine and Fresh Air* (New York, 1931).

24. Emily Post, *The Personality of a House* (New York, 1930), 3.

CHAPTER 4: *Growing Up, Going Out, Getting Old*

1. Borchert, *Alley Life in Washington*, 98; McDaniel, *Hearth and Home*, 22.

2. Levenstein, *Revolution at the Table*, 133, 122, 124, 128, 134.

3. Terkel, *Hard Times*, 207.

4. Marquis, *Hopes and Ashes*, 103, 109.

5. Cited in Wright, *Building the Dream*, 210.

6. American Country Life Association, *Proceedings* (Chicago,

1929), 2, 1. See also Liberty Hyde Bailey, *The Country Life Movement in the United States* (New York, 1911).

7. Terkel, *Hard Times*, 187.

8. "A Taste of Not-So-Flaming Youth," *Literary Digest* 105 (May 10, 1930), 70; Gay Head (pseud.), "Boy Dates Girl Jam Session," *Senior Scholastic* 15–20 (December 1941), 35, quoted in Beth Bailey, *From Front Porch to Back Seat*, 66–67.

9. Anna S. Richardson, "Dates in Christmas Socks," *Woman's Home Companion* (January 1940), 7; Elizabeth Woodward, "Sub-deb: Bargain Buys," *Ladies' Home Journal* (May 1942), 8, quoted in Bailey, *From Front Porch to Back Seat*, 29, 95.

10. Floyd Dell, "Why They Pet," *Parents* (October 1931), 18.

11. Margaret Sanger and others got into trouble with the law for disseminating information about birth control. But in many parts of the country it was legal to manufacture and purchase contraceptives.

12. Kiowa Costonie, *How to Win and Hold a Husband* (New York, 1945), 45, quoted in Beth Bailey, *From Front Porch to Back Seat*, 90; Emily Post, *Etiquette* (New York, 1937), 355.

13. Paula Fass, *The Damned and the Beautiful* (New York, 1977), 262–68; Jackson, *Crabgrass Frontier*, 254; G. V. Hamilton and Kenneth Macgowan, "Marriage and Love Affairs," *Harper's*, CLVII (August 1928), 281.

14. Bailey, *From Front Porch to Back Seat*, 124–26.

15. Bodnar, *Workers' World*, 52, 20.

16. Bodnar, *Workers' World*, 17.

17. Terkel, *The Good War*, 133.

18. *Ibid.*, 34.

19. *Ibid.*, 31–33.

20. *Ibid.*, 335.

21. *Ibid.*, 109.

22. Edward A. Strecker, *Their Mothers' Sons* (Philadelphia, 1946), 32, cited in Baritz, *The Good Life*, 173.

CHAPTER 5: *The Healthy Table and the Healthy Home*

1. Harvey Levenstein, *Revolution at the Table: The Transformation of the American Diet* (New York, 1988), 170–71.

2. *Ibid.*, 194. Of course, the statistics do neglect the recession that gripped the farm community in the 1920s, which would have decreased that sector's intake of beef and increased their consumption of vegetables and grains they could grow. The same is true for many

of the working class, who struggled with uneven and undependable working lives and incomes in the twenties.

3. Corporate financier Edward F. Hutton married C. W. Post's daughter in the early 1920s and immediately embarked upon expanding and consolidating the Postum Corporation. He sunk capital into the firm and acquired fourteen other food-producing companies to form General Foods. The steel and finance giant J. P. Morgan Company added food industries to its portfolio in the 1920s, including Chase and Sanborn Coffee and Royal Baking Powder, to form Standard Brands.

4. This preference was often a seed for generational conflict in the immigrant home. The children of immigrants attending American schools often were embarrassed by the different "immigrant" bread used for their sandwiches, wishing instead for the white bread of their American peers.

5. *Sixteenth United States Census of Manufactures,* 1939, volume 2, part 1 (Washington, D.C., 1940), 164. Raisin bread, popular by the end of World War I, was relatively unknown until large raisin manufacturers began to advertise their goods as a bread additive in 1916.

6. David Brownstone, *Island of Hope, Island of Tears* (New York, 1979), 17, quoted in Levenstein, *Revolution at the Table,* 106.

7. J. C. Kennedy et al., *Wages and Family Budgets in the Chicago Stockyard District* (Chicago, 1914), 72; Lucy Gillette and Penelope Rice, *Influence of Education on the Food Habits of Some New York City Families* (New York, 1931), 15–19, cited in Levenstein, *Revolution at the Table,* 175; Maurice Leven et al., *America's Capacity to Consume* (New York, 1934), cited in Marquis, *Hopes and Ashes,* 196; Velma Phillips and Laura Howell, "Racial and Other Differences in Dietary Customs," *Journal of Home Economics* (September 1920), 397, quoted in Levenstein, *Revolution at the Table,* 106.

8. Dora B. Somerville, "A Study of a Group of Negro Children Living in an Alley Culture," M. A. Thesis, Catholic University of America (1941), quoted in James Bochert, *Alley Life in Washington: Family, Community, Religion, and Folklife in the City, 1850–1970* (Urbana, 1980), 206.

9. Jesse Stene and Lydia Roberts, "A Nutrition Study of an Indian Reservation," *Journal of the American Dietetic Association* 3, no. 4 (March 1928), 217–21.

10. Levenstein, *Revolution at the Table,* 181.

11. *Ibid.,* 181–82, 201.

12. Advertisement in the *Berkshire Eagle,* 1 January 1920, 3.

13. Levenstein, *Revolution at the Table,* 185–89.

14. *Ibid.*, 116–17, 96–99.

15. *Ibid.*, 115–16; Bodnar, *Workers' World*, 24.

16. The Fleischmann Yeast Company, "The Healing Power of Compressed Yeast" (New York, 1919), 3, 7.

17. Even Standard Oil profited from the autointoxication scare. Nujol, a mineral oil distillate that allegedly lubricated the internal plumbing system, was advertised in newspapers, women's magazines, and more specialized periodicals such as Bernarr MacFadden's *Physical Culture* as the cure for intestinal sluggishness.

18. "That Coated Tongue . . ." *Time* 22, no. 10 (September 4, 1933), 5.

19. Louise P. Benjamin, "What Is Your Dream Girl Like," *Ladies' Home Journal* (March 1942), 114; Curt Reiss, "Beauty is a Bore," *Esquire* (March 1940), 27.

20. Levenstein, *Revolution at the Table*, 180.

21. *Historical Statistics of the United States* (Series B.107), 25; Cowan, *More Work for Mother*, 84–85.

22. Bodnar, *Workers' World*, 26.

23. *Ibid.*, 49–50.

24. Martin Melosi, *Garbage in the Cities: Refuse, Reform, and the Environment, 1880–1980* (Chicago, 1981), 100, 112–13, 144, 146–47.

25. McDaniel, *Hearth and Home*, 162.

26. Fitchburg *Sentinel*, 6 January 1919, 6; "More Influenza Cases Reported," Fitchburg *Sentinel*, 2 January 1919, 1; *Ibid.*, 6 January 1919, 5, 6.

27. Bodnar, *Workers' World*, 61.

28. In England, the other country most clearly affected by the "declining race" idea, the surprising number of physically unfit recruits for the Boer War led to the creation of the Boy Scouts and much gnashing of teeth about the fate of the empire.

29. See, for example, *Physical Culture* 58, no. 6 (December 1927).

30. Irving Fisher, "Impending Problems of Eugenics," *Science Monthly* 13 (1921), 214–31; John Fiske, *The Critical Period in American History, 1783–1789* (New York, 1916), 101, 106.

31. Albert Wiggam, "Can We Make Motherhood Fashionable?" *Physical Culture* 45, no. 5 (May 1921), 22–23, 93.

32. See, for example, " 'Read this little book *carefully*, dear. . . . It explains things so much better than I can,' " ad for Lysol in *Woman's Home Companion* (February 1927), 53; *Good Housekeeping* (March 1933), 157; *Ladies' Home Journal* (October 1927), 11.

CHAPTER 6: *Playing*

1. Quoted in Marquis, *Hopes and Ashes,* 15.

2. Foster Rhea Dulles, *A History of Recreation: America Learns to Play* (New York, 1965), 333–34; Baritz, *The Good Life,* 155. According to nearly every survey conducted during the 1920s and 1930s, the middle class had the largest percentage of listeners, followed by the working class and the wealthy. By 1930 between 37 percent and 55 percent of all households in Chicago's working-class neighborhoods owned radios, as did 67 to 83 percent of the city's middle-class neighborhood households. The U.S. census for 1930 revealed that one-half of all American households owned radios. When broken down by race, urban-rural residence, and immigrant status, the census showed that 56 percent of all native-born whites, 14 percent of all African-Americans, and 46 percent of all foreign-born whites owned radios. Only 21 percent of American rural farm families owned sets, and 34 percent of rural nonfarm households were equipped with them.

3. Lizabeth Cohen, "Encountering Mass Culture at the Grass Roots: The Experience of Chicago Workers in the 1920s," *American Quarterly* 41 (March 1989), 16–20.

4. Paul Lazarsfeld and Frank N. Stanton, eds., *Radio Research 1941* (New York, 1979), 110–39, quoted in Marquis, *Hopes and Ashes,* 40.

5. Terkel, *Hard Times,* 206.

6. "Amos 'n Andy: The Air's First Comic Strip," *Literary Digest* 105 (April 19, 1930), 37, 40–43.

7. J. Fred MacDonald, *Don't Touch That Dial* (Chicago, 1979), 243.

8. Statistics quoted in Marquis, *Hopes and Ashes,* 47.

9. Kathy Ogren, *The Jazz Revolution: Twenties America and the Meaning of Jazz* (New York, 1989), 91, 98.

10. Bruce Smith, *The History of Little Orphan Annie* (New York, 1982), 35.

11. Figures from Marquis, *Hopes and Ashes,* 92. In 1932 Curtis's net income had fallen to $5.5 million; in 1930 it had been $19.1 million dollars.

12. *Time*'s clientele was wealthy and educated. A survey conducted in 1938 revealed that 72 percent had some college education, including 64 percent of the women surveyed; 54 percent had servants; 53 percent owned listed stock; 63 percent owned their homes; 18 percent owned a second home; and 23 percent owned two or more cars. These were not the exactly the "Okies" and the residents of "Hoovervilles." Many of those in the New York City area that read

Time probably also read another of the smart magazines of the period, *The New Yorker*, which also appealed to the literate and consciously urbane. Fifty percent of the latter's subscribers lived within fifty miles of the metropolis in 1934.

13. "Raise Giant Frogs," *Modern Mechanix* 15, no. 2 (December 1935), 139. The magazine also featured a contest with a grand prize of $1,750 for the reader who could identify the faces in a series of composite photographs.

14. *New York Times*, 18 December 1937, quoted in Aaron et al., *The Strenuous Decade*, 385.

15. Ogren, *The Jazz Revolution*, 67.

16. *Ibid.*, 11, 44, 46.

17. Cited in *Ibid.*, 84.

18. Willie Smith, *Music on My Mind: The Memoirs of an American Pianist* (New York, 1964), 39, quoted in *Ibid.*, 64

19. Bodnar, *Workers' World*, 105–6.

20. *Ibid.*, 18.

21. Terkel, *Hard Times*, 36, 377.

22. Dulles, *A History of Recreation*, 378.

23. Bodnar, *Workers' World*, 26–27.

24. *Ibid.*, 105.

25. In 1907, for example, average annual expenses for car owners included new tires, $100; minor parts, $96; engine repairs, $70; and gas, $45. The car itself cost between $500 and $7,000. In addition, the smart driver had to carry an investment in tire-changing apparatus, water cans, gas cans (both filled), extra spark plugs, chains, and dusters, raincoats, goggles, and clothes for repair work on the road.

26. In 1915 only 300,000 of the nearly 3 million miles of roads in the United States were paved, and nearly all of those were in cities. Approximately 600,000 of the 3.3 million miles of roads were paved in 1925, and the paved mileage doubled to 1.3 million miles by 1935. In 1945 1.6 million of the 3.5 million miles of roads in the United States were paved.

27. Albert Maltz, "Man on a Road," *Proletarian Literature in the United States* (New York, 1935), 116–22, in Aaron et. al., *The Strenuous Decade*, 242.

28. Jackson, *Crabgrass Frontier*, 253–54.

29. McEvoy, *The Fisherman's Problem*, 142.

30. Bodnar, *Workers' World*, 139, 138.

31. In May 1920 the Berkshire *Eagle*, which served Pittsfield and the rest of western Massachusetts, provided standings for the major leagues, but devoted most of its space to the local Eastern League team, as well as the local school and industrial league sporting

scene. Weeklies had virtually no reporting on the majors. The Ux-
bridge, Massachusetts, *Times* of June 11, 1931, for example, devoted
space to high school baseball results only.

32. Jackson, *The Ku Klux Klan in the City,* 41.

33. *Jewish Civic Leader* 7, no. 4 (January 29, 1932), 5.

34. Fitchburg *Daily Sentinel,* 2 April 1938, 5.

35. Elmer Davis, "Miniature Golf to the Rescue," *Harper's* 162
(December 1930), 4–9, quoted in Aaron et al., *The Strenuous Decade,*
361.

36. Lynd and Lynd, *Middletown,* 484–87.

37. Bodnar, *Workers' World,* 54.

38. *Recreation Yearbook* (*Recreation* 33 [June 1939]), 124ff.